The Sum is Greater than the Parts

Doubling Shared Prosperity in Indonesia
Through Local and Global Integration

The Sum is Greater than the Parts
Doubling Shared Prosperity in Indonesia
Through Local and Global Integration

HARVARD Kennedy School
ASH CENTER
for Democratic Governance
and Innovation

Penerbit PT Gramedia Pustaka Utama, Jakarta

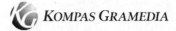
KOMPAS GRAMEDIA

THE SUM IS GREATER THAN THE PARTS
Doubling Shared Prosperity in Indonesia
Through Local and Global Integration

GM 20401130100

First published in 2013
by Harvard Kennedy School Indonesia Program
and
Gramedia Pustaka Utama
Kompas Gramedia Building Lt. 5
Jl. Palmerah Barat 29–37
Jakarta 10270
Indonesia

Cover design by Hendy Irawan

ISBN 978-979-22-9961-8

www.gramediapustakautama.com

Printed and bound in Indonesia by
Percetakan Gramedia, Jakarta, Indonesia

Table of Contents

Preface   xi
Abstract   xv
Executive Summary   *x*vii

CHAPTER ONE   1
Indonesia's Development Challenge:
Doubling Shared Prosperity by Accelerating Sustainable, Inclusive
    Growth

    Cukup Baik Tidak Cukup – Good Enough is Not Enough   1
    How fast has Indonesia grown?   4
    How competitive is Indonesia's growth?   18
    How fairly has Indonesia grown?   23
    Comparative Growth Performance   26
    Study Context and Organization   37

CHAPTER TWO   41
A Strategy for Accelerating Sustainable, Inclusive Growth:
Local and Global Economic Integration

    The Binding Constraint in Accelerating Sustainable, Inclusive
    Growth   42

Local Economic Fragmentation   42
Global Economic Marginalization   49
Local and Global Economic Integration   51

CHAPTER THREE   60
Improving Hard and Soft Infrastructure:
Reducing the Costs of Logistics and Transactions

Indonesia's High Cost Economy   60
The Context of Logistics and Transactions Costs   64
Indonesia's Hard Infrastructure Deficit: Logistics Costs and
    Efficiency   71
Indonesia's Soft Infrastructure Deficit: Transaction
    Costs and Productivity   85
Lessons and Policy Prescriptions   118

CHAPTER FOUR   123
Developing and Utilizing Human Resources:
Promoting Productive Employment and Livelihoods

Productive Work, Employment, Livelihoods, and
    Economic Growth   125
Boosting Productive Work in Indonesia   135
Raising Labor Productivity by Improving the Quality of
    Higher Education   150
Synergies in Broad-Based Initiatives   164

CHAPTER FIVE   167
Getting Things Done:
The Politics of Doubling Shared Prosperity

Political Benefits of Inclusive Growth   169

The Horizontal Politics of Getting Things Done:
Executive-Legislative Relations   173
The Vertical Politics of Getting Things Done:
Intergovernmental Relations   185
Promoting Local Investment: The Mining Sector   190
Politics, Investment, and Effective Decentralization   196

CHAPTER SIX   201
Moving Forward:
Reactive, Proactive, and Transformative Policy Alternatives

Three Development Paths   201
Reactive: Policy by Exception   203
Proactive: Sporadic Reform   206
Transformative: Fundamental Metamorphosis   209
The Road Not Taken   212

Annexes

Annex 1: Indonesia – Selected Indicators   217
Annex 2: Labor, Capital and Total Factor Productivity in Indonesia   218
Annex 3: What are Public Private Partnerships?   224
Annex 4: Where Has All the Garlic Gone?   229
Annex 5: State Capacity, Governance, and Credibility   233
Annex 6: "HE Drives Growth" – Empirical Issues   237

References   241

Figures

Figure 1.1: Indonesia's YoY GDP Growth – With Focus on *Krismon*   7
Figure 1.2: Indonesia and Regional Peers – GDP Growth Rates
(CAGR, %)   9

Figure 1.3: Indonesia and Country Peers – GDP Growth Rates
          (CAGR, %)   9
Figure 1.4: Manufacturing Value-Added per Employee (USD)   22
Figure 1.5: Saving and Investment Rates among Regional Peers   27
Figure 3.1: Domestic Credit Provided by Banking Sector
          (% of GDP)   88
Figure 3.2: Broad Money (% of GDP)   89
Figure 3.3: CPI Inflation Rates (%)   89
Figure 3.4: Nominal Prime Interest Rate (%)   94
Figure 3.5: Nominal Exchange Rate Against USD   107
Figure 3.6: Share of Manufacturing Output (% by Region)   115
Figure 3.7: Share of Manufacturing Output – Zoom in on the AFC
          (% by Region)   116
Figure 4.1: Population 15 Years of Age and Over by Main Industry
          (% Pop)   128
Figure 4.2: Population 15 Years of Age and Over by Main
          Employment Status (% Pop)   128
Figure 4.3: Arable Land and Agricultural Output   142
Figure 4.4: Employment in Agriculture (% of total) vs. Agriculture
          Output (% GDP)   143
Figure 4.5: HDI Index Trend Over Time   151
Figure 4.6: HDI Index Regional Benchmark, 2012   151

Text Boxes

Box 1.1: Government of Indonesia's Development Plans   3
Box 1.2: Indonesia's Middle Class as a Driver of Economic Growth 11
Box 1.3: "Stability" and "Balance" in the Indonesian Economy   17
Box 1.4: Total Factor Productivity in Indonesia   22
Box 1.5: Measures and Trends of Inequality in Indonesia   25
Box 2.1: Why Is There So little Support for MP3EI?   55
Box 3.1: Improvements in Personal Transport as a Negative Sum
          Game   67

Box 3.2: Corruption and Growth   91

Box 3.3: Indonesia's Banking System   95

Box 3.4: Dutch Disease   109

Box 3.5: Garlic, Salt, and Oranges – A Taste of Declining
         International Competitiveness   112

Box 4.1: Informal Work   127

Box 4.2: Labor Productivity and Long-Term Growth and
         Development   130

Box 4.3: Agricultural Workers and Output on Java and Outer
         Islands, 2007-2011   140

Box 4.4: The Educational Effect of Economic Growth   154

Box 5.1: Sources of Violence in Indonesia   170

Box 5.2: Legislative Leadership Constellation in Indonesia's
         Emerging Democracy   174

Box 5.3: Consensus in Indonesian Politics   179

Box 5.4: The Capacities of the DPR Secretariat General   183

Box 5.5: The Political Economy of Reform in Southeast Asia   196

Preface

In 2011, the Harvard Kennedy School Indonesia Program (HKSIP) published *From Reformasi to Institutional Transformation: A Strategic Assessment of Indonesia's Prospects for Growth, Equity and Democratic Governance*. This was our first effort to understand Indonesia's progress, opportunities, and challenges as it commenced its second decade as a democratic nation. In this study, we noted Indonesia's remarkable emergence under *Reformasi* as the world's first majority Muslim, multi-party democracy despite its geographic, ethnic, and religious diversity and the destabilizing turmoil that accompanied the end of Suharto's New Order. We also noted Indonesia's steady economic growth during the global financial crisis and subsequent economic recession experienced by most countries.

However, despite this impressive progress, we highlighted a number of problems as well that were preventing Indonesia from achieving its full potential. These impediments all pointed to the need for fundamental institutional transformation: continuation of patrimonial politics, perpetuation of an economic oligarchy, high barriers to entry in a wide range of industries, a dysfunctional legal system, disempowered citizens, and insufficient investment in infrastructure, health, and education. Thus, in comparison with its regional neighbors and global competitors, Indonesia was falling behind in many crucial measures of economic and social well being.

The Sum is Greater than the Parts: Doubling Shared Prosperity in Indonesia Through Local and Global Integration is a sequel to our first study. It further examines constraints to robust, sustainable, and equitable growth in Indonesia, and presents alternative develop strategies to achieve the government's primary development objective of joining the ranks of upper middle-income countries by 2025.

In addressing these issues, we ask:

1. Is Indonesia growing fast enough to double real per capita income over the next decade?
2. What is the quality of Indonesia's growth? Is it sustainable? Is it equitable?

The findings are discouraging. The growth rate is far below the level necessary to reach upper middle-income status by 2025, and this modest growth has been characterized by lack of job creation, declining competitiveness, and rising inequality. This is primarily because Indonesia has neither reaped the full benefits of being a large country nor positioned itself well in the global supply chain.

But our recommendations leave us cautiously optimistic. Although adhering to the current growth strategy does not bode well for Indonesia's future, the constraints to achieving high levels of sustainable, inclusive growth can be addressed, even in Indonesia's current challenging political landscape. The key to both local and global integration is the same: greater investment in enabling hard infrastructure such as roads, ports, and power; improved soft infrastructure in the form of better government and governance; and development of human resources through more effective education and training. If Indonesia's leaders take the proactive policy path outlined in this study, prospects for more rapid and higher quality growth over the next decade are good; they are even better if a more transformative approach is adopted.

Like our first study, this report was written by an interdisciplinary team from the Ash Center for Democratic Governance and Innovation at the Harvard Kennedy School, and it benefitted enormously from the insights and guidance of numerous Indonesian colleagues. Its purpose is to contribute to a public discussion of critical decisions Indonesia's leaders must make to move Indonesia onto a development trajectory that is more likely to meet the nation's needs and aspirations. It complements our other efforts to enhance the quality of public policy formulation, implementation, and evaluation in Indonesia by bringing Indonesian students, faculty, and practitioners to Harvard, and engaging in collaborative research between Harvard and Indonesian scholars. We look forward to continuing our joint efforts to improve the current lives and future prospects of all Indonesians.

ANTHONY J. SAICH
Daewoo Professor of International Affairs
Director, Ash Center for Democratic Governance and Innovation
Harvard Kennedy School
Harvard University
Cambridge, Massachusetts, United States

Abstract

The GOI's primary development objective is to join the ranks of upper middle-income countries by 2025. If Indonesia could double shared prosperity over the next decade, that is, generate an annual real GDP per capita growth rate of 8.5 percent for the next ten years, it would be well on the path to achieving this objective. However, at the present maximum per capita annual growth rate of 4.5 percent, not only will Indonesia fall well short of its target, but it will also continue to experience jobless growth, declining competitiveness, and rising inequality. Clear indicators of current trends, in addition to the modest GDP per capita growth rate, are the long-term decline in total factor productivity and more recent fall in manufacturing value added per employee, as well as steadily rising measures of inequality such as the Gini coefficient. The binding constraint to accelerating sustainable, inclusive growth is that Indonesia exploits neither the benefits of being a large country nor its international dynamic comparative advantage. Indonesia is beset by local economic fragmentation and global economic marginalization. At present, the sum is worth less than the parts – Indonesia does not have an integrated domestic economy. Instead, it is a collection of disconnected local and regional markets. The country has also undergone a significant disengagement from global production and distribution value chains. Its growth is dependent on commodities and old industries instead of high value-added products. Extending and integrating the domestic market, and linking it better to global value chains, will reduce economic distance and diminish barriers to trade and exchange. The key to addressing both domestic and international market problems is essentially the same, namely better hard infrastructure (ports, power, roads), soft infrastructure (government and governance), and wet infrastructure (human resources). This will reduce the costs of logistics and transactions, and promote productive employment and livelihoods. A requirement for effective implementation of new development policies is adroit management of both the horizontal politics (executive-legislative relations) and vertical politics (intergovernmental relations) of getting things done. Based on Indonesia's historical context and its current economic, political, and social environment, the nation has a choice of three future development paths: reactive, proactive, and transformative. Reactive, or policy by exception, best describes the GOI's current "muddling through" modus operandi; proactive, or sporadic reform, refers to policies pursued in response to past major crises such as widespread malnutrition and rural poverty in the 1960s and the collapse of oil prices in the 1980s; and transformative, or fundamental metamorphosis, characterizes the policies over the past half-century that have morphed the "Four Asian Tigers" (South Korea, Taiwan, Hong Kong, and Singapore) into high-income nations. The reactive approach will produce the same performance as the last decade – steady but unspectacular and largely jobless growth with declining competitiveness and growing inequality. The proactive approach will stimulate rapid growth in Indonesia for at least a decade, and inequality will not worsen – it might even decline. The transformative approach would, for the first time in Indonesia's history, move the economy onto a robust, sustainable, and equitable development trajectory.

Executive Summary

I. Indonesia's Development Challenge: Doubling Shared Prosperity by Accelerating Sustainable, Inclusive Growth

Cukup Baik Tidak Cukup – Good Enough is Not Enough

When Indonesians are asked how well their economy is performing, they often say *"cukup baik"* ("good enough"). There is a widespread sense of complacency that Indonesia's economic development policies must be generally sound, because although not spectacular, GDP growth has been steady over the fifteen years since Indonesia's recovery from *Krismon* (the East Asian Financial Crisis), including strong performance throughout the recent Global Economic Crisis.

This confidence has been supported by praise from international aid agencies, private consulting firms, and academics for Indonesia's macro-economic performance since *Krismon*, its status as a fast-growing MIST member, its potential as a new BRIC, and its imminent emergence as a "giant of Asia." They also project that Indonesia's growth will continue, supported by its expanding middle class and continuing external demand for natural resources.

However, even the GOI acknowledges that the current development trajectory will not achieve its own objectives. The GOI has been promoting double-digit growth in order to create an upper middle-income country by 2025, and although growth in Indonesia might indeed continue for some time, if it remains on its present path, it will fall short in three fundamental dimensions:

- **Job Creation**: It will not be rapid enough to create sufficient employment opportunities for Indonesia's quickly growing labor force. It will be characterized by *jobless growth*.

- **Competitiveness**: It will not be diversified, productive, or economically integrated enough to be sustainable. It will be characterized by *declining competitiveness*.

- **Equity**: It will not be inclusive enough to ensure shared prosperity from Indonesia's growing national wealth. It will be characterized by *rising inequality*.

Jobless growth, declining competitiveness, and rising inequality will not thrust Indonesia into the ranks of high-income countries, thus thwarting the government's own policy objective. Instead, it is a recipe for rising unemployment and underemployment, increased counterproductive protection of local businesses, and growing political and social unrest. Rather than potentially propelling Indonesia on a virtuous cycle of rapid, sustained, and inclusive growth, it threatens to send the country into a downward spiral of economic stagnation and popular discontent.

How fast has Indonesia grown?

When compared to other lower middle income countries, Indonesia's growth over the last two decades has been relatively strong but not outstanding. From 1990-2000 and 2000-2010, Indonesia's annual growth averaged 4.2 percent and 5.3 percent, respectively. During the most recent decade, Indonesia's growth was lower than both comparator groups and regional peers.

Despite lower comparative growth, Indonesia has benefited from a combination of strong external demand for its natural resource exports and prudent internal macroeconomic management such as its conservative approach to budgeting, official reluctance to borrow, legislated upper bound on the debt/GDP ratio, and hyper-accumulation of foreign exchange reserves. This has produced the "macroeconomic stability" about which there is much favorable comment, characterized by budget balance, relatively low inflation, a declining debt to GDP ratio, and a stable nominal exchange rate.

In addition, the financial system has been recapitalized and the large banks are extremely liquid, solvent, and profitable. The expansion of consumer credit has enabled the country's middle class to raise its living standards significantly over the last decade. One of the principal drivers of economic growth has been the rising incomes and expenditures of this "new consumer class," underpinned by the boom in natural resource exports and increased borrowing.

Indonesia's political and administrative situation has stabilized as well. The challenges posed by democratization and decentralization are being met in ways that create opportunities for peaceful social change and economic development. Indonesia's highly inter-connected and increasingly mobile citizens are gaining experience in the values of openness and freedom, and are now insisting on higher standards of transparency and accountability from their representatives.

Nonetheless, recent performance has fallen far short of the GOI's economic targets. For example, the National Medium-Term Plan Development Plan (RPJMN 2004-2009) was formulated to be "pro-growth, pro-jobs, and pro-poor" but: real aggregate GDP increased at an average annual rate of only 5.5 percent (or 4.3 percent per capita); formal sector employment grew by only 2.8 million, in contrast to an increase in the aggregate labor force of 7.2 million; and measured against the national benchmark, poverty increased from 16.7 percent of the population in 2004 to a peak of 17.8 percent in 2007, and then declined to 14.2 percent in 2009.

It is easy to find deficiencies and problems. Nonetheless, a reality check is a useful counter-weight to the widespread extravagant commentary about Indonesia's performance. The GOI's economic management has created serious distortions. Three areas stand out: budget expenditure is misallocated with consumption favored at the expense of investment; Indonesia is significantly under-taxed relative to its comparators, especially upper middle income countries; and Bank Indonesia has been allowed to misinterpret what an "independent" central bank is meant to accomplish. That misinterpretation has left the economy with inflation chronically above comparable international levels and an increasingly misaligned real exchange rate.

The stark truth is that not only is Indonesia's growth structurally flawed, but the country's growth rate is not high enough to double prosperity within the next decade, an aspiration held by many Indonesian leaders. According to the "Rule of 70," the most common metric for estimating how long it would take to double a country's GDP, Indonesia's real growth rate must be at least 7 percent per year to double real GDP within 10 years ($70 \div 7 = 10$). Indonesia's 5 to 6 percent growth rate of the past decade falls well short of this target, as it will take 12 to 14 years to double Indonesia's GDP at this pace. Given Indonesia's increasing population, the growth rate would have to be even higher to double GDP per capita within the next decade, an important component of shared prosperity – it would have to be at least 8.5 percent per year.

How competitive is Indonesia's growth?

Indonesia's current positive economic performance and upbeat assessments of Indonesia's future prospects mask serious adverse trends and their long-term implications for economic growth, primarily because they confuse static with dynamic comparative advantage:

- Static comparative advantage reflects the economy's performance given its existing structure, accumulated technology, skills, knowledge, and government policies.

- Dynamic comparative advantage (also referred to as "multi-period competitiveness") takes into account modifications in productivity and competitiveness as a result of changes over time in the prices of outputs and inputs, shifts in the social opportunity costs of productive resources, and variations (positive or negative) in technology.

Indonesia has a static comparative advantage in the production of raw and semi-processed agricultural and mineral products. This reflects its large cost advantage in these commodities, even after allowing for diminished profitability due to the over-valued exchange rate. The revenues from these products have supported a boom in mine and plantation investment, boosted government receipts, stimulated thriving real estate and urban services markets, increased formal sector incomes, and raised consumption expenditure.

Indonesia also has static comparative disadvantages. Its contribution to international manufacturing production and distribution value chains has declined due to the high comparative costs for producers of complying with labor regulations, as well as dealing with infrastructure deficiencies, elevated borrowing costs, and diminished export returns from the over-valued rupiah. Formal sector employment has expanded slowly because of labor market restrictions and the cost savings available when imported capital equipment, bolstered by exchange rate over-valuation, is substituted for labor. The economic costs of travel and transport have risen due to fuel subsidies, low taxation on vehicles, and limited public investment in transport infrastructure. Markets for goods and services across different regions are weakly integrated because of the low levels of effective demand in outer regions and inefficient inter-island transport. Utilization of formal financial services is limited because of their high real cost, poor service offered by formal credit institutions, and limited trust in the integrity and soundness of the financial system.

Two good indicators of Indonesia's decreasing long-term competitiveness are changes in total factor productivity (TFP) and manufacturing value added per employee. The long-term trend in annual TFP changes is negative: from 1970 to 2007, growth in inputs has exceeded GDP growth, subtracting rather than adding value through the application of additional resources. Although the short-term trend has been positive, the changes are still too small to support the 8.5 percent GDP growth rate required to double GDP per capita in a decade: since 2000, TFP has increased by an average of 1.7 percent per year, which, if continued, would support annual GDP growth of 6 to 7 percent. The steady decline in manufacturing value added per employee since 2008, despite the increased cost of labor and thus, the shift to the use of relatively more capital-intensive inputs, is a clear sign of falling rather than rising labor productivity. This decreases Indonesia's international competitiveness and reduces the likelihood it will move up the global value chain.

How fairly has Indonesia grown?

Not only has Indonesia's growth performance been based on static rather than dynamic comparative advantage, but it has also been non-inclusive as inequality has risen sharply. Income inequality, measured by the Gini coefficient, has increased, and both the Java/Off-Java divide and the urban/rural gap have intensified. With 120 million people left behind, roughly half of Indonesia's population is not sharing the nation's growing prosperity.

Despite the positive impact of expanded government social protection programs, they have had minimal effect on inequality. Moreover, none of them addresses the underlying causes of food insecurity, the starkest indication that exclusion persists despite robust economic growth.

The implication is that if Indonesia is to be transformed by high, sustained, and inclusive growth, much more than recent rates of economic expansion supplemented by social protection programs will be needed. Conditions need to be created so that all Indonesians can substantively and continuously participate in, contribute to, and benefit from economic growth. That will require the whole nation, persistently and determinedly, to raise the productivity with which it uses all of its productive factors, especially labor, as it becomes and remains more competitive.

II. A Strategy for Accelerating Sustainable, Inclusive Growth: Local and Global Integration

The Binding Constraint in Accelerating Sustainable, Inclusive Growth

The binding constraint to doubling shared prosperity in a decade through the acceleration of sustainable, inclusive growth is that Indonesia exploits neither the advantages of being a large country nor its dynamic comparative advantage. Indonesia does not reap the benefits of being a large country because it is a collection of disconnected local and regional markets rather than an integrated single market – it is beset by *local economic fragmentation*. Indonesia fails to exploit its dynamic comparative advantage because its growth is dependent on commodities and old industries instead of high value-added products in the global supply chain – it is characterized by *global economic marginalization*. The key to addressing both of these problems is essentially the same, namely better *hard infrastructure* (ports, power, roads), *soft infrastructure* (government and governance), and *wet infrastructure* (human resources).

Local Economic Fragmentation

Indonesia has made great strides in building a unified political national identity out of an archipelago of incredible cultural, ethnic, and religious diversity. However, there is no national policy to create a single economic entity from many regional markets.

At present, the sum is worth less than the parts. Indonesia does not have an integrated domestic economy. Domestic economic activity consists of a weakly connected set of loosely overlapping market domains, readily illustrated by the sharp divergence across regions in labor market conditions, financial depth, and price differentials for key staple commodities. This feature is the most prominent enduring structural deficiency in Indonesia's development activities.

It is evident in numerous ways: shipping costs; limited inter-regional trade; price differentials and market fragmentation; barriers to transport and trade; and substantial regional differences in average earnings.

Without an integrated dynamic domestic market, Indonesia has systematically missed the opportunity to benefit from having a large population. More importantly, much of the country's large population has been systematically excluded from the benefits of growth and development.

The original "patterns of growth" literature distinguished countries with large populations precisely because of the advantages of scale and scope derived from their large internal market. Indonesia has failed to take advantage of its large population and generally has few inter-regional demand spillovers. This has undermined the country's capacity for income generation and employment creation.

The losses have been enormous. First, lack of internal connectedness implies that a significant share of Indonesia's increasing incomes directly spills over to benefit Malaysia, Singapore, Vietnam, and China. Second, weak market integration is self-reinforcing; constraints on market size and its limited spread reduce the incentive to specialize. Third, restricted opportunities for employment expansion keep the domestic labor market fragmented and incomes low, thereby reducing the growth of inter-island commerce. Fourth, the rudimentary nature of the current division of labor in Indonesia, as well as the limited capacity to raise productivity through specialization, reinforce the existing unequal distribution of income and opportunity across the country's different regions. Fifth, the limited spread of electrification due to inadequate public investment reaffirms the perception that labor productivity is "normally" low. Sixth, macroeconomic management fragments the domestic market because the major economic institutions attempt to manage the economy as if one-size-fits-all.

Although the lack of attention to extending the domestic market in Indonesia has been a drag on growth and development, that situation need not persist. Extending and integrating the domestic market – systematically, coherently and sustainably – provides Indonesia with the prospects of rapid inclusive growth for decades to come.

Doing this requires: the creation of *spatially-blind institutions* that avoid regional or location biases; the promotion of *spatially-networked investments* to integrate more closely regions and districts; and the formulation of *spatially-targeted interventions* that encourage social and human development throughout the country. These conclusions provide a compelling case for inclusive growth and development derived from extending and integrating the domestic market.

Some of the above activities are already underway in Indonesia. Resources are being raised in high density regions and disbursed to lower density regions through the national budget: the decentralization of administrative authorities has resulted in a growing number of nationwide interventions, primarily with respect to health, education, and social protection. But when viewed more broadly, Indonesia is falling well short of having spatially-blind institutions as well as spatially-networked and spatially-targeted investments. It is these deficiencies, especially the latter, which keep transport and communication costs high throughout the country and keep the domestic market fragmented. These deficiencies directly limit productivity growth and undermine the capacity of workers, firms, and regions to improve their competitiveness.

Global Economic Marginalization

Although Indonesia's connections with international manufacturing production and distribution value chains broadened and deepened substantially following the acceleration of manufacturing activity in the mid-1980s, Indonesia has undergone a steady and significant disengagement from these international value chains. This trend, like local economic fragmentation, undermines Indonesia's efforts to achieve rapid, sustained, and inclusive growth.

Perhaps the most dramatic evidence of Indonesia's increasing integration with the international economy, as described in detail in the Harvard Kennedy School prequel to this study as a major source of growth, is the sharp rise in Indonesia's contribution to trade in manufactured products. World Bank data show that in 1990, Indonesia's share of world-wide manufactured exports was 0.4 percent. By 2000, that share had doubled to 0.8 percent. Relative to lower middle income countries, Indonesia's share was 7 percent in 1990 and 24 percent in 2000. Data for manufactured imports (the flip side of the value chain) show similar trends.

Recent changes in Indonesia have run counter to those trends. This is evident in the country's systematic disengagement from international production and distribution value chains during the resource boom. From 2000 to 2010, the share of manufacturing in GDP declined from 27.7 percent to 24.8 percent, and manufacturing exports as a share of total exports fell from 57.1 percent to 37.5 percent. This low growth, in both absolute and relative terms, is reflected in the drop in Indonesia's contribution to merchandise exports both world-wide and relative to lower middle income countries: in 2010, it had dropped to 0.6 percent and 12 percent, respectively.

Indonesia's disengagement from these international value chains would have few consequences if the manufacturing output had been displaced by the expansion of high-value services. That has not been the case. Furthermore, Indonesia is unlikely to have much success in promoting high-value services until it raises the quality of the education system and the capacity of its population for learning and knowledge generation. The most disconcerting aspect of the declining economic contribution of manufacturing in Indonesia is that it has been replaced by resource extraction which, despite the extraordinary though temporary increases in prices over the last decade, does not provide a viable foundation for rapid, sustained, and inclusive growth.

Local and Global Economic Integration

Extending and integrating the domestic market, and linking it better to global value chains, can promote and sustain rapid, sustained, and inclusive growth by reducing economic distance and diminishing barriers to trade and exchange.

In Indonesia, public policy can extend markets by improving the transport system. This will require investments in ports, roads, railways, bridges, airports, ferries, freighters, telecommunication linkages, and electrification. It will also require the removal of anti-competitive regulations so that cost-effective travel, transport, and movement of goods and services are possible throughout the entire country. By making such investments, Indonesia would be following the well-worn paths of upper middle-income countries. To stimulate their growth and development, these countries invested heavily in building a modern transport system.

III. Improving Hard and Soft Infrastructure: Reducing the Costs of Logistics and Transactions

Indonesia's High Cost Economy

There is an abundance of evidence that logistic and transaction costs are high in Indonesia. The downside is that, because the costs are so high, they have been inhibiting growth and development, as well as distorting the distribution of activities across sectors and regions. The upside is that because the costs are so high, they provide Indonesia with the opportunity to make major sustained gains in productivity, competitiveness, and inclusive growth, through measures that systematically and sustainably reduce these costs.

The Context of Logistics and Transactions Costs

High logistics and transaction costs undermine productivity because they absorb time and effort in moving both goods and people around, pre-empting resources that might be used more efficiently in alternative activities. Such a rise in productivity is essential if Indonesia is to gain the full benefits from extending and integrating its domestic market, and linking this market to global value chains. Since current policies are largely responsible for keeping those costs high, the challenge for the GOI is to foster the "constructive politics" that would help lower them. Current projections suggest that by the middle of the present decade, most of the large urban areas of the country will experience sharply rising explicit and implicit costs due to inadequate infrastructure. If this were to materialize, Indonesia's domestic market would have difficulty expanding. This would scuttle the prospects of sustained, rapid, and inclusive growth.

Indonesia's Hard Infrastructure Deficit: Logistics Costs and Efficiency

The World Bank's 2012 Logistics Performance Index ranks Indonesia 59th out of 155 countries, behind Thailand's 38th place and Malaysia's 29th place. The World Economic Forum's 2011-2012 Global Competitiveness Report ranks Indonesia 46th overall amongst 142 countries. For its infrastructure pillar, Indonesia ranked 90th for the quality of its roads and 103rd for quality of port infrastructure. The country's road density, at 25 km of road per 100 sq.km of land, is among the lowest in the region. Congestion due to a shortage of large-scale ports that are capable of receiving trans-oceanic vessels has made shipping costs in Indonesia the highest amongst the ASEAN countries. Shipping costs comprise around 15 percent of the final prices of goods, and high port infrastructure costs reduce Indonesia's ability to compete globally.

Indonesia's infrastructure bottlenecks are intensifying and its regional development is becoming more unbalanced. The country's main port, Tanjung Priok, which handles about 70 percent of Indonesia's total trade, is clogged well past its capacity. Similarly, congestion has brought average speed on Java highways to a crawl, confounding attempts to develop the region.

Infrastructure investment has been grossly inadequate. While the country spent almost 6 percent of GDP on infrastructure development before the Asian crisis, it has failed to reach even half that level since 2000. Estimates from BAPPENAS suggest that roughly $150 billion is required for infrastructure development during 2010-2014 to meet the plan target of 6-7 percent growth per annum. The state budget will only cover 30 percent of that total, or $45 billion. The 70 percent shortfall, totaling $105 billion, would need to come from private funds and this is unlikely.

This has not been due to lack of effort on the part of the government or donor institutions. Nor has it been a result of lack of policy leadership from the government. Instead, it has been the result of muddled processes that have resulted in a lack of understanding on how to balance the role of the existing state-owned agencies with those of private developers. The government has undercut its own efforts as it has sought to engage outsiders to join in the process of infrastructure development by failing to focus adequately and deploy its own substantial resources for that purpose. This point is illustrated in how Indonesian policymakers have chosen to develop two of the most significant infrastructure projects undertaken in recent times: the Solo-Kertosono segment of the Trans-Java toll road, the most important highway in Indonesia; and the expansion of Jakarta's Tanjung Priok Port (the Kalibaru Project).

Energy policy in Indonesia is inefficient and inequitable. It is inefficient since higher national income and welfare could be achieved with the same inputs of energy and budget support. It is inequitable because the richest groups in society benefit the most from the controlled prices and quantitative restrictions on energy use. Current energy policy subsidizes the better-off, encourages over-consumption, absorbs close to 20 percent of the government budget, leads to fuel smuggling, exacerbates macroeconomic instability, and encourages consumption of socially expensive liquid fuels. It adds to the import bill, creates blackouts, and keeps tens of millions of Indonesians from gaining access to electricity. Current energy policy therefore undermines inclusive growth and significantly lowers worker productivity, undercutting Indonesia's ability to become and remain competitive.

Indonesia is not deficient in energy – natural resources are plentiful. However, the GOI has not devised and implemented policies that would create incentives to expand efficiently and effectively the capacity to use the country's broad combination of energy sources to support inclusive national development. As in the case of transport, the public sector has not undertaken the investment that would ensure all Indonesians have basic access to reliable energy sources. This has kept their productivity low. Moreover, energy policy in Indonesia is still based on confusion between price and cost, with policy makers continuing the pretense that a low private price for fuel, mainly petrol and electricity, implies a low social cost.

That is the downside. The upside is that Indonesia's energy policy is so convoluted and inefficient, and so many opportunities to reduce wasteful practices have been ignored, that were the policies to change, the country could take advantage of the efficiency gains for decades.

Indonesia's Soft Infrastructure Deficit: Transaction Costs and Productivity

Indonesia is beset by high transaction costs that divert resources from potentially more rewarding pursuits. The result is that productivity of all activities, including those being used to facilitate transactions, is lower and workers are less competitive. Three areas of concern are a shallow financial sector, mistrust of Indonesia's financial system, and ineffective monetary and exchange rate policies. Although pervasive corruption in Indonesia also raises transaction costs, much of what is recommended here can be done despite the high level of corruption, and if implemented, will reduce opportunities for corruption. The Government does not have to "eradicate corruption" to make a significant reduction in transaction costs – the existence of corruption should not be used as an excuse for inaction in reducing other transaction costs.

Indonesia has an exceptionally narrow financial system for its per capita income, pattern of development, and the growth ambitions of its leaders. The rural areas remain grossly under-served by financial services. The major banks concentrate their activity in the urban areas and the use of credit and effective demand for locally-denominated financial assets are both low. The ratios of both money and domestic credit to GDP, common measures of financial depth, are low. In 2010, market capitalization of the Indonesian stock market was equivalent to 51 percent of GDP; the strength of creditors' legal rights on a scale of 0 to 10 (weak to strong) was 3.

Two primary indicators of Indonesia's shallow financial sector are high borrowing costs and the large numbers of Indonesians who continue to have no access to formal financial institutions. Financial exclusion exacerbates inequality because it denies large numbers of Indonesians the opportunity to use credit to expand their productive capacities or more efficiently allocate their consumption over time. Producers and consumers use cash or, if they borrow, they typically pay significantly higher rates than those advertised in formal institutions and have access to credit for short periods. Each of these reduces efficiency which, in turn, lowers productivity and welfare.

A low level of confidence and lack of trust in Indonesia's financial system is indicated by the: premium on foreign exchange; discount on government or central bank bills relative to a recognized international

asset; difference between the prime lending rate and the "riskless" Treasury Bill or bond rate; share of wealth held in local financial assets
relative to foreign alternatives; time-horizon of the average investment;
willingness to hold financial as opposed to real assets; extent contracts
are honored, reflected in the degree to which creditors expect to gain
control of collateral in the event of default; average length to maturity of
bank or other loans; volatility of asset values to changes in financial market "news"; degree to which borrowers can obtain loans on the financial
merits of their project rather than their political and other connections;
and time taken for the financial system to recover from a major shock.

Each of these indicators highlights particular weaknesses within
Indonesia's financial system. Taken together they reaffirm that many, if
not most, asset holders remain exceedingly skeptical of the capacities of
the GOI to meet its responsibilities. This leaves the Government with
a binary choice: maintain its current policies, implicitly accepting that
the financial system will remain shallow and thus, most Indonesians will
either be excluded or have limited engagement because of their minimal
trust in its operational integrity and stability; or introduce policies that
deepen the financial system and lower financial transaction costs.

The contribution of Bank Indonesia (BI) to Indonesia's development
has been undermined in two ways: its ineffective handling of inflation
targeting, and the adverse effects of a one-size-fits-all monetary and
exchange rate policy.

BI's general lack of success in containing inflation has resulted in a
serious credibility problem. Given its track record, few people expect BI
to meet its inflation target. This induces behavior, such as the increased
velocity of circulation and flight to foreign currency, which makes it even
more difficult for the BI to meet its target. Moreover, BI has supported
its attempts to reduce inflation by large sales of foreign exchange. This
has insulated the economy from exchange rate movements, which under
normal circumstances would have flowed through to domestic prices.

BI also manages the Indonesian economy as if it were an integrated entity that looks and behaves much like the Jakarta greater metropolitan area. The implication is that while BI cannot avoid a one-size-fits-all approach, its monetary policies need to be appropriate to the whole economy, especially in view of the limited degree to which the domestic market is extended, its low level of regional integration, and the fragmentation of money and financial markets. Indeed, the surest means the Government can block extension of the domestic market and hinder further integration of the national economy is to continue its current practice of treating Indonesia as a unitary monetary and exchange rate entity that behaves and responds like the country's richest region.

IV. Developing and Utilizing Human Resources: Promoting Productive Employment and Livelihoods

Productive Work, Employment, Livelihoods, and Economic Growth

Productive work of all types and labor at all skill levels are central to the task of promoting rapid, sustained, and inclusive growth. Workers receive income for their services. Workers are also consumers and their expenditure comprises a major component of aggregate demand. Workers are investors as well, obtaining resources by borrowing from others or saving unconsumed income. Moreover, workers are the largest group in society for whom economic development is intended, and to whom the benefits of inclusive growth will accrue. Finally, workers' skills are major components of the economy's human capital stock. When viewed in this way, workers - their absolute number, economic behavior, and productivity - are integral to the economy's circular flows of output, expenditure, and income.

Boosting Productive Work in Indonesia

There is now ample evidence that increased labor productivity is a key to achieving long-term economic growth and development. The link from rising labor productivity to improving standards of living, derived from productive employment and remunerative livelihoods, is central to promoting rapid, sustained, and inclusive growth. The challenges associated with strengthening this link are formidable, especially since data from the last three decades show that labor productivity in Indonesia has risen in spurts but at a relatively low rate, especially when compared to other lower middle-income countries and to most of Indonesia's Asian neighbors.

The majority of employment growth in Indonesia occurs in the non-organized, non-structured, informal sector. No doubt the Government, in its pursuit of upper middle-income status for Indonesia, would prefer that all future employment be created in the formal sector. That will not happen. The policy challenge is to expand productive work irrespective of where it is located or however it is designated. That will happen when all work throughout the country generates earnings that exceed each worker's reservation wage.

Inclusive growth is a mirage when a large share of the population remains food insecure, and many Indonesians are presently chronically food insecure when viewed from both supply and access. Roughly 110 million Indonesians, or around 46 percent of the population, subsist on less than the international benchmark of $2 per day. Research reveals that income poverty, as represented by this $2 benchmark, poses greater risks of insecurity and vulnerability for the poor than consumption poverty. Malnourished adults cannot work productively, and under-nourished children will not grow up to be healthy, productive future workers.

Existing policies will not materially or rapidly mitigate food insecurity in Indonesia. Although welfare is essential for the destitute and those who cannot help themselves, productive work is the only sustainable means of raising living standards for the remainder. Food insecurity results from poverty and rising inequality. It is perhaps the most obvious indication that growth is non-inclusive. Reducing food insecurity requires simultaneously increasing the overall supply of food and ensuring that real wages are sufficient to access the food.

The Government has numerous ways to increase food security: boost investment in relevant infrastructure such as roads, bridges, storage, irrigation, wharves, and ports; remove counterproductive restrictions on agricultural activity; ensure rehabilitation of mining areas; and move beyond stop-gap measures such as food distribution and cash transfers that do not address the underlying problems of low food consumption and inadequate income.

Several scholars have analyzed food budgets and consumer surveys in Indonesia and concluded that higher food prices will undermine food security. This conclusion directly contradicts decades of experience showing that the best antidote to high food prices is high food prices.

Since *Krismon*, poverty has become increasingly concentrated in the agricultural sector and rural areas. This is the result of the sharp decline in the contribution of agriculture to GDP, combined with lagging adjustment of the rural labor force. The rural-urban income gap, which had been closing during the 1980s and 1990s, has widened over recent years. Major efforts to boost agricultural output in Indonesia need to be made. It will help reduce rural poverty. It will also enable Indonesia to take advantage of the expanding world demand for agricultural products.

Over the last decade, the brisk pace of urbanization, with 60 percent of the population now classified as urban, has not been associated with commensurate output growth in the urban-industrial sector. Indeed, by the standards of the 1980s and 1990s, the expansion of manufacturing employment and related high value-added services has been low.

This situation need not persist. Special attention will be needed by the GOI to help manufacturing regain its lost dynamism, such as: promoting value-added exports via an appropriately valued exchange rate rather than by selective and counterproductive protectionist measures; and dismantling employment regulations that have raised the costs and reduced the incentives for formal, large-scale employers to expand labor-intensive activities.

Raising Labor Productivity by Improving the Quality of Higher Education

Indonesia has made impressive gains by extending the benefits of education throughout the country. Low family income is the main barrier to remaining in school and thriving while there.

However, the low skill level of graduates hinders employment expansion and increased productivity. The education system inadequately prepares high school graduates for the rigors of university education, while the universities, in turn, have lowered their standards in ways that fail to prepare graduates for their professional careers. Despite increased access to higher education (HE), the quality of HE in Indonesia is significantly lower than most other Asian countries. Components of HE needing improvement include the quality of curriculum, teaching, research, and academic management. The GOI could also give HE a major boost by initiating a program to educate a generation of Indonesians abroad in advanced skills.

V. Getting Things Done: The Politics of Doubling Shared Prosperity

Political Benefits of Inclusive Growth

Implementing policies that encourage inclusive growth throughout the whole of Indonesia would benefit both the poor and marginalized, largely excluded from the gains of recent growth, and the elites who control Indonesia and need peace and stability to govern sustainably and continue gaining access to the benefits of rapid growth.

A threat to effective implementation of policies to promote rapid, sustained, and inclusive growth is inequality between groups and poverty in ethnically divided contexts, which have been major sources of ethno-communal and secessionist violence. Empirical evidence from Indonesia and other parts of the world has shown that relative deprivation and exclusion from political and economic resources along ethnic lines have increased the prospects of violence. The resultant clashes have been deadly, costly, and have seriously disrupted economic growth and political development. They create distrust and division amongst the local population. Competitive elections in this environment can encourage politicians to manipulate ethnic loyalties in order to mobilize voters. In doing so, they increase the likelihood of ethno-communal violence. Delineating new jurisdictions by ethnicity exacerbates these tendencies.

The Horizontal Politics of Getting Things Done: Executive-Legislative Relations

The reality of multiparty politics in the DPR is that all policy making and implementation in Indonesia requires participants to conform to democratic norms. That conformity occurs as they accommodate the interests of multiple actors, especially potential veto players, whose exchanges largely determine how the executive and legislative bodies interact, and includes: inducing agreement between the Executive and the Legislature on the substance of development policies and strategies; ensuring that the policies are acceptable to all parties in the Legislature; establishing mechanisms so that the policies will be implemented over extended periods; and achieving the above within the context of the short-term orientation of DPR members.

Indonesia is a new, messy democracy that is still coming to grips with the opportunities and limitations of participation and representation as it seeks to develop operational procedures, acceptable to the voting public, on how to respond to emerging events. The whole democratic exercise, particularly the decentralization of administrative responsibility, is still unfolding. However, electoral reform that addresses the most grievous aspects of Indonesia's current worst combination of electoral systems could have an immediate and dramatic positive impact.

DPR technical capacity is low. This contrasts with the demanding

nature of the DPR's lawmaking authority and its extensive oversight responsibilities. For the DPR to derive and formulate substantively better
policies *and* increase the efficiency of the lawmaking process itself, its
members require the appropriate expertise and technical support. Much
of the institutional assistance for the DPR was established before the
advent of democracy. In principle, the Secretariat General of DPR plays
this role, but in practice, it has not. Members have far more personal
assistance than technical and professional support. DPR members have
difficulty gaining access to well-informed analysis on relevant subjects
and related policies.

Many of Indonesia's implementation difficulties are compounded
by inefficient bureaucracy. Much of this inefficiency can be traced to
unclear, overlapping and conflicting regulations, low compensation,
weak incentives for cooperation, and limited oversight. Some of it can
be traced to the arbitrary nature of public sector recruitment, non-merit
based appointments, and the transactional nature of advancement. Dealing with these problems will involve fundamental bureaucratic reform
(BR), such as open recruitment, promotion based on merit, and broader
oversight and accountability. Most important, effective implementation
at all levels of government also requires appropriate incentives. Providing them on a sustained basis entails a sound monitoring and evaluation framework so that the progress of policy implementation can be
regularly reviewed. A special effort is needed to improve data quality
and timeliness.

The Vertical Politics of Getting Things Done: Intergovernmental Relations

Few leaders at the national and local levels have an incentive to promote
BR. The first five years of the reform would be full of problems that are
politically unpopular, while the outcomes would only be enjoyed after
their terms end. For BR to be supported and successful, it will be nec-

essary to create incentives for the relevant politicians. At present, the principal advocates of BR have been from civil society rather than the government – researchers, NGOs, engaged academicians, and the media.

Despite these difficulties, several local governments—headed by reform-minded leaders—have implemented some aspects of bureaucratic reform, such as: establishment of the one-stop shops for business licensing; open and transparent staff recruitment; participatory formulation of standard operating procedure and service standards; transparency of licensing requirements; e-procurement; and establishment of a complaint response mechanism.

The over-riding issue of BR is to reconfigure central-subnational roles and responsibilities. Some specialists in government highlight the devolution of authorities to the district level, bypassing the provincial governments, as a major weakness in the Indonesian decentralization architecture because it Balkanizes public policy and public administration. Others claim that it is efficient and effective for most basic services to be provided at the local level, as it fosters government transparency and accountability through participatory governance.

Nonetheless, there are some services and, more importantly, particular activities related to the promotion of economic growth, such as watershed management, pollution abatement, environmental mitigation, and electrification, which require the attention of provincial governments or some other type of cross-jurisdictional authority. Although the autonomy law is currently being revised, rather than clarifying and rationalizing intergovernmental relationships, the draft legislation instead makes the provincial governments more accountable to the central government as an extension of the central government apparatus. As now structured, the revised law on sub-national autonomy is likely to be a significant setback to decentralization and democratization, leaving district and municipal officials convinced that the national government is seeking to re-centralize control. An alternative would be to enhance the decentralization architecture by keeping the existing law but revising its implementing regulations to enhance the facilitative and coordinating role of provincial governments.

Politics, Investment, and Effective Decentralization

Decentralization has profoundly affected the distribution of power and benefits. The central government appears to have recognized that regional voices need to be heard and that their concerns deserve attention. To ensure effective operation of the decentralized political system, the central and local governments need to reach an "equilibrium" reflected in institutional arrangements that are consistent with their particular interests. An essential component of this is recognition that under a democratic regime, state capacity cannot be exercised through force and control. As a result, there has been more attention paid to negotiation and the distribution of incentives in the devolution of power to subnational levels of government.

Superficially, it appears that the settlements reached through democratic processes are fragile. The reverse is true. Those processes are resilient and adaptable. The incentives are negotiated and distributed in a manner that participants perceive to be fair. The enforcement of rules is the joint responsibility of local leaders and the central government. The process avoids unnecessary political conflicts. So long as the political players and other actors negotiate feasible outcomes, the investment climate will stabilize. Accommodation by the central government does not represent a weakening of its role or authority relative to local political actors.

With Indonesia now democratic and decentralized, its prospects for an effective outcome hinge on the collective endeavors and aspirations of its population and their representatives. Indeed, some governance specialists reverse the emphasis by stressing the quality of citizen "follow-ship" in achieving national objectives. A related perspective is that politics is the art of helping to open up the path along which the general population is already headed. Indonesia's recent history, with popular support for anti-corruption efforts and the change of leaders in the 2012 elections for the governor of Jakarta, are highly positive developments. They signal a desire by the population at large and some of their leaders for a different approach to development, one under which the current pattern of transactional politics is recalibrated so that it is consistent with, or at least not antagonistic to the promotion of rapid, sustained, and inclusive growth.

VI. Moving Forward:
Reactive, Proactive, and Transformative Policy Choices

Three Development Paths

Based on Indonesia's historical context and its current economic, political, and social environment, the nation has a choice of three future development paths: reactive, proactive, and transformative. *Reactive* best describes the GOI's current "muddling through" policies; *proactive* refers to reform policies pursued by the GOI in response to major crises such as widespread malnutrition and rural poverty in the 1960s and the collapse of oil prices in the 1980s; and *transformative* characterizes the policies over the past half-century that have morphed the "Four Asian Tigers" (South Korea, Taiwan, Hong Kong, and Singapore) into high-income nations and that would be adaptable to Indonesia's development strategy. Each of these development paths is summarized below.

Reactive: Policy by Exception

There is little difference between reactive policies and "muddling through." It is akin to "policy by exception," whereby leaders ride on past accomplishments, and overcome their inertia to formulate new policies only when existing policies can no longer be continued.

This approach to economic and social policy-making has been evident in Indonesia at three points in the last four decades. It has typically followed a period of intense, fruitful change, namely: the push for improved food security in the late 1960s; the manufacturing export boom of the 1980s; and post-*Krismon* democratization and decentralization.

There has been no clear pattern to the policy regression. Reform fatigue, complacency, and political gridlock have all been involved. A feature common to the reactive approach has been the re-emergence of exaggerated rates of "surplus extraction" by the political and business elites and their enablers. The three episodes have coincided with the rising oil affluence of the 1970s, the financial excesses of the mid-1990s, and the resource boom that began in 2003. In each of these phases, the increased availability of finance and government revenues eroded and largely scuttled the reforms that had been adopted when the economy was under stress.

Current policy in Indonesia is reactive. Complacency has re-surfaced among political, business, and civil society leaders. Although they understand that the country's current development path is unsustainable, they also believe that neither President Yudhoyono nor his administration will actively promote economic reform during the remainder of his term. The current policy stasis parallels the final years of the Suharto regime.

This reactive approach has placed Indonesia on its present development trajectory: still growing, but not fast enough, unsustainable, with intensifying inequality, and 120 million Indonesians outside the economic mainstream.

The next policy changes are predictable. There will be some reorganization of expenditure when the deficit hits its three percent legal limit, and some emergency reductions in credit growth in response to balance of payments and inflationary pressures. Fuel subsidies will be adjusted a bit as oil prices rise. Social protection expenditure is likely to increase, particularly with the roll-out of the anti-poverty program MP3KI, and there may even be some limited borrowing to jump-start infrastructure projects. This option will become more attractive as Government officials increasingly realize that the public-private partnerships upon which MP3EI's major activities are based will not materialize. Yet, this patch-work response will not foster and sustain rapid, inclusive growth.

Proactive: Sporadic Reform

A second potential policy path for the Government is to promote vigorously selected changes that will raise the rate of economic growth and reduce inequality, or at least prevent inequality from worsening. Such changes should be relatively attractive to political and business leaders. Raising the rate of growth will enable Indonesia to remain a dynamic member of the G-20, while simultaneously defusing the possibility of urban disruption that might accompany a growth slow-down. Avoiding a further deterioration in inequality would deflect agitation at the subnational level for additional transfers from the center, or for increased local autonomy.

Indonesia is familiar with proactive responses, especially in response to crisis. It was how the New Order regime dealt with the hyperinflation and food shortages at the end of the Sukarno era. It was also how the Suharto regime handled the collapse of oil prices in the early 1980s. Similar fundamental economic and political changes were adopted in the aftermath of *Krismon*.

Proactive reforms need to be selective if they are to be implemented. This approach creates the "political space" for change. International experience shows that both politicians and the public lose their willingness to continue reforms once the basic responses to the crisis have been made. Selective reforms are the easiest to defend and, if appropriately packaged, can be sold politically. Broad-based reforms offer the prospect of dramatic change, but they quickly encounter widespread resistance. Too many changes are difficult to organize and implement and, being disruptive, they are more easily diluted and deflected.

Four changes would significantly boost Indonesia's productivity and competitiveness and raise its rate of growth:

- sharply increase public investment in infrastructure and sustain it for the next decade;
- re-focus attention on agriculture as a means of raising the productivity of work and improving rural welfare, including the elimination of food insecurity;
- rationalize center-subnational relations so that each level of government works for, and not against, *national* development; and
- raise the quality of higher education, as well as learning more generally.

The problem with this package of reforms is there is no pressure for action. The economy is still growing robustly, international admiration for Indonesia's performance remains full-throated, and local voters continue to work around the economy's bottlenecks.

Nevertheless, there are several potential tipping points.

One possible trigger is fiscal. The 2012 rejection of efforts to reduce the fuel subsidy and other distortions in government expenditure is placing stress on the budget. The stresses will intensify as commodity prices soften. As the budget deficit approaches its three percent limit, the Government will be forced to cut other budget items or raise additional revenue, both of which will encounter political resistance.

A second trigger could be an adverse shift in the flow of foreign investment in response to local restrictions. Combined with the rapidly rising demand for imports to satisfy the "new consumer class," this will result in what senior officials are likely to see as an "unacceptable" erosion of foreign reserves.

A third trigger could be the realization among residents of Greater Jakarta (and other increasingly cluttered urban areas) that rising traffic congestion, increased commuting times, and worsening pollution represent economic regression rather than economic progress and are due to ineffective government.

Transformative: Fundamental Metamorphosis

Neither of the first two options will fundamentally modify Indonesia's economic structure and administrative arrangements. They will not substantively change the present allocation of public expenditure or revenue generation, significantly raise the amount of productive work being undertaken, or meaningfully modify the coherence of what each level of government is attempting to achieve. Both approaches involve the minimal amount of change consistent with avoiding major social disruptions, alienating the powerful, or forcing the most vocal and potentially troublesome urban-based groups to moderate their demands.

By contrast, transformative change seeks to sustain the reforms that extend and integrate the domestic market through measures that raise and sustain productivity and competitiveness. The critical difference between proactive and transformative change is that the latter involves the regular recalibration and redirection of the reforms as experience accumulates and learning occurs. Transformative change explicitly builds upon the initiatives identified in the proactive scenario. Unlike in the proactive case where changes are one-off, the transformative approach regularly modifies and adapts them in ways that enable rapid inclusive growth to continue. Proactive reform aims to avoid troubles; transformative reform embraces the costs of reform to create a better future. It requires an energized coalition with a vision.

In short, a transformative development policy would comprise integrated, evolving, and sustained reforms to promote synergistic, dynamic, and lasting change.

It would include the following six key elements:

- Adopt economically and socially feasible measures to extend and integrate the domestic market, and progressively to link this expanded and unified national market to global production and distribution value chains.

- Reduce logistics costs by expanding public investment in roads, bridges, ports, harbors, water, power, and sanitation facilities through budget reallocation from consumption to investment.

- Reduce transaction costs by normalizing operations of the financial system, modifying regulations that entrench privilege and reinforce economic discrimination, and persevering in the campaign against corruption and public waste. Reducing judicial arbitrariness and bureaucratic discretion would complement this process.

- Stimulate productive work for all Indonesians through expansion of the private sector.

- Increase worker productivity by enhancing the quality of knowledge and learning.

- Realign center-subnational administrative and fiscal arrangements in a most appropriate allocation of respective roles and responsibilities.

The Road Not Taken

The *reactive* approach will produce much the same performance as the last decade—steady but unspectacular and largely jobless growth with declining competitiveness and rising inequality.

Average GDP growth would likely remain in the range of 5-6 percent per annum, or 4 percent per capita. This implies that it will take 12-15 years to double GDP, and that by 2025-28, real per capita income will be around $5,300, significantly below the $14,000 plus envisioned in MP3EI. Indonesia will be well short of its goal of being among the 10 largest economies in the world. This tepid performance will also undercut Indonesia's status within the G-20.

The *proactive* approach will stimulate rapid growth in Indonesia for at least a decade. Inequality will not worsen, and might even decline.

Such one-off reforms typically boost economic performance at several levels. A large-scale effort in infrastructure would have multiple payoffs. Construction activity would expand the opportunities for productive work and boost incomes. The additional investment would have multiplier effects in related industries. The increased employment would raise consumer welfare and well-being. By reducing the real resource costs of moving goods and people, and of providing services, the increase in capital stock would have productivity-enhancing and income-generating effects that reverberate throughout the economy. The induced expenditure would further stimulate industry and enterprise, producing additional rounds of expenditure.

The major challenge with pushing a few reforms in response to a crisis such as a sharp deterioration in the balance of payments or rising inflation is that, once undertaken, the effects of the reforms tend to fade and are often reversed as special interests stiffen their resistance.

The advantage of the *transformative* approach is that it would, for the first time in Indonesia's history, move the economy onto a robust, sustainable, and equitable development trajectory.

None of the Asian countries that have attained middle or high income status over the last four decades—Japan, Korea, Taiwan, Hong Kong, Singapore—have done it through truncated, stop-start, or tentative reforms. Indonesia will not be the exception. The country's well-publicized and thoroughly commendable goals of reaching upper middle-income status by 2025 will only be achieved through sustained, deep-rooted reform. The reactive and proactive approaches outlined above, or some version of them, are inadequate to this purpose.

The goal determines the strategy. If political and business leaders want Indonesia to double shared prosperity over the next decade, the required strategy is transformative. None of the difficulties the GOI will face in promoting and sustaining the reforms needed to achieve rapid and inclusive growth is insurmountable. The key challenge will be to seriously pursue robust, sustained economic reform in the interests of the whole population, while getting influential stakeholders to support both transformative policies and government resistance to special interest pushback. Meeting this challenge offers the opportunity to launch the nation on a development trajectory that will enable it to join the ranks of upper middle-income countries by 2025. This would be the finest legacy Indonesia's leaders could bequeath to future generations.

CHAPTER ONE
Indonesia's Development Challenge: Doubling Shared Prosperity by Accelerating Sustainable, Inclusive Growth

The trick is to make sure you don't die waiting for prosperity to come.

LEE IACOCCA

Cukup Baik Tidak Cukup – Good Enough is Not Enough

When Indonesians are asked how well their economy is performing, they often say *"cukup baik"* ("good enough"). There is a widespread sense of complacency that Indonesia's economic development policies must be generally sound, because although not spectacular, GDP growth has been steady over the fifteen years since Indonesia's recovery from *Krismon*,[1] including strong performance throughout the recent Global Economic Crisis (GEC).

This confidence has been supported by numerous reports from international aid agencies, private consulting firms, and academics[2] praising

---

[1] *Krisis Moneter* (Monetary Crisis), the Indonesian term used to describe the Asian Financial Crisis, or AFC.

[2] *Economist* (2009); Woo and Wong (2009); IMF (2011, 2011a, 2012); Reid (2012);

Indonesia's recovery from *Krismon*, its macroeconomic performance, its status as a fast-growing MIST member, its potential as a new BRIC, and its imminent emergence as a "giant of Asia".[3] These reports also project that Indonesia's growth will continue, supported by its expanding middle class and continuing external demand for natural resources.

However, even the GOI acknowledges that the current development trajectory will not achieve its own objectives (see Box 1.1). The GOI has been promoting double-digit growth to create an upper middle-income country by 2025, and although growth in Indonesia might indeed continue for some time, if it remains on its present path, it will fall short in three fundamental dimensions:

- **Job Creation**: It will not be rapid enough to create sufficient employment opportunities for Indonesia's quickly growing labor force. It will be characterized by *jobless growth*.

- **Competitiveness**: It will not be diversified, productive, or economically integrated enough to be sustainable. It will be characterized by *declining competitiveness*.

- **Equity**: It will not be inclusive enough to ensure shared prosperity from Indonesia's growing national wealth. It will be characterized by *rising inequality*.

Jobless growth, declining competitiveness, and rising inequality will not thrust Indonesia into the ranks of high-income countries, thus thwarting the government's own policy objective. Instead, it is a recipe

---

Rumbaugh (2012); Oberman *et al.* (2012); OECD (2012); ADB (2012); Hendar (2012); World Bank (2012) Some reviews are not so upbeat – Saich *et al.* (2010); Olivia and Yamauchi (2012); Nasution (November 9, 2012, 2013); Buehler (2013).

[3]MIST: Mexico, Indonesia, South Korea, Turkey. BRIC: Brazil, Russia, India, China. Emmerson (2012) examines the different designations and how they relate to Indonesia.

for rising unemployment and underemployment, increased counterproductive protection of local businesses, and growing political and social unrest. Rather than potentially propelling Indonesia on a virtuous cycle of rapid, sustained, and inclusive growth, it threatens to send the country into a downward spiral of economic stagnation and popular discontent.

Box 1.1: Government of Indonesia's Development Plans

Promoting rapid, sustained, and inclusive growth has been part of the GOI's development agenda for the last decade. The National Medium-Term Development Plan (RPJMN) 2004-2009 was "pro-growth, pro-jobs, and pro-poor." Its successor, RPJMN 2010-2014, has sought to raise annual growth to 7-8 percent and "...involve the largest possible number of Indonesian people... " (BAPPENAS 2010, Book 1, 18). The Master Plan for the Acceleration and Expansion of Indonesia's Economic Development 2011-2025 (MP3EI) is designed to "...transform the Indonesian economy into a developed nation...through high, inclusive, and sustainable economic growth" (CME 2011, 15).

Rapid inclusive growth (and development) is also featured in the programs of several international agencies (IMF 2011; Aryo 2011; Hill, Khan and Zhuang 2012; ADB 2012). The UNDP asserts that it "... works to support Indonesia's fight against poverty, promote inclusive economic growth ... [and]...reduce inequalities between groups and regions..." (www.undp.or.id/general/). The World Bank's logo for Indonesia is "Investing in Indonesia Institutions for Inclusive and Sustainable Development" (World Bank July 2012, 2).

This emphasis might suggest that the GOI already has in place the measures needed to move the economy onto a rapid inclusive growth path. It does not. In the Preface of MP3EI, President Yudhoyono states: "...we must also acknowledge that our economic growth thus far has not yet reached advanced, inclusive, and sustainable ... levels" (CME 2011, 9).

How fast has Indonesia grown?

Indonesia's Historical Performance[4]

The late Sukarno period was characterized by declining output, hyperinflation, crumbling physical infrastructure, widespread hunger, and pervasive poverty. Under Suharto, many of these trends were reversed. The Indonesian economy grew at an average rate of 6.7 percent per annum between 1967 and 1996, until the *Krismon* shock of 1997-98. Annual GNP per capita growth of 4.7 percent was one of the highest rates among the world's fast-growing, emerging economies.[5] Per capita GNP was around US $100 in the mid-1960s. It reached US $580 in 1982, and by the early 1990s it was close to US $1,000, enabling Indonesia to move into the ranks of the lower middle-income economies.[6] Suharto's "New Order" government also introduced a family planning program that reduced population growth from an annual average of 2.4 percent in the 1960s to 1.8 percent from 1980 to 1996.[7] It promoted education throughout the country and provided broad-based access to health care as well.[8]

Indonesia's economic performance was underpinned by the expansion of gross domestic investment, including investment in human capital. From 1966 to 1996, that growth averaged 9.2 percent per annum, on a par with two other fast-growing Southeast Asian economies, Malaysia and Thailand.[9] It was accompanied by steady increases in total factor productivity.[10] An important outcome of this performance was the marked reduction in absolute poverty—from 40.1 percent of the population in 1976 to 11.3 percent in 1996.[11]

---

[4]This section draws on Perkins (2012) and Thee (2012).
[5]World Bank (1998, p. 25).
[6]Thee (2002, p. 198; 2010).
[7]World Bank (1992, p. 268; 1998, p. 43).
[8]Sumarto and Suryahadi (2010, pp. 234-5).
[9]World Bank (1999, pp. 16-19).
[10]World Bank (1993); van der Eng (2009).
[11]BPS online "Trends of Poverty Incidence in Indonesia 1998-2011."

Despite its initial successes, the shortcomings of the "developmental state" began to emerge. Corruption intensified and the acronym KKN (corruption, collusion, and nepotism) became increasingly synonymous with the New Order regime. Corruption was widespread at all levels of government, stemming from collusive relationships between political power holders and their business cronies. The post-New Order regime has been affected by the legacies of this system in what the Harvard Kennedy School's precursor to this study refers to as "unfinished institutional transformation."[12]

It was supported by the proliferation of policy-generated barriers to domestic competition in the form of restrictive regulations and restraints on domestic competition and international trade. The regulations were issued by the central and regional governments, and sometimes by officially-sanctioned trade and industry associations. They raised the costs of doing business in Indonesia, reduced efficiency, and limited productive economic opportunities for entrepreneurs, including small and medium-scale enterprises (SMEs).[13]

In addition, KKN practices distorted market incentives through the rent-seeking opportunities they provided to well-connected businessmen and their political patrons. These practices led to an increase in the number of large conglomerates. But, unlike their Korean counterparts, the *chaebols*, the conglomerates were not internationally competitive. Their expanding interests in sectors such as forestry, plantation agriculture, manufacturing, banking, and real estate began to dominate the economy.[14]

The activities of the conglomerates widened the economic gap between rich and poor, and between the Sino-Indonesian minority and the indigenous (*pribumi*) majority. It began to undermine the social cohesion

[12]Saich *et al.* (2010, pp. 103-151).
[13]Thee (2006, p. 141).
[14]Thee (2002, p. 213).

required for political stability and national development.[15] The market power and institutional connections of the conglomerates slowed down the development of a more broad-based entrepreneurial class which would have been representative of the country's diverse ethnic groups.[16]

A key feature that supported the New Order's growth performance was the ability of economic technocrats, led by Professor Widjojo, to maintain appropriate macroeconomic policies. They did this with strong support, particularly during times of economic distress, from Suharto, who had progressively consolidated his position as Indonesia's undisputed leader. By the early 1990s, the financial discipline that had been maintained since the late 1960s eroded, largely due to the waning influence of the economic technocrats, some of whom by that time had retired. Although their successors were equally capable, this younger group had neither the trust nor the rapport with Suharto that their predecessors had enjoyed.[17]

The loss of influence by the economic technocrats was reflected in rising off-budget expenditures, outside the control of the Ministry of Finance but under the direct control of Suharto. These off-budget expenditures were allocated to ailing state-owned enterprises, the companies of well-

---

[15]Thee (2002, pp. 213-214).

[16]Scholars debate the extent to which the emergence of a local entrepreneurial class was hindered by the inadequacy of efforts to promote small-scale, indigenous Indonesian enterprises (Booth 1998, p.322). In 1986, the number of medium and large manufacturing establishments was 12,765 with average employment per establishment of 132 workers. By 2004 there were 20,685 medium and large manufacturing establishments of which 71 percent were in food and beverages, textiles, garments, furniture, rubber and plastic products, and wood products. These are mostly labor-intensive manufactures. Average employment per establishment was 209 workers. There were also many small and household manufacturers. Since most of the deregulation affecting manufacturing began around 1986, much of the increase in manufacturing establishments would have occurred prior to the AFC. That is, there were a significant number of manufacturing establishments that were not large conglomerates and their numbers increased substantially in the 1985-1995 period.

[17]Thee (2003, p. 35; 2010).

connected businessmen, and "strategic industries," including the aircraft sector controlled by Dr. B.J. Habibie, the Minister of State for Research and Technology. They also included the companies owned by Suharto's children.

In late 1997, the period of rapid growth ended abruptly with the contagion effect of *Krismon*, as foreign investors and creditors scrambled to reduce their financial exposure to Indonesia (and other Asian countries). GDP fell by 13.1 percent (Figure 1.1). The inability of the Government of Indonesia (GOI) to deal effectively and speedily with the financial melt-down precipitated a political crisis that ended Suharto's 32-year rule. In the aftermath of *Krismon*, Indonesia's poverty rate increased from 11.3 percent of the population in 1996 to 23.4 percent in 1999.[18]

Figure 1.1: Indonesia's YoY GDP Growth – With Focus on *Krismon*

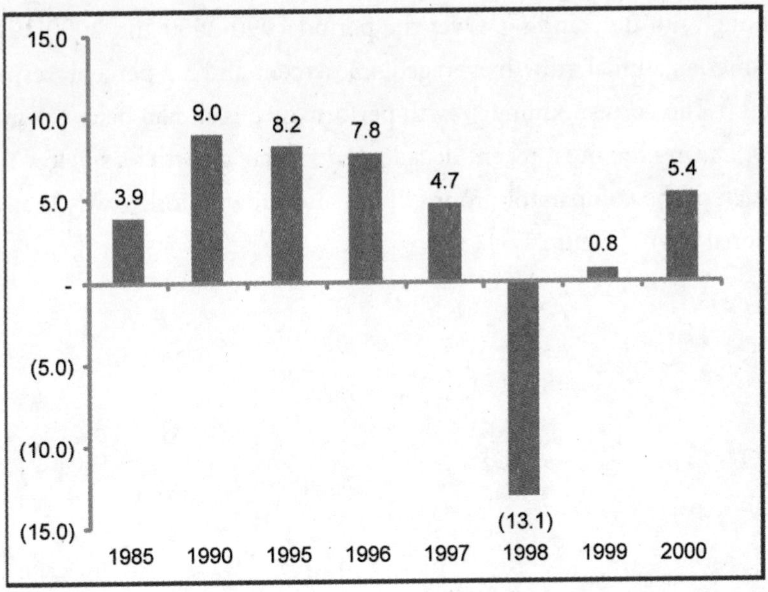

Source: BPS

---

[18]The 1996 datum is from a UNESCAP report (www.unescap.orga/stat/meet/povstat/pov7_ido.pdf). The poverty rate in 1998 was 24.3 percent, equivalent to 49.5 million people (BPS online "Trends of Poverty Incidence in Indonesia 1998-2011").

Subsequent democratic governments steadily reduced the economy's imbalances, bringing expenditures into line with revenues and lowering the burden of external debt. Economic growth recovered from 0.8 percent in 1999 to 5.4 percent in 2000 and to 6.5 percent in 2011. The commitment to balance the budget, rationalize the financial system, reduce the ratio of debt to GDP, and rebuild foreign exchange reserves – fortuitously supported by the boom in natural resource exports – left the Indonesian economy relatively unscathed by the GEC of 2008.[19]

Indonesia's Recent Growth Experience

When compared to lower middle income countries in general – including countries in East Asia and the Pacific, and South Asia – Indonesia's growth performance over the last two decades has been noteworthy, although not outstanding. Over the period 1990-2000 and 2000-2010, Indonesia's annual growth averaged 4.3 percent and 5.2 percent, respectively.[20] The corresponding growth performance is shown below (Figure 1.2). During the most recent decade, Indonesia's growth was below that of each of the comparator groups. It has also grown more slowly than its regional peers (Figure 1.3).

---

[19]Kuncoro, Widodo, and McLeod (2009, p. 151); Rumbaugh (2012). Indonesia was also spared the full impact of the GEC because its meltdown during *Krismon* essentially excluded it from international financial markets.

[20]*WDI* (2012, Table 4.1); Indonesia's annual growth rate averaged 5.5 percent from 2000 to 2012.

Figure 1.2: Indonesia and Regional Peers - GDP Growth Rates (CAGR, %)

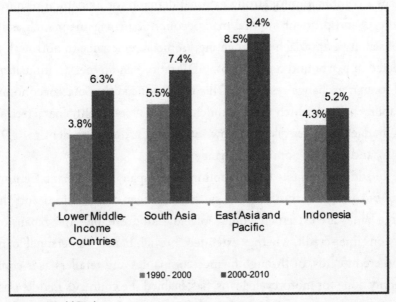

Source: World Bank

Figure 1.3: Indonesia and Country Peers - GDP Growth Rates (CAGR, %)

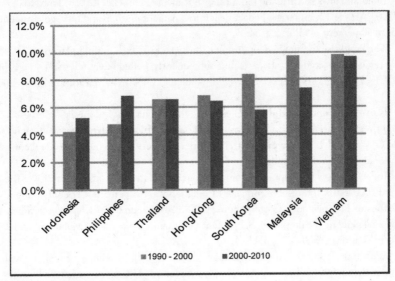

Source: World Bank

Despite lower comparative growth, Indonesia has indeed benefited from a combination of strong external demand for its natural resource exports and prudent internal macroeconomic management such as its conservative approach to budgeting,[21] official reluctance to borrow, legislated upper bound on the debt/GDP ratio,[22] and hyper-accumulation of foreign exchange reserves.[23] This has produced the "macroeconomic stability" about which there is much favorable comment, characterized by budget balance, relatively low inflation,[24] a declining debt to GDP ratio, and a stable nominal exchange rate.[25]

In addition, despite the disruptions accompanying the Bank Century bail-out in 2008, the financial system has been recapitalized and the large banks are extremely liquid, solvent, and profitable. The expansion of consumer credit, whether extended through banks via personal loans and credit cards, or through finance companies and retailers as is commonly done for motorcycle loans, has enabled the country's middle class to raise its living standards significantly. Over the last decade, one of the

---

[21]Blondal, Hawkesworth and Choi (2009); Kuncoro *et al.* (2011, p.16) Law No. 17/2003 Article 12, limits the budget deficit to 3 percent of GDP and total government debt to 60 percent of GDP.

[22]The rapid rise in foreign debt during *Krismon* to $152 billion (143 percent of GDP) has been counteracted by a sharp decline subsequently. Foreign debt fell to 34.4 percent of GDP ($125 billion) in 2006. It was 22.1 percent of GDP ($187 billion) in 2011 (EIU 2012).

[23]Ruiz-Arranz and Zavadjil (2012) examine the adequacy of Indonesia's reserves given their potential costs and returns (loss of output, risk of sudden reversal of capital inflows, low yields). They conclude that Indonesia's reserves generally exceed all conventional prudential benchmarks.

[24]Inflation is low by Indonesian standards but not relative to comparators. Over the period 2000-2010, Indonesia's annual CPI inflation was 8.7 percent. (The GDP implicit deflator was 11.1 percent.) Corresponding CPI inflation data were: 1.6 percent (Singapore); 5.4 percent (Philippines); 8.2 percent (Vietnam); 2.4 percent (Malaysia); and 2.4 percent (China) (*WDI* 2012, Table 4.16).

[25]With Indonesia's rate of inflation above that of its major trading partners, the real value of the rupiah has become increasingly overvalued. This point is discussed further in Chapter 3.

principal drivers of economic growth has been the rising incomes and expenditures of this "new consumer class"[26] (see Box 1.2), underpinned by the boom in natural resource exports and increased borrowing.[27]

Indonesia's political and administrative situation has stabilized as well. The challenges posed by democratization and decentralization are being met in ways that create opportunities for peaceful social change and economic development. Indonesian voters and citizens, who are highly interconnected and increasingly mobile, are gaining experience in the values of openness and freedom. They are learning how to insist upon higher standards of transparency and accountability from their representatives.

Nonetheless, recent performance has fallen far short of the GOI's economic targets, due largely to the role that incomplete institutional transformation has played, as described in detail in our first study.[28]

Box 1.2: Indonesia's Middle Class as a Driver of Economic Growth

Numerous studies suggest that the expanding middle class is a major source of economic growth in Indonesia. The World Bank defines the middle class as people with expenditure ranging from $2 to $20 per day. Basri (2012, p. 32) refers to the group as the "new consumer class," suggesting that expenditure between $10 and $100 per day is more representative. The National Socio-Economic Survey (Susenas) data show that more than half the Indonesian population fit into the expenditure range identified by the World Bank, while only 2 percent,

---

[26]Basri (2012, pp.32-33).

[27]Over the period 2000-2010, household final consumption grew annually by 4.3 percent and government consumption by 8.1 percent. Gross fixed capital formation expanded by 6.1 percent per annum. A recent IMF study (IMF 2011, Table I.3) attributed the main source of growth over that period to capital services (reflecting rising rates of investment), supported by some recovery in total factor productivity, particularly in the first part of the decade (2000-2005).

[28]Saich *et al*. (2010, pp. 103-151).

or 4.8 million people in 2010, have daily expenditure above $20 per day. That number is roughly the population of Costa Rica, Singapore, or Turkmenistan.

With private consumption in Indonesia in 2010 at 57 percent of GDP, a generous estimate of the size of annual expenditure by the "new consumer class" is around $300 billion. Over the period 2000-2010, private consumption expenditure grew annually at 3.1 percent per capita (or 4.3 percent overall). This expenditure is far too small and lacks the dynamism to drive economic growth at the rates envisioned by Indonesia's leaders.

Even if the expenditure totaled $300 billion (the annual national income of smaller countries like South Africa or Denmark) and could grow at double-digit rates, Indonesia's weakly integrated and often non-overlapping markets dissipate the benefits of consumer expenditure. Much of the excess consumer demand would spill over to imports rather increase the demand for providers of goods and services within Indonesia.

For example, the "new consumer class" in West Java (the most economically dense market in Indonesia) boosts some key domestic industries, but local supply is regularly supplemented by imports from China, Vietnam, Japan, and Korea. Similarly, the emerging middle class in Riau and other parts of northern Sumatra draw on some locally produced goods (including some from Java), but depend heavily on imports from Malaysia, Singapore, and other external markets. The emerging middle class in Makassar (South Sulawesi) and the urban areas of East Kalimantan draw far more extensively for their consumption on foreign than local markets.

It would be a mistake to discount the potential impact on growth of rising local demand for locally produced consumer goods and services, especially if policies were changed to extend and integrate the do mestic market. But given current circumstances (especially the present exchange rate regime, high transport costs, and high costs of credit), it is equally mistaken to believe that all the expenditure of Indonesia's emerging middle class reflects effective demand for locally produced goods and services. A significant share leaks to imports.

For example, the National Medium-Term Plan Development Plan (RPJMN 2004-2009) was formulated to be "pro-growth, pro-jobs, and pro-poor,"[29] but:

- Real aggregate GDP increased at an average annual rate of only 5.5 percent (or 4.3 percent per capita), less than Suharto-era per capita growth.[30]
- Formal sector employment grew by only 2.8 million (or 9.8 percent), in contrast to an increase in the aggregate labor force of 7.2 million (or 8.6 percent), while informal sector employment rose by 8.2 million (or 12.5 percent).[31]
- Measured against the national benchmark, poverty increased from 16.7 percent of the population in 2004 to a peak of 17.8 percent in 2007, and then declined to 14.2 percent in 2009. The drop in poverty resulted from the economic recovery and support provided through the GOI's social protection programs.[32]

---

[29]BAPPENAS (2010, Book 1, pp.16-18).

[30]The data in this section are from the WDI online 2011 and the Economist Intelligence Unit, 2012.

[31]The difference in growth rates implies that measured unemployment (both open and under-employment) fell.

[32]Social protection was 3.8 percent of the GOI budget in 2004; by 2009, it was 7.5 percent. Numerous commentators (e.g., Thee 2002, pp. 225-226) have noted that Indonesia's national poverty line is significantly lower than that of neighboring countries (such as Philippines). That is, national poverty rates are understated. Nonetheless, the reduction in poverty achieved in the late 2000s was impressive.

The jobs situation was especially disappointing. Despite robust economic growth, there was no shift in the balance between the formal and informal employment.[33] In this sense, the GOI's policies were non-inclusive.[34] Most of the country's poor continued to eke out livelihoods in self-employment or informal sector activity.

Another example is the Medium-Term Plan for 2010-2014, which was designed to achieve inclusive growth of 7-8 percent per annum, but over the period 2010-2012, aggregate real GDP increased by only 6.2 percent per annum (or 4.9 percent per capita). Furthermore, since the growth resulted mainly from middle income consumption and the natural resource boom, inequality increased.[35]

More recently, the Master Plan for the Acceleration and Expansion of Indonesia's Economic Development (MP3EI) has been superimposed on the Medium-Term Plan with the expectation that it will markedly accelerate growth and expand development. Under MP3EI, real per capita income is projected to increase by at least 10.5 percent per annum over the period 2010 to 2025.[36] So far, MP3EI has encountered two problems. One is widespread skepticism (and even rejection) of its basic premises. The other is that actual per capita income growth has been

---

[33]In 2004, formal employment was 30.3 percent of all employment; by 2009, it was 29.8 percent.

[34]As noted in Chapter One, President Yudhoyono acknowledged this point.

[35]Some perspective is needed on the extent to which income has been driven by natural resources (especially their rising prices). Over the period 2000 to 2011, the quantity of exports increased by 114 percent; for imports it was 123 percent. Corresponding increases in export and import prices were 54 percent and 85 percent. The trade data show that the current US dollar value of exports (imports) increased by 288 percent (320 percent) over the same period while the dollar value of GDP increased by 413 percent. Since the corresponding increase in the real value of national output in local currency units was only 77.2 percent, there has been a major disconnect between the dollar values of trade and output and the growth of the real economy (Source: World Bank WDI 2012, online). This is one (of several) manifestations of Dutch Disease, a topic discussed further in Chapter Three.

[36]This is based on the low end target for 2025 of $14,250 per capita.

below target,[37] with IMF projections suggesting an increase of roughly 5.0 percent in 2012 and 5.3 percent in 2013.[38] Initial shortfalls means subsequent growth would have to be even higher.

It is easy to find deficiencies and problems. Nonetheless, a reality check is a useful counter-weight to the widespread extravagant commentary about Indonesia's performance. The GOI's economic management has created serious distortions (see Box 1.3). Three areas stand out: budget expenditure is misallocated with consumption favored at the expense of investment; Indonesia is significantly under-taxed relative to its comparators especially upper middle income countries;[39] and Bank Indonesia has been allowed to misinterpret what an "independent" central bank is meant to accomplish. That misinterpretation has left the economy with inflation chronically above comparable international levels[40] and an increasingly misaligned real exchange rate.

Still, the stark truth is that not only is Indonesia's growth structurally flawed, but the country's growth rate is not high enough to double prosperity within the next decade, an aspiration held by Indonesian leaders. According to the "Rule of 70," the most common metric for estimating how long it would take to double a country's GDP, Indonesia's real growth rate must be at least 7 percent per year to double real GDP within 10 years (70 ÷ 7 = 10). Indonesia's 5 to 6 percent growth rate

---

[37]"By utilizing the MP3EI, Indonesia aims to earn its place as one of the world's developed countries by 2025 with expected per capita income of USD 14,250-USD 15,500 with total GDP of USD 4.0-4.5 trillion. To achieve the above objectives, real economic growth of 6.4-7.5 percent is expected for the period of 2011-2014. This economic growth is expected to coincide with the decrease in the rate of inflation from 6.5 percent in 2011-2014 to 3.0 percent in 2025. The combined growth and inflation rates reflect the characteristics of a developed country" CME (2011, p. 15).

[38]IMF (September 25, 2012).

[39]WDI (2012, Tables 4.12 and 4.14); Cornwell and Anas (2013).

[40]Palomba (2012) examines why Indonesia's inflation rate has been (and remains) chronically above that of its neighbors and international competitors. Rapid credit growth is a major factor. This area is the responsibility of Bank Indonesia. The implications are examined in Chapter 3.

of the past decade falls well short of this target, as it will take 12 to 14 years to double Indonesia's GDP at this pace. Given Indonesia's increasing population, the growth rate would have to be even higher to double GDP per capita within the next decade, an important component of shared prosperity – it would have to be at least 8.5 percent per year.

Box 1.3: "Stability" and "Balance" in the Indonesian Economy

Stability and balance have been recurrent themes in describing the trajectory of Indonesia's economy, particularly since its recovery from Krismon. The World Bank and IMF regularly highlight the degree to which macroeconomic balance has been restored, and many academicians concur in this positive assessment of Indonesia's economic performance.

These views, however, reflect only one dimension of reality. In practical terms, Indonesia's economic balance is an unstable transition with growing distortions disguised by the natural resource-driven revival of aggregate economic growth.

Three sets of data illustrate. The first, described in Box 1.3, is the sharp increase in inequality across individuals and provinces, between the rural and urban areas, and between the West and the East of the country. The second is the internal allocation of the budget which is dominated by subsidies, transfers and wage payments, with minimal amounts (relative to the GOI's ambitions for rapid growth) allocated to public investment. The third imbalance is the sharp appreciation of the real exchange rate relative to Indonesia's comparators and competitors.

If the macro economy were balanced, inequality would not be increasing because growth would be inclusive; the budget would allocate expenditure in ways that meet current priorities and expand the capacity for future growth; and the real exchange rate (supported by the overall stance of monetary, fiscal, and debt management policies) would enable Indonesia to remain internationally competitive. That is, the macroeconomic stance as reflected in budget and monetary policies, debt dynamics, and exchange rate management would stimulate rapid, inclusive growth. That is not now the case; moreover with present policies, it cannot be the case.

There are other obvious imbalances. One is the juxtaposition of large coal exports with limited electrification throughout Indonesia. Another is the contrast between Indonesia as the world's largest exporter of palm oil and a major exporter of cocoa, coffee, rubber and several other agricultural-based products, and the 43.5 percent of children under five who are malnourished. Countries with large populations and significantly lower per capita income, such as Vietnam, Ethiopia, Nigeria, and Bangladesh, have lower shares of children under five who are malnourished. In the case of Vietnam and Nigeria, it is significantly lower even though GDP per capita is less.

One trend which reflects the lack of balance more prominently than others has been the relative decline in manufacturing. This reflects economic regression rather than progress since other fast growing countries have increased their manufacturing share. Labor productivity growth has been low. Agricultural output has increased but not in a way that enables food insecurity to be eliminated in the foreseeable future. The persistent real overvaluation of the rupiah has boosted the fortunes of the "new consumer class" which has become increasingly dependent upon subsidized energy and "cheap" imports. Moreover, the majority of jobs created is in the informal sector of the economy. None of these trends reflects balance; nor will any of them foster or sustain inclusive growth.

How competitive is Indonesia's growth?

Indonesia's current positive economic performance and upbeat assessments of Indonesia's future prospects mask serious adverse trends and their long-term implications for economic growth, primarily because they confuse static with dynamic comparative advantage:[41]

- *Static comparative advantage* reflects the economy's performance given its existing structure,[42] its accumulated technology, skills, and knowledge, and the government's policy stance.

- *Dynamic comparative advantage* (also referred to as "multi-period competitiveness") takes into account modifications in productivity and competitiveness as a result of changes over time in the prices of outputs and inputs, shifts in the (social opportunity) costs of productive resources, and variations (positive or negative) in technology.[43]

---

[41]Fedchun (1995); Redding (1997); Findlay (1998); Chinn (2006).

[42]The economy's structure reflects the current: distribution of income and wealth; regional distribution of effective demand/purchasing power; educational accomplishments and skill base of the labor force; risks and costs of gaining access to finance; resources and time required to travel and ship goods and provide services across and between regions; quality of professional and legal services; value of contracts and predictability of their enforcement; degree of access by the ultra-poor to public assistance; functional allocation of public expenditure; incidence and level of taxation; quality of infrastructure, including the reach and reliability of electrification; appropriateness and spread of existing technology; and general state of confidence and trust throughout the economy.

[43]A basic difference between the two is the role of public policy. Static comparative advantage takes the existing policies as given. By contrast, public policy has positive and negative effects on dynamic comparative advantage. Policies directly affect the overall context within which markets operate and the incentives and disincentives which determine how readily and in what direction producers and consumers change their economic behavior.

Relative to its global competitors, Indonesia has a significant static comparative advantage in the production of raw and semi-processed agricultural and mineral products. This reflects its large relative cost advantage in these commodities (even after allowing for diminished profitability due to the overvalued exchange rate). The revenues derived from these products have supported a boom in mine and plantation investment, boosted government receipts, stimulated thriving markets for real estate market and urban services, increased formal sector incomes, and raised consumption expenditure among the middle and upper income groups. This is the economic performance that has received such favorable comment.

But Indonesia has serious static comparative disadvantages. Several dimensions stand out:

- The country's contribution to international manufacturing production and distribution value chains has declined[44] due to the continued high comparative costs for producers of complying with labor regulations and dealing with infrastructure deficiencies, elevated borrowing costs, and the diminished export returns from the overvalued rupiah.
- The slow expansion of formal sector employment is related to labor market restrictions and the cost savings available when imported capital equipment is substituted for labor, stimulated (in part) by exchange rate over-valuation.[45]

---

[44]Nasution (December 5, 2012), Buehler (2013). The resurgence of natural resource exports and declining share of manufactured exports illustrates the interplay of static and dynamic comparative advantage. The incentive structure shifted in ways that favored the immediate rewards from extraction over the longer-term gains from continued industrialization, technology adaptation, and human resource development. Chapter 3 addresses this in detail.

[45]The flip-side of this trend is that the majority of jobs in Indonesia continue to be created in the informal sector because of its flexibility with respect to hours of work, location, activities, benefits, wage rates, and the ease of avoiding/evading labor regulations.

- The rising resource costs of travel and transport can be traced to the combined effects of fuel subsidies and low taxation on vehicles (which increases the number of vehicles) and limited public investment in infrastructure (which leads to congestion).

- The weak integration of markets for goods and services across different regions (and especially between the West and East of Indonesia) results from the low levels of effective demand in regions away from Java/Sumatra and inefficient inter-island transport. The latter is accentuated by regulations that discourage competition.

- The limited use by Indonesians of formal financial services is explained by their high real cost (including risk and time), the poor service offered by formal credit institutions, and the limited public trust in the integrity and soundness of the financial system.

The lavish assessments of the economy's performance referred to earlier exaggerate the economy's comparative advantages and downplay (or ignore) its comparative disadvantages. These assessments especially miss the point when it comes to providing guidance about the economy's future prospects.[46] For that, policy makers and others need to shift their attention to Indonesia's dynamic comparative advantage.

An example will illustrate. Based on relative cost considerations, Indonesia exports in excess of 300 million tons of coal annually. While this activity is fully consistent with the country's static comparative advantage, the countries that import the coal are far more intensively (and reliably) electrified that Indonesia. Among other things, this provides them with the capacity to raise the incomes and welfare of their respec-

---

[46]Asian countries are an obvious example. Writing in the early 1960s, few experts on Singapore, Hong Kong, Korea or Taiwan imagined that these countries would attain upper income status within a generation. Non-Asian examples are Mauritius and Chile. In the early 1970s, both were considered basket cases.

tive populations more rapidly and more inclusively than Indonesia has been (and is) doing. Indonesia would use more of its coal domestically if local effective demand – derived from both the level and distribution of income – were higher.[47] That outcome is precluded in part because of the limited expansion of electricity generation and distribution throughout Indonesia, the direct result of under-investment by the public sector and regulations that deter private investment in these activities.

The result is that while the short-term gains from digging and hauling coal (and other commodities) provide Indonesia's leaders (and visiting commentators) with immense pride in current achievements, the strategy is a dead-end for the country as a whole and the majority of Indonesian people. Similar examples appear throughout this study.

There are two good indicators of Indonesia's decreasing long-term competitiveness.

The first indicator is changes in total factor productivity, or TFP (see Box 1.4 and Annex 2.). The long-term trend in annual TFP changes is negative: from 1970 to 2007, growth in inputs has exceeded GDP growth, subtracting rather than adding value through the application of additional resources. Although the short-term trend has been positive, the changes are still too small to support the 8.5 percent GDP growth rate required to double GDP per capita in a decade: since 2000, TFP has increased by an average of 1.7 percent per year, which, if continued, would support annual GDP growth of between 6 and 7 percent – precisely its recent level.

The second indicator is manufacturing value added per employee (Figure 1.4). The steady decline in this indicator since 2008, despite the increased cost of labor and thus, the shift to the use of relatively more capital-intensive inputs, is a clear sign of falling rather than rising labor

---

[47]Countries often export large amounts of raw materials because of the underdevelopment of their domestic markets, in part because of low effective demand. This is clearly the case in Indonesia with respect to coal.

productivity. This decreases Indonesia's international competitiveness and reduces the likelihood it will move up the global value chain.

Figure 1.4: Manufacturing Value-Added per Employee (USD)

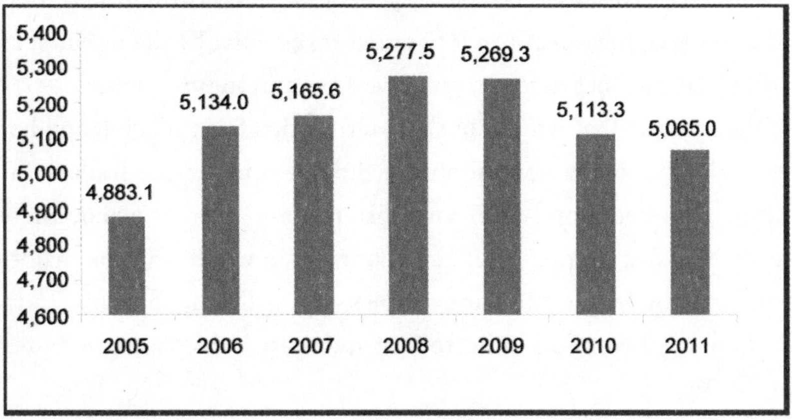

Source: World Bank

Box 1.4: Total Factor Productivity in Indonesia

Total Factor Productivity (TFP) is GDP growth resulting from neither labor nor capital increases. Instead, it is growth from the combined productivity of labor and capital, and can be attributed to better education, improved technology, economies of scale and scope, higher rates of utilization, and removal of cost-increasing regulations.

TFP changes in Indonesia are not encouraging. Given that growth in capital and labor (including the effects of education) in Indonesia is likely to support annual GDP growth of about 5 percent over the next decade, TFP would have to grow at an annual rate of approximately 3.5 percent to double GDP per capita during this period. Not only would such a high TFP growth rate exceed South Korea's annual TFP growth of 3.1 percent during its 1960 to 1989 boom, but as depicted below, changes in TFP from 1970-2007 were actually negative, i.e., GDP growth was less than the growth of inputs. Even the modest 1.7 percent average annual TFP growth since 2000, if continued, would support annual GDP growth of only 6-7 percent.

The movement of additional new workers into high-productivity sectors might raise total GDP growth to 7-8 percent, still not sufficient to achieve the vision of doubling prosperity in a decade.

Annex 2 provides a detailed analysis of TFP trends in Indonesia supporting these conclusions.

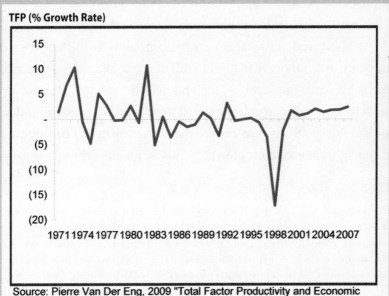

TFP (% Growth Rate)

Source: Pierre Van Der Eng, 2009 "Total Factor Productivity and Economic Growth in Indonesia" - BPS and National Accounts

How fairly has Indonesia grown?

Not only has Indonesia's solid growth performance been based on static rather than dynamic comparative advantage, but it has also been non-inclusive as inequality has risen sharply. Income inequality, measured by the Gini coefficient, has increased, and both the West/East divide and the urban/rural gap have intensified (see Box 1.5). In practical terms, large numbers of people, estimated by the National Statistical Service (Badan Pusat Statistik, BPS) at around 120 million, are being left behind – roughly half of Indonesia's population is not sharing in the nation's growing prosperity.[48]

The GOI has responded by expanding social protection programs, providing supplementary credit, and increasing support for education and health services.[49] Despite their positive impact, these efforts have had minimal effect on inequality. Moreover, none of them directly addresses food insecurity, which is perhaps the most obvious indication that exclusion persists despite robust economic growth.[50]

The implication is that if Indonesia is to be transformed by the "... high, inclusive and sustainable economic growth" as the Government anticipates, much more than recent rates of economic expansion supplemented by social protection programs will be needed. For inclusive growth to materialize, conditions need to be created so that all Indonesians can substantively and continuously participate in, contribute to, and benefit from economic growth.[51] That will require the whole nation,

---

[48]BAPPENAS (2010, Bk 1, p.18). Dervis (2012) noted that exclusion has a global dimension. Per capita incomes for the richest cohorts in developed and emerging countries have converged over recent decades. They have diverged for the poorest cohorts.

[49]These include National Health Insurance for the Poor (Jamkesmas), School Operational Assistance (BOS), Family Hope Program (PKH), Unconditional Cash Transfers (BLT), National Program for Self-Reliant Community Empowerment (PNPM), credit guarantees for micro/small/medium enterprises (UMKM), Microenterprise Credit (KUR), and Temporary Community Direct Assistance (BLSM). In addition, subsidized rice has been distributed to low-income families via the Rice for the Poor Program (RASKIN).

[50]World Bank data show that during the period 2005-2010, 17.5 percent of children under 5 years in Indonesia were malnourished (i.e., below weight-for-age). For upper middle income countries as a group, the corresponding datum was 3 percent (*World Development Indicators* 2012, Table 1.2, pp.25-26). The *Jakarta Globe* (March 27, p.5) reported that "child rights organizations" in Indonesia estimated that 5.4 million children have been abandoned by their families. Few of these are likely to be food secure.

[51]Economic growth is a sustained increase real income per capita. Hill, Khan

persistently and determinedly, to raise the productivity with which it uses all of its productive factors (especially labor) as it becomes and remains more competitive. This study suggests how that might be done.

Box 1.5: Measures and Trends of Inequality in Indonesia

Inequality has worsened in Indonesia, especially since *Krismon*. According to BPS, the national Gini coefficient was 0.31 in 1999, 0.32 in 2004, and 0.37 in 2009. By 2011, it had risen to 0.41. World Bank data show that in 2005, the income share of the lowest 20 percent of the population was 8.3 percent, while the share of the highest 20 percent was 42.8 percent. As the chart below shows, this trend was interrupted by *Krismon* but has continued since then. Estimated Gini coefficients also reveal that income inequality has increased in all provinces. The trend of increasing inequality is reflected in BPS estimates of the Gini ratio for western Indonesia (Sumatra, Java, Bali, Kalimantan) and eastern Indonesia (Sulawesi, NTB, NTT, Papua, Maluku). In the West, it was 0.31 in 2008 and 0.35 in 2010, while in the East it was 0.34 in 2008 and 0.38 in 2010. Income differences are stark within some provinces as well.

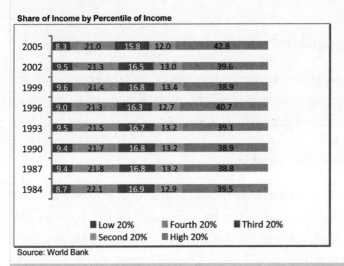

Share of Income by Percentile of Income

Source: World Bank

and Zhuang (2012, p.2) define inclusive growth as "… growth that not only generates economic opportunities, but also ensures equal access to them by all members of a society…." For the World Bank, inclusive growth comprises sustained (economic) growth, the broad sharing of opportunities and benefits of growth, and growth that involves the coherent interaction among all sectors of the economy. For the ADB, inclusive growth combines rising income and equal opportunities (Rauniyar and Kanbur 2010, p. 457).

Growing inequality is evident in other measures. The agriculture/non-agriculture income gap initially narrowed but has increased recently. This was the result of the slow rate of decline in the agricultural workforce and the sharper fall in the contribution of agriculture to GDP. During the period 1981-1990, agricultural employment was 55.2 percent of total employment while the sector's contribution to GDP was 22.7 percent. That is, average per worker income in non-agriculture was 4.2 times above that of agricultural workers. For the period 1991-2000, the multiple was 4.0, but over the decade 2001-2010, it rose to 4.3.

Finally, there are inequalities in the access of both men and women to employment and income. An International Labor Organization study, *Decent Work Country Profile Indonesia* (ILO 2011), highlighted the male/female gaps within particular sectors. Women have a much lower measured labor force participation rate than men. From 1995 to 2010, the national average participation of women was below 40 percent, although for some sectors such as manufacturing, hotels, restaurants, wholesale/retail trade, and personal services it was close to 50 percent. Reported wage inequality was higher for women than for men. The ratio of the top 10 percent to the bottom 10 percent (P90/P10) for men was 5.2 in 2000, 4.7 in 2005, and 6.0 in 2010. Corresponding data for women workers were 9.0, 6.8, and 8.3, respectively.

Comparative Growth Performance

Although Indonesia has experienced periods of elevated growth, as summarized above, it has not attained rapid, sustained, and inclusive growth. Are there comparative experiences that might provide a useful guide?

The Asian Giants: China and India

Since China has had an extended period of double-digit growth, it has been regularly cited as the appropriate comparator by officials, scholars, and business leaders who believe that because of its "demographic dividend" and expanding middle class, Indonesia is poised to grow at rates approaching double digits.[52] China is the only country to have surpassed double digit

---

[52]Indonesia's population structure in 2010 was: 0-14 years, 27 percent; 15-64 years, 67 percent; and 65+ years, 6 percent (*WDI* 2012, Table 2.1). This indicates that Indonesia is already partaking of its "demographic dividend." In less than two decades, the main effect will be over and Indonesia will face the "longevity transition" (i.e., increased survival among the older population). Recent studies show this holds back growth (Eggleston and Fuchs 2012).

growth rates (averaging 10.8 percent per annum from 2000 to 2010) while India, the next highest, had an annual growth rate of 8 percent. Some of the factors that supported China and India's rapid growth were high savings and investment rates. Figure 1.4 provides comparisons among savings and investment rates for China, India, and Indonesia covering the decade 2000 to 2010.

Figure 1.5: Saving and Investment Rates among Regional Peers

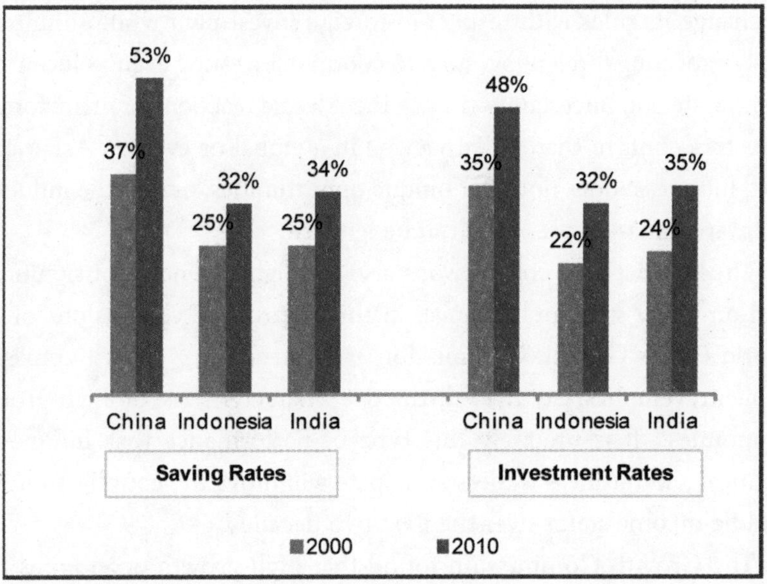

Source: BPS, World Bank

These data show that high sustained growth was associated with rising savings and investment rates. Indonesia clearly had the capacity to raise both rates. Yet, even with an investment rate matching India's, Indonesia's growth rate was lower by more than two percentage points. The implication is that for Indonesia to raise and maintain higher rates of growth above its recent rates, it will have to save and invest a higher share of GDP while simultaneously improving the efficiency of investment and using all of its resources more productively. (Annex 2 considers how this might be done.)

The above comparisons are compelling. China and India combined have ten times Indonesia's population and fewer resources per capita yet have grown at significantly higher rates. In addition to the need for high rates of saving and investment, the comparison serves at least one further purpose. It forcefully dispels the notion – held widely by many policy makers, business leaders, and scholars—that Indonesia is unique and, as such, can selectively ignore the economic measures that sustain rapid growth. A recent example is the resurgent theme of "economic nationalism" (including "food sovereignty"), which has induced the GOI to change its rules with respect to foreign investment while simultaneously expecting foreign investors to continue investing even as incentives deteriorate and uncertainty rises.[53] The adverse reactions of many foreign investors confirm that, when viewed in a global or even an Asian context, Indonesia does not offer unique opportunities, or that the influence of external market pressures can be ignored.

The international comparisons also highlight the need for significant and on-going structural change. In this regard, the conclusions of the World Bank's Growth Commission are instructive.[54] The Commission explicitly emphasized the "distinctive characteristics of high-growth economies." It is precisely this type of performance that Indonesia's political and business leaders anticipate will move the country to upper middle-income status over the next two decades.

The Growth Commission found that high-growth economies had many (but not all) of the following features: close engagement with the global economy; macroeconomic stability; an orientation to the future; high levels of savings and efficient public and private investment; market incentives and decentralization; rapid diversification and emphasis on productive employment; continuing structural transformation; high rates of urbanization; and resource mobility across sectors—especially of labor.

---

[53]Other examples appear elsewhere in the study. They include the decision to close the Jakarta port to horticultural imports, the dispossession of Churchill Mining, and the banning of raw rattan exports.

[54]World Bank (2008), with Supplementary Report by Brady and Spence (2010).

These changes were supported by improving governance; a stable and functional investment environment; decisive political leadership and effective, pragmatic and (when needed) activist government; a multi-decade vision, which reflected appropriate development strategies and priorities; the willingness to experiment, act in the face of uncertainty about policy impacts, and avoid (policy) paralysis; sequential decision-making under uncertainty with learning; a persistent and determined focus on inclusive growth; and a government that acts in the interests of all the citizens of the country—as opposed to the interests of its officials, or selected subgroups of the population. When viewed in broad terms, these features reflect a pragmatic combination of sensible economics and constructive politics.

This is an extensive agenda. A major conclusion of the Growth Commission's study is that the changes do not have to (and, indeed, cannot) be made simultaneously. Indonesia has many of the financial, human, institutional, and organizational capacities to make progress. Implementing the agenda will help strengthen the relevant capacities over time. It is here that specific examples of the development experience of selected Asian countries, especially those that made the transition to sustained, rapid, and inclusive growth, illustrate the issues that should be stressed and how they can be effectively sequenced.

The East and Southeast Asian Development Experiences

Countries in East Asia (Japan, South Korea, and Taiwan) achieved sustained growth at close to double digit rates over extended periods. There are many examples elsewhere in the world where rapid economic growth occurred for a decade and more, but no other major region has seen some of its countries progress from low to high income status in less than a generation.[55]

---

[55]Saich *et al.* (2010, pp. 11-17, 27-44).

For a country to move from a Purchasing Power Parity GDP of $2,000 per capita to over $20,000 within three decades, its GDP per capita needs to grow at an annual rate of 8 percent. Rates of growth of this magnitude over a period of three decades in countries starting at $2,000 or even $4,000 per capita will only materialize through the rapid rise of industry generally, and manufacturing in particular. Agriculture needs to expand but it can never grow at sustained rates anywhere near 8 percent per annum. Modern business and financial services need to grow as well, but services cannot (and do not) lead growth in the early decades of this transformation.[56]

The following discussion concentrates on the experience of South Korea, with occasional references to Japan, Taiwan, Singapore, and Hong Kong. Japan's industrialization experience was well advanced by WWII. The years between 1914 and 1945 were a period when foreign trade was inhibited by trade wars and shooting wars, a sharp contrast with the era that began in the late 1940s, when the world economy was open and international trade was expanding rapidly.[57] Singapore and Hong Kong were major international ports long before WWII, so the infrastructure and institutions needed to support international trade were in place. Moreover, both had a long history of free trade.

South Korea was different. It had suffered total destruction of its urban housing and national infrastructure during the Korean War and was heavily dependent on foreign aid, mainly from the United States, for its survival. The policies of the government were geared to maximizing

---

[56]Services only begin to lead economic growth when an economy surpasses $20,000 per capita, and no country at that level of income has managed to sustain a GDP per capita growth rate of more than 4 percent per year. In East Asia, services growth has begun to dominate in Hong Kong, Singapore, and increasingly in Japan, South Korea, and Taiwan. Indonesia is nowhere close to their stage of development.

[57]This limits the relevance of Japan's experience since much of their early stage growth occurred during the inter-war period. Lockwood (1954) has an analysis of this period.

the dollar amount of foreign aid and included an overvalued exchange rate. Politics governed key economic policies in that trade with Japan was prohibited.

All of this changed in 1960-61 with the fall of the Syngman Rhee government, a brief democratic interlude, and a military coup that ushered in 26 years of authoritarian rule by former generals. Our interest here is what these governments did to promote industry because, as history has shown, the policies pursued were for the most part highly successful.

The Park Chung Hee government started from the political proposition that it did not want to have the country's sovereignty limited by dependence on foreign aid. To end aid dependence, it was necessary to earn foreign exchange through exports. South Korea lacked natural resources and the rice exports of the Japanese colonial period disappeared with land reform (with Koreans consuming all locally produced rice). That left only manufactures as a realistic basis for export expansion.

The steps that Korea took to promote manufactures, and manufactured exports in particular, illustrate how a country can accelerate industrial growth.[58] These included:

- Devaluing the exchange rate. For the most part, the Korean won was undervalued for the next three decades.
- Ending the prohibition of trade with Japan, even although this was politically unpopular.
- Utilizing regulations to promote business in general and exports in particular, rather than simply sweeping away these regulations and creating a level market-driven playing field.[59]

---

[58]Eichengreen *et al.* (2012) have an up-to-date study of the Korean growth experience.

[59]This was in response to a government bureaucracy that was riddled with rules and regulations that made it difficult for business to gain access to foreign exchange to im-

- Giving government leaders a high degree of discretionary authority over the economy, without the decisions being dominated by rent-seeking and outright corruption. This was possible because economic failure would have threatened the country's existence. When that threat receded in the 1990s, rent-seeking played an increasing role in industrial policy decisions and contributed to major losses during the 1997-1998 AFC.

- Partially rebuilding the country's basic infrastructure with foreign aid after the end of the Korean War in 1953, although that infrastructure was poor. By the early 1970s, there was one high-speed limited access highway from Seoul to Pusan, but most of the other roads outside the major cities were dirt and rocks where speeds above 25 kph were difficult.[60] Electric power generation, however, increased by 19 percent a year from the end of 1962 through 1978 and the share of electric power going to manufacturing rose from 52 percent in 1964 to 72 percent in 1978.[61]

- Imposing restrictions that made it difficult for Foreign Direct Investment (FDI) to enter and play an important role in the development of the country's manufacturing sector and in manufactured exports. The argument for these restrictions was that any liberalization of the rules would lead to the return of Japanese dominance over the local economy, something that was politically unacceptable. This policy did not begin to change until after the AFC.[62]

---

port needed inputs. Many rules and regulations were rewritten so that exporters gained favored access to foreign exchange. Moreover, the President made special efforts to reduce barriers resulting from government bureaucracy. Companies successful in meeting the government's production/export goals were given favored access to bank loans. This approach created weak banks, which in turn led to periodic financial crises requiring regular restructuring of the banks.

[60]Dwight Perkins, personal experience. See also Keidel (1981).

[61]Economic Planning Board, Major Statistics of Korean Economy (1982, p.117); Economic Planning Board, Handbook of Korean Economy (1980, p. 329).

[62]Elsewhere in Northeast Asia, notably in Hong Kong and in China, FDI has been

What do the industrial development experiences of South Korea and the other economies of Northeast Asia reveal about achieving rapid growth? The first thing to note is that Korea (and Taiwan, Japan, and China) got some of the most important things right:[63]

- **_Exchange rate_**: They made sure that the exchange rate was favorable to the export of manufactures—it was never overvalued and most of the time it was probably significantly undervalued.

- **_Infrastructure_**: Improvements in infrastructure were made over time. Korea had a poor transport system until the middle of the second decade of its industrial push. China's infrastructure from roads to railroads to electric power lagged well behind domestic demand during the first two decades of its post-1978 reform period. In the late 1990s, however, China introduced an expansion program that has transformed its infrastructure to first world status.[64] Essentially, when the transportation infrastructure is inadequate, the growth of manufacturing tends to concentrate in limited parts of the country (in and around Seoul in Korea, and on the coast in China). As the quality of transport infrastructure improves throughout the country, the other areas are able to join in the industrial boom. Electricity shortages, on the other hand, lead to blackouts in factories, lost production, and rising costs.

---

welcome and has played an important role in upgrading the quality and technology of Chinese manufactures, in improving business practices, and in providing access to foreign markets (with over half of Chinese manufactured exports coming from foreign-owned companies.).

[63]Dwight H. Perkins (forthcoming 2013) has an in-depth discussion of the development strategies pursued by East and Southeast Asia economies.

[64]In the 1980s and 1990s, electric power production lagged behind GDP growth at around 8 percent per year and shortages were common. Since 2000, however, the growth rate of electric power has increased to 12 percent per year (Perkins 2013).

- *Doing business*: The methods used by Japan, Korea, and Taiwan to create a favorable low-cost environment for doing business worked for them, but similar practices will not work well where rent-seeking and corruption characterize government intervention. Most governments that actively intervene at the discretion of individual officials have a high level of corruption with concomitant high costs of doing business. For most countries, it makes much more sense to limit government intervention in business and rely as much as possible on market forces to stimulate investment, production, and sales.[65]

- *FDI*: There were costs to the interventionist approach in Northeast Asia that did not derail growth but caused periodic crises and recessions. Probably the most serious was government-directed bank lending that typically led to high levels of non-performing loans, weak banks, and a shallow financial system. These accentuated Korea's problems during the AFC.[66] FDI can be a powerful force for increasing the quality of output, improving technology, and gaining access to foreign markets.[67] Singapore, Hong Kong, and China have all encouraged FDI.[68]

---

[65]The methods often used by Japan, Korea, and Taiwan for intervening to support particular industries and firms now contravene the rules of the World Trade Organization.

[66]It also explains (in part) Japan's stagnation since the stock market and real estate crash in 1991.

[67]As Korea, Taiwan, and Japan demonstrated, there are substitutes that can replace some of what FDI offers (large trading companies as in Japan, connections between domestically-owned firms and foreign wholesale and retail outlets, etc.), but these arrangements require close ties between domestic producers and foreign purchasers. It is sometimes more efficient to encourage FDI rather than develop these links.

[68]Governments find FDI to be a problem only when they are unable to regulate the foreign firms in ways that meet the needs of the country rather than the corrupt needs of particular individuals in the government and in the foreign enterprises.

The general point is that an effective industrial development and manufactured export expansion strategy has to get some things right, but it does not have to get everything right at the same time. Most of the Northeast Asian economies did some things in this area either immediately (in the case of exchange rate policy) or over time (in the case of infrastructure). Although all of the countries could have done better, they eventually did what was necessary to induce and sustain high rates of growth. The other general point is that the relationship between the government and the private (or state-owned) business sector needs to create a level and low-cost playing field for the participating firms. Some governments can accomplish this through a high level of intervention in the economy, but most cannot.

What Might Indonesia Learn?

Even though its economy in 2013 differs from that of the Northeast Asian comparators, Indonesia could benefit from these international experiences, as follows:

- *Exchange rate*: Over the last decade, Indonesia has allowed high natural resource prices to seriously overvalue its exchange rate. This has contributed to two adverse trends: manufacturing exports have stagnated, and industrial growth overall is less than half what it was in the 1980s and early 1990s.[69]

- *Infrastructure*: Little has been done to improve infrastructure. Transport infrastructure is poor—seaports are overcrowded and inefficient, and trunk roads between major cities are narrow, dangerous, and congested. It is far cheaper for most parts of Indonesia to

---

[69]Manufactured exports were 57 percent of total exports in 2000 and 37 percent in 2010 (*WDI* 2012, Table 4.4, p.227).

ship to Singapore than to Jakarta or any other destination within Indonesia. The state-owned electric power production, transmission, and distribution system requires a major overhaul and expansion.

- **Doing business**: The World Bank Ease of Doing Business Index ranks Indonesia 129 out of 183 countries.[70] Much of the liberalization achieved during the 1980s is still in place and though formal impediments have increased, they have not blocked trade. In contrast, Transparency International's Corruption Perceptions Index rates Indonesia's law courts, local governments, and politicians as among the most corrupt in Asia.[71]

- **Education**: Indonesia has rapidly expanded education at all levels, but started from one of the weakest human capital bases in all of East and Southeast Asia. This expansion has involved a large increase in the quantity of education. Education quality, however, is well below that of most of the region.

Drawing on these observations, Indonesia could make more progress in achieving its development objectives of moving to higher rates of inclusive growth and sustaining them (see Box 1.1) by taking decisive action to improve its overall productivity and competitiveness.

This will require action to revamp its infrastructure, to realign its exchange rate, re-integrate the economy with international production/ distribution value chains, strengthen its internal economic integration, boost opportunities for productive work, and raise the quality of its education.

---

[70]The recently released Global Competitiveness Report showed that Indonesia continues to slide in world competitiveness rankings (Schwab 2011, 2012; WEF 2012).

[71]Transparency International ranks Indonesia 100 out of 183 countries reviewed (TPI 2011, p.4). See also Buehler (2012).

There are many proposals as to how the various technical requirements might be met. The challenge, which this study addresses, is how to ensure that what is technically feasible will be politically acceptable and accepted. In this regard, the most demanding element will be to generate and sustain the political arrangements to formulate and sustainably implement the policies and programs (such as upgrade the country's infrastructure, improve the quality of education, and so on) that will raise the productivity and competitiveness of all Indonesians so that the country can grow more rapidly and inclusively.

Study Context and Organization

This study is a sequel to Saich *et al.* (2010). It builds on the previous report's assessment of Indonesia's growth trajectory and identifies possible policy responses to Indonesia's current and anticipated development challenges. It is the product of collaboration between scholars from Harvard University and Indonesia, including a considerable amount of empirical field research.

Each team member was asked to identify the factors likely to promote rapid, sustained, and inclusive growth in Indonesia over the coming decades, and those that are likely to hinder it. Team members visited numerous districts, municipalities, and provinces and met with members of civil society, scholars, government officials, and business men and women to elicit their views on the prospects for promoting rapid, sustained, and inclusive growth. The team has benefited from discussions with mayors (*walikota*) and district heads (*bupati*), as well as with their planning agency heads (*ketua bappeda*) who attended the Harvard Kennedy School Indonesia Program (HKSIP) Transformasi (Leadership Transformation in Indonesia) Executive Education Program. Members of the international donor community and commercial legations from several countries generously contributed their perspectives as well. The team also benefited from valuable insights of Indonesia specialists based at the Australian National University.

The research and this report have been organized around three inter-related themes and one cross-cutting sub-theme. The themes are: reducing the resource costs of transactions and logistics; extending and integrating the domestic market; and promoting productive work. A cross-cutting theme is effective implementation. Supplementary discussions on related topics are included in boxes and annexes throughout the text. This additional material has enabled us to include ideas, notions, and issues that emerged during the discussions by team members with the (several hundred) Indonesians interviewed during the course of the research.

This study evaluates the short-term success and long-term prospects of Indonesia's growth to date, applying the metrics of speed, sustainability, and equity; drills down into the weaknesses of Indonesia's current growth path; and offers policy alternatives to address these weaknesses.

The study is arranged as follows:

* **Chapter 2** proposes an agenda for accelerating sustainable and inclusive growth via local and global economic integration. This will require integration and extension of Indonesia's domestic market and broad-based expansion of productive employment opportunities. Both of these have been done at different times in Indonesia's history, but never simultaneously and never on a sustained basis. Together, they will support rapid, sustained, and inclusive growth because they will create the conditions that will enable all Indonesians in all regions to productively participate in, contribute to, and benefit from economic development. The chapter concludes by identifying policy initiatives that will support integration and extension of the domestic market. These are a pragmatic blend of sensible economics and constructive politics: reducing logistics and transaction costs by improving hard and soft infrastructure; boosting productive work by investing in human capital and enabling optimization of human resources; and improving implementation capabilities by enhancing intergovernmental administrative and fiscal relations.

- *Chapter 3* analyzes how logistics and transaction costs can be reduced through improved hard and soft infrastructure, that is, better physical infrastructure and better government. Roads, ports, and energy, with a special focus on electrification, are examined to demonstrate the improvements in hard infrastructure will reduce logistics costs. The financial system and improvements in governance designed to enhance trust and confidence are examined to indicate how transaction costs can be lowered.

- *Chapter 4* examines productive work in Indonesia, and how it both benefits from and contributes to activities that integrate and extend the domestic market. Productive work is also boosted through improvements in hard infrastructure, diminished food insecurity, the revival of manufacturing, and the expansion of enterprise and entrepreneurship. This chapter discusses some of the factors that diminish employment opportunities, such as regulations and restrictions on market access, and suggests ways to mitigate these factors. It concludes by reviewing how higher quality education and intensification of "extracurricular learning" can support improvements in productivity and competitiveness.

- *Chapter 5* discusses key dimensions of the political system and governance arrangements in Indonesia. Topics examined include the relationship between the executive and the legislature, efforts being made to promote bureaucratic reform, and negotiations between the central and local governments to resolve jurisdiction issues involving mining rights. This chapter concludes with suggestions on reorganizing center-province-local administrative and fiscal arrangements that would help promote rapid inclusive growth.

- *Chapter 6* closes out the study by delineating reactive, proactive, and transformational policy alternatives, with only the third option providing a path to rapid, sustained, and inclusive growth in Indonesia. This third option highlights the need to shift policies from the current focus on static comparative advantage to the growth-related aspects of dynamic comparative advantage and multi-period competitiveness.

- *Annexes* provide additional data and analysis that supplement and support the main text.

CHAPTER TWO
A Strategy for Accelerating Sustainable, Inclusive Growth:
Local and Global Economic Integration

Rwâneka dhâtu winuwus Buddha Wiswa,
Bhinnêki rakwa ring apan kena parwanosen,
Mangka ng Jinatwa kalawan Siwatatwa tunggal,
Bhinnêka tunggal ika tan hana dharma mangrwa.

It is said that the well-known Buddha and Shiva are two different
substances.
They are indeed different, yet how is it possible to recognize their dif-
ference in a glance,
since the truth of Jina (Buddha) and the truth of Shiva is one.
They are indeed different, but they are of the same kind, as there is no
duality in truth.

MPU TANTULAR

The Binding Constraint in Accelerating Sustainable, Inclusive Growth

The binding constraint to doubling shared prosperity in a decade through the acceleration of sustainable, inclusive growth is that Indonesia exploits neither the advantages of being a large country nor its dynamic comparative advantage. Indonesia does not reap the benefits of being a large country because it is a collection of disconnected local and regional markets rather than an integrated single market – it is beset by *local economic fragmentation*. Indonesia fails to exploit its dynamic comparative advantage because its growth is dependent on commodities and old industries instead of high value-added products in the global supply chain – it is characterized by *global economic marginalization*. The key to addressing both of these problems is essentially the same, namely better *hard infrastructure* (ports, power, roads), *soft infrastructure* (government and governance), and *wet infrastructure* (human resources).

Local Economic Fragmentation

Bhinneka Tunggal Ika – Unity in Diversity

The quotation cited above is taken from the 14th century Javanese poem, Kakawin Sutasoma, written during the "Golden Age" of the Majapahit Kingdom. This poem is well known for promoting tolerance between Buddhists and Hindus. It is also the source of Indonesia's national motto, *"Bhinneka Tunggal Ika,"* or "Unity in Diversity," which is included in both the Indonesian national symbol (Garuda Pancasila) and the Constitution (Article 36A).

Indonesia has made great strides in building a unified political national identity out of an archipelago of incredible cultural, ethnic, and religious diversity. However, there is not a similar aspiration to integrate the Indonesian archipelago economically, no national policy to create a single economic entity from many regional markets. Historically, the goal of political unity has been pushed without a concomitant recognition that the country's future also depends on economic integration: while the unity of Indonesia has been a political imperative, it has not been an economic one. Consequently, at present, the sum is worth less than the parts.

Lack of an Integrated Domestic Economy

Indonesia does not have an integrated domestic economy.[72] Domestic economic activity consists of a weakly connected set of loosely overlapping market domains. It is readily illustrated by the sharp divergence across regions in labor market conditions, financial depth, and price differential for key staple commodities. This feature has been, and remains, perhaps the most prominent enduring structural deficiency in Indonesia's development activities.

It is evident in numerous ways:

- shipping costs;[73]
- limited inter-regional trade;[74]
- price differentials and market fragmentation;[75]
- barriers to transport and trade;[76] and
- substantial regional differences in average earnings.[77]

---

[72]The statement by Dick *et al.* (2002, p.244) that "…Java and the Outer Islands are no longer just a collection of island or sub-island economies but a single economic unit" has no basis in fact, when it was written, or now.

[73]Dick (1985); LPEM-FEUI (2010); ESCAP (2011).

[74]Firdaus and Widyansanti (2010); Sandee (2011).

[75]Alexander and Wyeth (1994); Istiqomah (2006); Sumantri and Lau (2011); Verala, Aldaz-Carroll and Iacovone (2012).

[76]Lubis *et al.* (2005); Sjafruddin *et al.* (2010); Strategic Asia (2012).

[77]Corwell and Anas (2013).

Without an integrated dynamic domestic market, Indonesia has systematically missed the opportunity to benefit from having a large population. More importantly, much of the country's large population has been systematically excluded from the benefits of growth and development.

The original "patterns of growth" literature distinguished countries with large populations precisely because of the advantages of scale and scope derived from their large internal market.[78] Indonesia has failed to take advantage of its large population and generally has few interregional demand spillovers. This has undermined the country's capacity for income generation and employment creation.[79]

The losses have been enormous.

First, lack of internal connectedness implies that a significant share of Indonesia's increasing incomes directly spills over to benefit Malaysia, Singapore, Vietnam, China, among others. Riau trades more with Malaysia and Singapore than with Java and Bali; Kalimantan trades more with China and Japan than with Java and Sumatra; Batam is more closely connected to Singapore and Korea than to Java.[80]

Second, as Adam Smith observed, weak market integration is self-reinforcing; constraints on market size and its limited spread reduce the incentive to specialize: "When the market is very small, no person can have an encouragement to dedicate himself entirely to one employment..."[81] This lowers the potential for productivity growth.

Third, restricted opportunities for employment expansion keep the domestic labor market fragmented and incomes low, thereby reducing

---

[78]Chenery and Syrquin (1975); Syrquin and Chenery (1989).
[79]Firdaus and Widyansanti (2010); BAPPENAS (2011).
[80]Firdaus and Widyansanti (2010).
[81]Smith (1776, p.17).

the growth of inter-island commerce. The unit costs of transport for both goods and people remain high, which further reduces the incentives for this type of exchange.[82]

Fourth, the rudimentary nature of the current division of labor in Indonesia, as well as the limited capacity to raise productivity through specialization, reinforce the existing unequal distribution of income and opportunity across the country's different regions. Too many of Indonesia's workers (more than 6 out of 10) are competing among themselves for low productivity informal work. Moreover, by having to split their time among several informal tasks to earn a livelihood, these workers cannot gain from specialization.

Fifth, following from the example of coal exports above, the limited spread of electrification due to inadequate public investment reaffirms the perception that labor productivity is "normally" low. This assessment reinforces the argument regularly made by public officials that scarce public resources should not be "wasted" providing public services where workers have low productivity.[83] This argument confuses static with dynamic comparative advantage.

Sixth, macroeconomic management fragments the domestic market because the major economic institutions, such as Bank Indonesia and the Ministry of Finance, attempt to manage the economy as if one-size-fits-all. Their approach to monetary, fiscal, and exchange rate policies is structured as if Indonesia were a coherent, integrated market.[84] This approach is misguided on two counts: all large integrated economies

---

[82]Sullivan and Diwyanto (2007); LPEM-FEUI (2010). The recent deregulation of the airlines has demonstrated the rapidity and breadth of the private sector response to improving regional connectivity in Indonesia, notwithstanding the problem or regulation and safety (Tedjasukmana 2007; Budhrani 2010; SMH 2012). These governance issues will be addressed as institutions strengthen (Saich *et al.* 2010; Andrews 2013).

[83]A senior official of BAPPENAS made this argument during a discussion of public investment with our team.

[84]Ridhwan (2011, 2011a).

(the European Union, the United States, Brazil, Australia, Canada) have nuanced policy stances so that all regions and sectors do not operate within a single policy strait jacket; and the basic operating assumptions of these key central agencies so far has been that, in policy terms, the whole of Indonesia behaves and responds largely like Java and Bali.[85]

Although the lack of attention to extending the domestic market in Indonesia has been a drag on growth and development, that situation need not persist. Extending and integrating the domestic market – systematically, coherently and sustainably – provides Indonesia with the prospects of rapid inclusive growth for decades to come.

One way of understanding why (and how) is to examine Indonesia's growth potential within an economic geography framework. A number of relevant sources are available.[86] One of these is the World Bank's 2009 World Development Report "Reshaping Economic Geography."[87] It provides fruitful insights on (a) why Indonesia's domestic market is so weakly integrated; (b) how the degree of integration can be strengthened; and (c) how national productivity and competitiveness can be boosted in the process.

The Report identifies three determinants of the spatial pattern of growth and development: economic density, economic distance, and economic and social division.[88]

Economic density refers to income or expenditure per unit area (e.g., gross domestic product per square kilometer). Income generation tends

---

[85]An example, discussed further in Chapter 3, highlights the inadequacy of this policy. During *Krismon*, Kalimantan, Sulawesi, and the resource-rich provinces in Sumatra (e.g., Riau) experienced rapid growth due largely to a much depreciated currency. Java, which was the epicenter of the financial chicanery and excess, collapsed.

[86]Krugman (1991); Grigg (1995); Wu and Gopinath (2008).

[87]World Bank (2009).

[88]"Rising densities of human settlements, migration of workers and entrepreneurs to shorten the distance to markets, and lower divisions caused by differences in currencies and conventions between countries are central to successful economic development" (World Bank 2009, p.12).

to concentrate in well-defined locations due to economies of scale and agglomeration effects - scale refers to the volume of economic transactions, while agglomeration effects result from the inter-connections among transactions. These produce cost advantages, such as lower input costs, particularly for information. They also increase the rewards, through higher output prices or wages, for those who operate in, or adjacent to, high density areas.

Economic distance is a measure of the resource cost of bridging the physical, time, and information gaps across space, particularly between areas of high economic density and lagging areas (i.e., those with low density). Distance is also measured as the resource cost (time, effort, equipment charges) of travel or transport between two locations.

Economic and social division relates to barriers and impediments to economic transactions between regions, or districts within regions, due to formal and informal restrictions on trade and commerce, regulatory obstacles, and ethnic differences. Other barriers include traditional rivalries, antipathy, and lack of trust. When applied to nation states, the cost and risk of currency conversion are relevant as well. That issue is important in Indonesia – the Singapore dollar is widely used in Batam, the US dollar is accepted everywhere, and the ringgit is common in Sumatra and Kalimantan.

Examining variations in patterns of growth and development using a density, distance, and division framework leads to several conclusions: [89]

- Economic development is spatially uneven. Particular locations tend to acquire an advantage as a market, transshipment point, port, raw material source, or administrative center. These advantages often cumulate over time.
- Markets shape the economic landscape. Markets take time to develop and deepen but once established, benefit from urban growth,

---

[89]World Bank (2009).

population mobility, and vibrant trade. These changes are consequences of extending the market referred to earlier. Once development is under way, the division of labor, and specialization it implies, is driven by and, in turn, leads to further extension of the market.

- Human capital moves to where it is abundant, not to where it is scarce. This is an outcome of knowledge and information spillovers. A person's knowledge and skills are more valuable in settings where there are many other people with knowledge and skills. This outcome is consistent with theories of collective action and teamwork. Adding a productive person to a team raises his/her output and that of the team.[90]

- Declining transport costs enhance the benefits of specialization and increased production scale. These benefits promote trade and exchange with neighboring regions (and countries) rather than with those that are more distant.

The Report concludes with a number of policy suggestions from which Indonesia could benefit. Since economic activity tends to concentrate geographically due to agglomeration effects, spillovers from skills and knowledge, and economies of scale in production, the quest for *national* development involves having the government generate resources in areas of high economic density and use them to promote development more broadly.

Doing this requires: the creation of **spatially-blind institutions** that avoid regional or location biases; the promotion of **spatially-networked investments** to integrate more closely regions and districts; and the formulation of **spatially-targeted interventions** that encourage social and human development throughout the country. These conclusions provide

---

[90]Olson (1965, 1998); Radner 1998).

a compelling case for inclusive growth and development derived from extending and integrating the domestic market.

Some of the above activities are already underway in Indonesia. Resources are being raised in high density regions and disbursed to lower density regions through the budget. In addition, the decentralization of administrative authorities has resulted in a growing number of nation-wide interventions, primarily with respect to health, education, and social protection. But when viewed more broadly, Indonesia is falling well short of having spatially-blind institutions as well as spatially-networked and spatially-targeted investments. It is these deficiencies, especially the latter, which keep transport and communication costs high throughout the country and keep the domestic market fragmented. These deficiencies directly limit productivity growth and undermine the capacity of workers, firms, and regions to improve their competitiveness.

Global Economic Marginalization

Although Indonesia's connections with international manufacturing production and distribution value chains broadened and deepened substantially following the acceleration of manufacturing activity in the mid-1980s, Indonesia has undergone a steady and significant disengagement from these international value chains. This trend, like local economic fragmentation, undermines Indonesia's efforts to achieve rapid, sustained, and inclusive growth.

The trends from 1985 to 2000 were quite encouraging, as the manufacturing as a share of GDP rose from 16 percent to 27.7 percent, and the share of manufacturing exports in total exports rose from 13 percent to 57.1 percent.[91]

Perhaps the most dramatic evidence of Indonesia's increasing integration with the international economy, as described in detail in the Har-

---

[91]World Bank MetaData series (online).

vard Kennedy School prequel to this study as a major source of growth [92] was the sharp rise in Indonesia's contribution to trade in manufactured products. World Bank data show that in 1990, Indonesia's share of world-wide manufactured exports was 0.4 percent. By 2000, that share had doubled to 0.8 percent. Relative to lower middle income countries, Indonesia's share was 7 percent in 1990 and 24 percent in 2000.[93] Data for manufactured imports (the flip side of the value chain) show similar trends.[94] This experience is entirely consistent with the patterns observed in North Asian countries discussed in Chapter One.

Recent changes in Indonesia have run counter to those trends. This is evident in the country's systematic disengagement from international production and distribution value chains during the resource boom.

Several trends stand out. From 2000 to 2010, the share of manufacturing in GDP declined from 27.7 percent to 24.8 percent, and manufacturing exports as a share of total exports fell from 57.1 percent to 37.5 percent.

A key reason for the drop in export share has been the slow growth of the volume of Indonesia's exports. At the same time as numerous other competitors and comparators were experiencing robust annual growth in the volume of exports, Indonesia recorded a growth rate of just 0.8 percent. In contrast, other growth rates were much higher:

- China (20.5 percent) and India (11.4 percent);
- South Korea (12.1 percent), Singapore (10.2 percent), and Japan (5.2 percent); and
- Vietnam (11.4 percent), Thailand (7.2 percent), and Malaysia (5.5 percent).[95]

---

[92]Saich *et al.* (2010, pp. 11-17, 27-44).

[93]Computed from WDI 2003, Tables 4.5, 4.6 and WDI 2012, Tables 4.4, 4.5.

[94]Indonesia's share of world merchandise imports was 0.7 percent in 1990 and 0.9 percent in 2000. Its share of LMIC merchandise imports was 8 percent in 1990 and 28 percent in 2000.

[95]WDI 2012, Table 6.1, pp.338-341.

This low growth, in both absolute and relative terms, is reflected in the drop in Indonesia's contribution to merchandise exports both world-wide and relative to lower middle income countries: in 2010, it was 0.6 percent and 12 percent, respectively, down from the 0.8 percent and 24 percent shares cited above.[96]

As noted in Chapter One, Indonesia's disengagement from these international value chains would have few consequences if the manu-facturing output had been displaced by the expansion of high-value services. That was not the case.[97] Furthermore, from the discussion in Chapter Four, Indonesia is unlikely to have much success in promoting high-value services until it raises the quality of its education and the capacity of its population for learning and knowledge generation. The share of people using the internet, for example, is half that of Vietnam.

The most disconcerting aspect of the declining economic contri-bution of manufacturing in Indonesia is that it has been replaced by resource extraction which, despite the extraordinary though temporary increases in prices over the last decade, does not provide a viable foun-dation for rapid sustained inclusive growth.

Local and Global Economic Integration

As noted at the beginning of this chapter, the antidote for both local economic fragmentation and global economic marginalization is the same: better hard, soft, and wet infrastructure. The crux of this premise is summarized below, and the next two chapters explore the strategy in detail.

---

[96]Indonesia's share of LMIC merchandise imports fell from 28 percent in 2000 to 13 percent in 2000.

[97]Although they grew rapidly (from a small base), Indonesia's "commercial service exports" lost share over the period 2000 to 2010 relative to LMIC, countries in East Asia and Pacific, and South Asia (WDI 2012, Table 4.6, pp.234-237).

Improved Inter-Connectivity and Better Governance

Extending and integrating the domestic market, and linking it better
to global value chains, can promote and sustain rapid inclusive growth
in several ways. All of them relate to activities (or actions) that reduce
economic distance and/or diminish the barriers to trade and exchange.
Increasing economic density has some spillover and multiplier effects
but these are typically weak.[98]

In Indonesia, public policy can extend markets by improving the
transport system, particularly its inter-connectivity. This will require
investments in ports, roads, railways, bridges, airports, ferries, freighters, telecommunication linkages, and electrification. It will also require
the removal of anti-competitive regulations so that cost-effective travel,
transport, and movement of goods and services are possible throughout
the entire country. Since the GOI already highlighted transport system
challenges when it formulated MP3EI, there should be little official hesi-
tation in making such investments, even if details need to be worked out
regarding source of financing and magnitude of investments, as well as
the specific timing and location of these investments.

By making such investments, Indonesia would be following the well-
worn paths of upper middle income countries. To stimulate their growth
and development, these countries invested heavily in building a modern
transport system. This strategy benefited all of them in numerous ways.
The investment stimulated economic activity, boosted employment, and
raised incomes. In the process, it created the physical capital or "back-
bone" for the economy which enabled it to progress in self-reinforcing

---

[98]A strategy to increase economic density is "trickle down" development. Its non-inclusive effects have been well demonstrated by Indonesia's historical pattern of growth.
Indeed, some of the first theories of the dualism between areas of high economic density
and low economic density were developed in Indonesia. The widening West/East divide
in Indonesia is an all-too-obvious contemporary example.

ways.[99] Perhaps the greatest advantage of such broad-based improvements in connectivity was that by lowering the costs of communicating, interacting, and transacting, infrastructure development expanded the opportunities for every citizen. In doing so, it enhanced the economy's capacity for inclusive growth.

The extension of the market can also be fostered by diminishing the barriers to exchange. Across Indonesia, participation in particular markets is restricted often arbitrarily. Examples include inter-island livestock sales, pharmaceutical compounding, steel production, and the importation of diesel fuel, rice, cloves, wheat, flour, and numerous other commodities. Indonesians were once highly critical (even if most of the criticism was muted) when Tommy Suharto was granted the clove monopoly.[100] That era of impunity, in principle, is meant to have ended. Removing the arbitrary restrictions on market participation in Indonesia would enhance competitiveness. This would expand the opportunities for local entrepreneurs, producers and distributors to increase their productivity and add value.

Many officials who promulgate regulations and restrictions can often point to public safety and security concerns. Influence peddling aside, the current system could readily be reformed through the use of negative lists and by allowing markets, especially for inter-island trade and exchange services to be openly and transparently contested. With this approach, the only remaining barriers to trade and exchange would be those which serve a transparently demonstrated and widely agreed public purpose.

Extending the market as suggested above would have a significant impact on productive work. It would raise the expected net returns to labor (i.e., the earnings of labor after deducting the associated produc-

---

[99]This is a major theme of the World Bank's 1994 World Development Report "Infrastructure for Development" (World Bank 1994).

[100]Thee (2012, pp. 233-234).

tion expenses, including logistics costs, and allowances for risk). These net returns would rise for several reasons: [101]

- The improved infrastructure and diminished barriers would increase the demand for locally-produced commodities. This would raise their price and profitability.
- The improved infrastructure would reduce the costs of importing output-enhancing inputs.
- The expansion of economic activity would provide local producers with the incentive to increase their scale of production, leading to learning-by-doing and learning-by-exchanging, and improve the quality of their output.
- With increased output and a growing range of profitable activities, every worker would be motivated to upgrade his/her skills. Some of this would take the form of specialized (formal) training. Much of it, however, would be "extra-curricular learning" that strengthens the knowledge base of the economy and benefits the whole population.

Indonesia's Master Plan for the Acceleration and Expansion of Indonesia's Economic Development (MP3EI) is the country's first attempt since the fall of Suharto to articulate a strategy for developing the connective infrastructure necessary to unify the country's fragmented domestic markets. However, there is considerable criticism of this initiative and to date, MP3EI has made scant progress in achieving its objectives (see Box 2.1).

---

[101]These points have been well understood from the early part of the 19th Century. Johan von Thunen provided a rationale for the location of production. David Ricardo described the productivity gains which accrue from extending the intensive and extensive margins of production. The same principles explain the gains in output and productivity from which Indonesia would benefit as economic distance diminished and barriers to trade and exchange were lowered.

Box 2.1: Why Is There So Little Support for MP3EI?

MP3EI (Master Plan for the Acceleration and Expansion of Indonesia's Economic Development) is an ambitious blueprint for the creation, between 2010 and 2025, of major infrastructure corridors across Indonesia. If implemented as planned, MP3EI is expected to raise real per capita GDP from its level of around $3,000 (in 2010 prices) to between $14,250 and $15,500 by 2025. This represents an annual growth rate of in excess of 10.9 percent. MP3EI's advantage is that it sets a high standard. Its disadvantage is that Indonesia's present economic structure and political arrangements cannot formulate and implement the measures necessary to achieve such a high rate of growth for such an extended period. Its over-ambition is an obvious strike against MP3EI.

Nonetheless, this is the first coherent scheme devised to physically integrate the country. MP3EI provides a pragmatic vision of what is required to develop the country as a whole. Indeed, with MP3EI, the GOI has finally identified the infrastructure investments needed to begin promoting economic unity of Indonesia.

MP3EI highlights the functional roles of each infrastructure corridor: natural resources and energy-related development in Sumatra; industry and services in Java; agriculture and mining in Kalimantan; agriculture and fisheries in Sulawesi; tourism and agriculture in Bali and Nusa Tenggara; and mining and fisheries in Papua and Maluku. Based on experience from other countries, e.g., the Trans-Amazon highway in Brazil, the road to the Northeast in Thailand, the Beira corridor in Mozambique, these functional roles are indicative at best. Enterprises and entrepreneurs will find multiple additional productivity and welfare-enhancing ways to exploit any improvements in connectivity.

Curiously, many Jakarta-based officials and commentators have a dim view of MP3EI. A committee (KP3EI) established to review the implications of MP3EI found at least six major problems—land-acquisition; the lack of coordination among government ministries, agencies and local governments; difficulties with licensing/permits, both at the central and local government levels; overlapping concession permits on the use of forest areas; and complications in re-designating land status, especially from nature reserves (Tampubolon, Osman, and Witular, 2012). Some economists have dismissed MP3EI as impractical given the GOI's weak record on implementation. Others argue that there are more pressing social problems that need attention.

The KP3EI concluded that a considerable amount of activity was under-way with more planned, although the overall rate of implementation was low. There is little agreement on how the GOI will find the resourc-es to jump-start the investments. There has been too much reliance and wishful thinking about using public-private partnerships to finance the investments, especially unrealistic expectations regarding magnitude of private sector financing and the private sector's appetite for risk. There is also a problem of phasing, with the first five years focused on "quick wins implementation"; the second five years on "strengthen[ing] eco-nomic and investment bases"; and the final five years (2020-2025) for "sustainable growth implementation." (BAPPENAS, 2011, Ch. 4) In practice, the three phases will need to overlap.

Yet, for all its shortcomings MP3EI is the only comprehensive plan Indo-nesia has for integrated national development. So far, it is the only plan that focuses on the comprehensive expansion of the national (multi-modal) transport system that will be essential for helping to promote rapid, sustained, and inclusive economic growth. On that point alone, MP3EI deserves attention and support.

A More Productive Workforce

To promote rapid sustained inclusive growth, Indonesia will need to take every available opportunity to become and remain competitive. Techni-cally, this means enhancing and exploiting the country's dynamic comparative advantage. That will happen if all Indonesians use their skills, capacities, physical resources, and knowledge to raise their productivity at rates comparable to their main competitors.

This does not mean throwing open the whole economy to the unfettered exercise of market forces, whatever that might mean in today's world. Critical public goods, services, and amenities have to be provided, collective risks have to be shared, and social objectives (peace, justice, equity, opportunity, regional development) have to be promoted.

But it also does not mean restricting access to formal sector jobs in current markets to insiders with connections, or maintaining secure positions for academics and other professionals who buy their degrees and bureaucrats who purchase their promotions. Nor does it mean granting exclusive rights to a particular market segment to state-owned enterprises, the military, or some other favored group.[102]

Many of these points are likely to be fudged in the negotiations and interactions that will help assemble and maintain the political coalitions needed to move the agenda forward. But whatever compromises are made and fixes are agreed, Indonesia will continue falling short of its potential for rapid inclusive growth unless there emerges a broad commitment to raising productivity throughout the country and stimulating competition in a setting that is transparent, accountable, contestable, and guided by due process.

It is difficult to become and remain competitive. Competitiveness and the ability to compete are defined in numerous ways.[103] They all

---

[102]Claessons, Djankov and Lang (2000) examined the excesses of Indonesia's meltdown during *Krismon* and some of its proximate causes. One of these was the insider lending in major financial institutions. Quoting their findings, Morales, Mahendra and Widyastuti (2012, p.81) noted that "…some 417 firms and 17 percent of market capitalization were traced back to a single family, and 10 families controlled more than half the corporate sector."

[103]Some examples include the following: "Competitiveness is defined by the productivity with which a nation utilizes its human, capital and natural resources" (Porter

translate into some measure of output per unit of input (i.e., productivity). Comparative advantage, both in its static and dynamic versions, derives from differences in relative productivities. Individuals, firms, and industries generate and retain their competitive advantage when their relative productivity in providing particular goods and services exceeds that of other individuals, firms, and industries.

As described in Chapter One, Indonesia's current circumstances reflect a static comparative advantage in coal, copper, oil palm, nickel, rubber, and several other raw and semi-processed materials. That is not the case with other goods and services, many of which have such a high opportunity cost for Indonesia, they are not produced locally.[104] In the former, Indonesia's relative productivity is higher than its competitors, while in the latter it is much lower. By boosting income and expenditure, and creating scale and scope economies as well as multiplier effects in the process, rising relative productivity enables individuals, firms, industries, and the country as a whole to become increasingly competitive across a broader range of activities and in a more geographically dispersed set of markets. As also explained in Chapter One, it is rising relative productivity – not the current ability to sell coal, nickel and palm oil – which will ensure that Indonesia enhances its capacities to grow rapidly, sustainably and inclusively.

2005); "Competitiveness is a measure of a country's advantage or disadvantage in selling its products in international markets" (OECD Sources and Methods of the Economic Outlook "Glossary of Statistical Terms" online); "Competitiveness pertains to the ability and performance of a firm, sub-sector or country to sell and supply goods and services in a given market, in relation to the ability and performance of other firms, sub-sectors or countries in the same market" (Wikipedia, accessed December 24, 2012). Paul Krugman (1994) conflated competitiveness with productivity arguing that nations, unlike corporations, do not have a "bottom line" that will put them "out of business" if they "cannot afford to pay...workers, suppliers, and bondholders..."

[104]In this case, the relative cost measured in terms of the domestic resources required to produce these goods and services is prohibitive under current technical and institutional arrangements, including availability of the necessary skills and managerial expertise.

The links between the ability to compete and productivity have been widely examined by economists. Adam Smith, for example, related productivity to the division of labor, i.e., the degree to which workers were induced to specialize.[105] The division of labor, in turn, was determined by the "extent of the market."[106] This last observation helps place in context Indonesia's growth performance while simultaneously providing guidance about its future growth potential. Rapid, sustained, and inclusive growth has not occurred so far in Indonesia because of the collective incapacity of the public and private sectors to create the conditions which engage all Indonesians in activities that fully extend the domestic market.

---

[105]Smith (1776, Cannan edition 1937, Book I, Ch. 1, pp.3-4) Economists have subsequently made a distinction between specialization and the division of labor. In Smith's example of the "pin-maker," one implied the other.

[106]Smith, *op. cit.* p.17. Griliches (1979, 2000) Krugman (1990, 1994) reinterpreted the connection when he argued that being productive enables individuals, firms, and ultimately nations to be competitive.

CHAPTER THREE

Improving Hard and Soft Infrastructure: Reducing the Costs of Logistics and Transactions

Price is what you pay. Value is what you get.
WARREN BUFFETT

Indonesia's High Cost Economy

Extending and integrating the domestic market, together with broadening and deepening engagement with international manufacturing production and distribution chains, will raise productivity. This will enable all Indonesian workers to become and remain competitive. Rising productivity and improving competitiveness, in turn, provide the foundation for rapid, sustained, and inclusive economic growth.

Policymakers can reinforce this virtuous cycle by shifting their focus away from the short-term (static) gains from trade and take the measures needed to enhance the country's dynamic comparative advantage, or its "multi-period competitiveness." Making that shift would involve several changes: increased investment in hard and soft infrastructure, which reduces logistics and transaction costs throughout the economy; use of incentives that stimulate productive work; and rationalization of central-subnational administrative and fiscal arrangements. The present chapter deals with the challenges of enhancing Indonesia's hard and soft infrastructure.

There is plenty of evidence that logistics costs are high in Indonesia:

- Sofyan Wanandi, Chairman of the Indonesian Employers Association (Apindo), believes that logistics costs comprise up to 17 percent of industrial costs, the highest in Asia. He says comparable costs are 8 percent in Malaysia and 5 percent in Japan.[107]
- According to representatives of KADIN, the Indonesian Chamber of Commerce and Industry, their members regularly expect trucks traveling between Jakarta and Surabaya, a distance of 670 km, to take three days and two nights. The cost per container for the journey varies from $1500 to $2000.[108]
- Individuals regularly report that travel time by car from Yogjakarta to Jakarta, a road distance of 434 km, can range from 12 to 32 hours.
- A 20-ft container shipped from Jakarta to Singapore (825 km) costs $185. By contrast, a similar container shipped from Padang (West Sumatra) to Jakarta, a shorter distance, costs $600.[109]
- Sending a 100 kg package to Tanjun Pinang in Riau Islands Province from Jakarta (825 km) costs Rp 2.5 million. A comparable package from Jakarta to Singapore (same distance) costs less than half (Rp 1.2 million).[110]

The same holds true for transaction costs, for example in the financial sector:

- Evidence from Bank Indonesia shows that "... around 60 percent of Indonesia's population has no financial access."[111]

---

[107]Hanifah (2013); BAPPENAS (2011); Sumantri and Lau (2011).

[108]FreshFruitPortal (2012).

[109]Baksoro (2011).

[110] Wardi and Wisnibroto (2012).

[111]Hadad (2010). The datum came from a 2007 World Bank Study "Finance For All." See also Wong and Yan (2010) and Samboh (2012).

- A 2010 World Bank household survey designed to determine the general population's access to financial services indicated that approximately 50 percent of households used formal financial institutions for saving, while a further 18 percent used informal institutions; 30 percent of households had no savings, or none in financial form.
- Fewer than 17 percent of households borrowed from banks, and 43 percent obtained their credit from non-bank sources. This left 40 percent of households who did not borrow through financial organizations.

The lack of access and fragmentation of credit markets is due largely to high transaction costs.

There are many more examples. They reaffirm the everyday experience of all Indonesians regarding the high private and social costs associated with gaps and deficiencies in both hard and soft infrastructure such as roads, ports, electricity grids, governance systems, and institutions.[112] The downside of this situation is that because the costs are so high, they have been inhibiting growth and development and distorting the distribution of activities across sectors and regions. The upside is that because the costs are so high, they provide Indonesia with the opportunity to make major sustained gains in productivity, competitiveness, and inclusive growth, through measures that systematically and sustainably reduce them.

The chapter is arranged as follows. A brief introduction sets the context. We then discuss four issues – roads, ports, energy, and finance – each of which illustrates different dimensions of the challenges of reducing logistics and transaction costs. These costs are inter-related. For

---

[112]The social costs are accentuated by inequalities in access to existing facilities. Buehler (2012), for example, notes that the rich in Indonesia have much stronger protection under the law than the poor. Hill and Thee (2012, pp.232-233) describe inequalities in access to higher education.

example, although roads and ports are largely about bulldozers, barges, and buildings their financing is directly related to institutional arrangements, such as contracts, conventions, codes of practice, confidence, and trust. Similarly, while finance depends on regulations, accounting procedures, and portfolio management, significant amounts of hard infrastructure, in the form of communication systems, buildings, and physical security are required to improve its efficiency.

The Context of Logistics and Transactions Costs

Why does Indonesia annually mine and ship more than 300 million tons of coal to countries (primarily China) that have broader electricity coverage?[113] Why does Singapore serve as Indonesia's principal transshipment port? Why do fewer than half of all Indonesians have access to formal banking institutions? And, why after decades of being guided by the principle of *Kesatuan Indonesia* ("Unity of Indonesia"), does the country still comprise a loose set of fragmented markets rather than an integrated economy?

There are many answers.[114] One is the lack of effective demand (i.e., demand backed by purchasing power) for local goods and services due to Indonesia's low per capita income and the unequal distribution of that income.[115] Another is the high risks associated with connecting markets

---

[113]Coal exports in 2010 were 316 million tons (www.indexmundi.com/energy.aspx/). According to BAPPENAS, 67 percent of Indonesia's population had regular access to electricity in 2010 with per capita average electricity consumption of 590 kwh. Corresponding data for lower middle income countries was 644 kwh; for upper middle income countries it was 2714 kwh (*WDI* 2012, Table 5.11, pp.324-6).

[114]Adam (2010) gave four reasons why Indonesia experienced major problems with its infrastructure: "relatively low" commitment by Government to infrastructure development; the poor allocation of infrastructure spending; slow implementation of planned expenditure; and (often inconsistent) regulations which impede the effective expansion and use of infrastructure.

[115]The most recent data show that the share of income/expenditure of the bottom 40

because of the limited trust among potential market participants, the low degree of confidence among asset-holders that their financial assets will retain their value, and regulatory barriers on electricity distribution, coal deliveries, and inter-island shipping that deter producers from offering alternative domestic sources of supply. A third answer is the systematic failure of the public sector to provide the public facilities (roads, ports, electricity grids) that would stimulate the complementary market-extending private sector response. Each explanation can be traced to some aspect of high logistics and transaction costs.

Logistics involve activities related to acquisition or procurement, security, material handling, transport, storage, packaging, distribution, re-shipment, replacement, and disposal of goods. *Logistics costs* refer to the public and private real resource cost of transporting and/or transferring goods, personnel, and information from one location to another, typically from the point of production to the point of purchase or consumption.

Transaction costs are the value of public and private resources, time, and information used to participate in economic exchange or, more broadly, economic and social interaction. [116] For some economists, development and transaction costs are inextricably linked. Nobel laureate Douglass North, for example, argued economic and social development has largely reflected the systematic reduction in transaction costs associated with the elaboration of institutions ("rules of the game") that allow the progressive broadening of human interaction and exchange. [117]

Each of these costs includes allowances for losses and risk. Logistics losses can be treated as a cost of doing business or they can be defrayed

---

percent of the population was 20.3 percent. For 2010, this represented average annual per capita income/expenditure of $1270. The average for the whole population was $2500 (*WDI* 2012, Tables 1.1, 2.9).

[116]Economists typically define "transaction costs" as arising "...from the transfer of ownership or, more generally, of property rights" (Neihans 1998). They typically involve the costs of search, bargaining, and enforcement.

[117]North (1990, 1997).

by the purchase of insurance (which is a transaction cost). Transaction costs also allow for risk, delay, or default.

Logistics and transaction costs link comparative (or competitive) advantage to the extension and integration of the market.[118] It is only by keeping these costs low that every contributor to the successive steps that add value between producers and consumers can improve their productivity (i.e., input per unit of output). Furthermore, it is only by their capacity to add value and benefit from it at each step that economic actors, from the smallest to the largest in the economy, are induced to participate more extensively in the country's markets.[119]

Techniques for analyzing these costs are widely available.[120] They are particularly useful in economic planning, which is a deeply embedded practice in Indonesia. Economic plans are convenient exercises for systematically attempting to understand how pre-established social goals can be achieved using the available public resources efficiently, effectively, and equitably.[121] They show how scarce resources can be used

---

[118]This point has been recognized in Indonesia. Adam (2010) noted: China's "... decision to allocate massive spending on infrastructure since the early 1980s has contributed significantly to the country's improved competitiveness. The resulting development helped various sectors to reduce transportation costs, strengthen distribution networks and improve efficiency in the production process."

[119]Phylis Deane (1965) argued that the United Kingdom had an advantage in exploiting emerging technology in the "First Industrial Revolution" because of its rapidly expanding expansion of its canal system and the fortuitous proximity of its major cities to the seas. Both of these reduced transport costs.

[120]A basic principle is the minimization of the resource/time costs of providing logistics and/or transaction services that underpins major areas of study, including the value of information (Hayek 1945; Spence 1973), market formation (Arrow 1959; Vernon Smith 1963), portfolio analysis (Samuelson 1970; Herschliefer 1989; Hakansonn 1998), and economic dynamics (Strotz 1956; Dorfman 1969; Arrow and Lind 1970).

[121]Efficiency refers to the absence of waste. Resources are being used efficiently when no other combination will raise output further, or for a given level of output no other arrangement of resource inputs will lower costs. Effectiveness is the degree of coherence between the goal of a policy and its actual outcome. Equity has two components – horizontal and vertical. Horizontal equity requires similar treatment/rewards for people (or

in ways that help overcome the most serious impediments to achieving national objectives.[122] In this respect, MP3EI has been a major breakthrough. On the negative side, it makes clear the high cost of overcoming the logistics deficiencies which block the broader integration of the Indonesian economy. On the positive side, it provides direct evidence of the exceedingly high returns, evident in the projected rates of economic growth, which can be expected if national resources are deployed to overcome those deficiencies.

Because of public under-investment, the potential social returns from expanding and upgrading hard infrastructure have been rising, particularly as congestion costs intensify and individuals seek their own decentralized, socially inefficient remedies. Box 3.1 discusses this point by illustrating how individual commuters have responded to the lack of public transport.[123]

Box 3.1: Improvements in Personal Transport as a Negative-Sum Game

The increasing cost of commuting in Indonesia's urban areas has individuals and authorities caught in a negative-sum game. Current policies such as fuel subsidies, low taxes on vehicles, low levels of public infrastructure

---

groups) in similar circumstances. Vertical equity is reflected in the differential distribution of benefits/costs. With respect to public goods/services, the better off receive fewer benefits (or incur more costs) than those who are less well-off.

[122]Ramsey (1928); Hotelling (1931); Tinbergen (1952); Dorfman, Samuelson and Solow (1958); Koopmans (1975).

[123]The discussion illustrates the adverse collective effects of individually rational responses. The World Bank's 1994 World Development Report "Infrastructure for Development" emphasized the complementarity between public investment in infrastructure and private economic activity (World Bank 1994). In aggregate, that effect is not working in Indonesia because public investment in infrastructure is so low.

investment, and weak provision of infrastructure services, have created adverse incentives. Individuals who find public transport limited and inconvenient have sought alternatives. With incomes rising and consumer credit increasingly available, a growing number of individuals have purchased automobiles and motorcycles. (Villikappen and Moestafa, 2013)

Recent changes have been dramatic: the total vehicle fleet has increased threefold between 2001 and 2010; the number of passenger cars, buses, and trucks registered growth of more than 20 percent annually between 2005 and 2010; and the number of motorbikes rose from 47.7 million in 2008 to 68.8 million in 2011. Indonesia's demographic road density (2.0 km per 1,000 people) and spatial road density (200 km per 1,000 km²) are below average when compared with regional and international benchmarks. (World Bank 2012) Travel times have risen both within urban areas and between them. Traffic is estimated to move at an average speed of less than 10 kph throughout the day in the Greater Jakarta region (Terziz 2010) and traffic congestion has reduced the efficiency of road-based public transport such as the trans-Jakarta system. Although some favorable behavioral change, such as car-pooling, is already occurring to accommodate increased vehicular traffic, a much more prevalent response is the hiring of seat fillers ("car jockeys") to avoid the "three-in-one" rush hour restriction for downtown Jakarta's main roads.

Buying a motorbike or car resolves the problem of personal transport, but it creates social problems. The limited capacity of Indonesia's roads, bridges, and ferries, combined with the rapidly rising volume of vehicles, has sharply increased traffic congestion. It is rational for individuals to take measures to reduce the inconvenience of travel. But the collective outcomes of their individual decisions raise the social costs of moving people and goods. One outcome is that total costs of travel and transport (time, fuel, wear and tear, and health including psychic costs) increase.

A further effect is that the high costs of commuting are capitalized into the rising value of property with locations close to work, entertainment, and schools.

Breaking out of this negative-sum game will require public sector initiatives such as those taken in Thailand, Malaysia, Mexico, Colombia, and Brazil. Numerous studies and plans suggest how this might be done but to date, action has been limited. For example, the 2004 Study on Integrated Transportation Master Plan for Jabodetabek (Jakarta, Bogor, Depok, Tangerang and Bekasi) was designed to deal with the transport problems beyond Jakarta's administrative borders. It proposed 172 transportation projects, including the expansion of the busway, MRT construction, and improvements in rail transport and the road network. Evaluations of progress in 2010 indicated that only 21 percent of the projects were on schedule; the rest were stalled. In the meantime, costs continue to mount. In 2011, the Jakarta Transportation Agency estimated that traffic congestion costs the city up to US$5 billion a year. Similarly, the Transportation Ministry claims that congestion costs Rp 28.1 trillion each year, including wasted fuel, lost productivity, and traffic-induced health problems. (Ardiansyah 2012) This failure to deliver by the public sector reinforces the downward spiral. When individuals and firms see the Government is not making the necessary effort, they make other arrangements, including the purchase of more cars, motorbikes, and trucks.

Large-scale miners and industrial firms such as those with petrochemical and cement enterprises at Gresik and mining enterprises in East Kalimantan and South Sulawesi have built their own ports and access roads. Indonesia has many similar examples where private investment substitutes for rather than complements public investment. The result is that private and public sectors are locked in a negative-sum

game with the nation as a whole losing through slower growth and diminished development.

High logistics and transaction costs undermine productivity because
they absorb time and effort in moving both goods and people around,
pre-empting resources that might be used more efficiently in alternative
activities.[124] Such a rise in productivity is essential if Indonesia is to gain
the full benefits from extending and integrating its domestic market.[125]
Since current policies are largely responsible for keeping those costs
high, the challenge for the GOI is to foster the "constructive politics"
that would help lower them. The urgency of the need is increasing.
Much of West Java is following the well-worn (and irrational) path of
large metropolitan areas in other countries, namely that of grinding to a
halt on a regular basis.[126] Current projections suggest that by the middle
of the present decade, most of the large urban areas of the country will
experience sharply rising explicit and implicit costs due to inadequate
infrastructure. If this were to materialize, Indonesia's domestic market
would have difficulty expanding. This would scuttle the prospects of
sustained, rapid, and inclusive growth.

---

[124]Relative to its comparators, Indonesia's (labor and capital) productivity is already
low. For the period 2000 to 2010, Indonesia grew annually by 5.3 percent and investment as a share of GDP averaged 27 percent. That is, the (incremental) capital-output
ratio was 5.1. Corresponding data for LMICs (Indonesia's comparators) were, respectively, 6.3 percent, 25 percent, and 4.8 (*WDI* 2012, Table 4.1, 4.8).

[125]Advantages would also accrue in international trade from improvements in
domestic efficiency. Some of the international disadvantage could be further offset by
devaluing the rupiah to compensate for high logistics costs. By changing the ratio of
tradable to non-tradable prices, the devaluation would raise local effective demand and
thereby help extend the domestic market.

[126]It is irrational because there has been no apparent learning. Officials in Jakarta
should not feel reassured that other large cities – Lagos, Sao Paulo, Bangkok, Beijing,
Hanoi, Delhi, Mexico City and numerous others – have similar congestion and pollution problems. Fundamental to the "convergence thesis" in economics is that countries
with low incomes can enjoy rapid "catch-up" growth because they avoid the mistakes
being made by other countries. Indonesia (or certainly Jakarta and West Java) have not
done that.

Indonesia's Hard Infrastructure Deficit: Logistics Costs and Efficiency[127]

To help place the high resource costs of transporting goods and people and transferring information throughout the country, the World Bank's 2012 Logistics Performance Index ranks Indonesia 59th out of 155 countries, behind Thailand's 38th place and Malaysia's 29th place.[128] The World Economic Forum's 2011-2012 Global Competitiveness Report ranked Indonesia 46th overall amongst 142 countries. For its infrastructure pillar, Indonesia ranked 90th for the quality of its roads and 103rd for quality of port infrastructure.[129]

This section focuses on two critical infrastructure components: roads and ports. The country's road density, at 25 km of road per 100 sq.km of land, is among the lowest in the region. Congestion due to a shortage of large-scale ports that are capable of receiving trans-oceanic vessels has made shipping costs in Indonesia the highest amongst the ASEAN countries. Shipping costs comprise around 15 percent of the final prices of goods, and high port infrastructure costs reduce Indonesia's ability to compete globally.[130]

Indonesia's infrastructure bottlenecks are intensifying and its regional development is becoming more unbalanced. The country's main port, Tanjung Priok, which handles about 70 percent of Indonesia's

---

[127]Based on Akash Deep (2012).

[128]"Pelabuhan II Has Big Plans for New Ports," *The Jakarta Globe*, June 25, 2012; www.lpisurvey.worldbank.org/international/global.

[129]Schwab (2012, pp.200-201). The rankings represent a slippage from 2011, in which Indonesia was 83rd and 103rd, respectively, out of 139 countries. The WEF was explicit about the problems: "The insufficient supply and quality of transport, energy, and telecommunications infrastructure seriously limit Indonesia's output capacity. The manufacturing and export sectors particularly suffer as this state of affairs translates into limited connectivity and handling capacity, high costs, delays in shipments, and production loss" (Geiger 2011, p.12).

[130]BAPPENAS (2011).

total trade,[131] is clogged well past its capacity. Similarly, congestion has brought average speed on Java highways to a crawl, confounding attempts to develop the region.

Historically, much of Indonesia's infrastructure investment has been channeled through the country's large state-owned-enterprises. In the road sector, Jasa Marga has been a successful builder and operator for over 40 years; the ports have been controlled by a network of state-owned agencies called Pelindos (*Pelabuhan Indonesia*). The lack of adequate high quality infrastructure confirms that the collective efforts of policy makers and these (and other) state-owned companies have not served the country well.

The amount of investment has been inadequate, made worse by the inefficient allocation of resources within the budget.[132] While the country spent almost 6 percent of GDP on infrastructure development before the Asian crisis, it has failed to reach even half that level since.[133] Estimates from BAPPENAS suggest that roughly $150 billion is required for infrastructure development during 2010-2014 to meet the plan target of 6-7 percent growth per annum. The government's budget will only cover 30 percent of that total, or roughly $45 billion. The 70 percent shortfall, totaling $105 billion, would need to come from private funds or partly from government funds financed with savings from reduced fuel subsidies.

In his first year in office, President Yudhoyono outlined an ambitious, far-reaching program to build infrastructure using public and private resources. In 2005, at the Indonesia Infrastructure Summit, he announced 91 new infrastructure projects worth $22.5 billion that would be eligible for private participation. "Infrastructure for all" was declared as one of the government's policy pillars, as it sought the dual aims of allaying concerns about an impending infrastructure crisis and reducing dis-

---

[131]"Ministry to get involved in Kalibaru Project," *The Jakarta Post*, (January 9, 2012).
[132]Referred to as "squandered fiscal space" in Saich *et al.* (2010, pp.87-89).
[133]OECD (2012, Table 5, p.16).

parities in the levels of development between the provinces. The more recent Master Plan for the Acceleration and Expansion of Indonesia's Economic Development (MP3EI) exceeds those plans not only in sophistication and ambition, but also its recognition of the imperatives of balanced growth and regional development.

Unfortunately, the ambitious array of projects planned by the administration has not been implemented despite seven years' of effort. Of the 91 projects that the President outlined at the 2005 Summit, few have even broken ground. Of those who do not reject the initiative out of hand (see Box 2.1 in Chapter 2), many fear that most of what MP3EI contains will meet a similar fate.

This has not been due to lack of focus or effort on the part of the government, its agencies, or donor institutions. Nor has it been a result of lack of policy leadership from the government. Instead, it has been the result of muddled processes that have resulted in a lack of understanding on how to balance the role of the existing state-owned agencies with those of private developers. The government has undercut its own efforts as it has sought to engage outsiders to join in the process of infrastructure development by failing to adequately focus and deploy its own substantial resources for that purpose.

This point is illustrated by discussing how Indonesian policymakers have chosen to develop two of the most significant infrastructure projects undertaken in recent times: the Solo-Kertosono segment of the Trans-Java toll road, the most important highway in Indonesia; and the expansion of Jakarta's Tanjung Priok Port (the Kalibaru Project).

Highways

Indonesia's size and geographical spread have always challenged its planners to place particular emphasis on the development of transport infrastructure, within which the road sector accounts for the major share of domestic freight and inter-urban passenger land travel.

The first toll road in Indonesia was built in 1978 using government and foreign funds and operated by the newly created government-owned company PT Jasa Marga, which was also its own regulator. In 2005, the Government announced that it intended adding almost 1500 kilometers of new toll roads across 38 projects over the period 2005-2009 at a cost of $9.4 billion.[134] To achieve this target, the Government significantly revised the policy and institutional framework for infrastructure public-private partnerships (PPPs), as well as the specific measures for development and regulation of toll road projects. Presidential Regulation 67 (*Perpres 67*) provided a comprehensive plan to facilitate participation of the private sector in the provision of infrastructure. The new framework demarcated a program of private concession contracts for projects that were economically and financially viable. The new policy defined the role of PPPs in the toll road sector.

To promote private participation, the Government also made several institutional reforms. A new toll road regulator, the Indonesian Toll Roads Authority (BPJT), was established in the Ministry of Public Works to prepare projects, facilitate land acquisition, supervise the implementation of concession agreements, and set tariffs. An Infrastructure Guarantee Fund was established to provide support through subsidies or risk sharing for specific projects that would encourage private investment. An infrastructure fund was proposed to co-finance commercially viable infrastructure projects in partnership with private investors and multilateral financial institutions. A Project Development Facility was established to improve project preparation in accordance with international best practices.

The role of Jasa Marga was transformed. The company retained its existing toll road concession rights but could no longer be appointed by the Government to develop new projects. It would compete for them

---

[134]JICA (2007, pp. 6-9).

with private bidders. In its new mission statement, Jasa Marga aimed at "continuously developing new toll roads to maintain its leading position of at least 50 percent of the total toll road length in Indonesia" and becoming a "highly competitive company in both national and regional scales." While formally under the Ministry of State-Owned Enterprises, Jasa Marga enjoys substantial independence, controlling over 80 percent of the operating toll roads in Indonesia.

Despite these policy and institutional reform efforts, the results to date have been disappointing.

Stalled highway construction on Java is a good example of Indonesia's current transportation predicament. Java is the most densely populated island in the world, almost twice as dense as Japan's main island of Honshu or the Philippines island of Luzon. With its population of 130 million, Java is the mainstay of socioeconomic activities, the nucleus of industrial development, and the contributor of 60 percent of Indonesia's GDP. Yet Java lacks a continuous major highway across its east-west axis.

A development plan for the Trans-Java Highway that had divided its 900 km stretch into 16 contiguous sections was prepared in 1996. Five of these sections were already in operation and most of the others were "appointed to owners" at that time. But none of these sections had reached "financial closure" even by 2005. One of the first tasks upon which the newly created regulator BPJT focused was to resume work on the toll projects that had been awarded earlier. Updated studies sponsored by the new government reaffirmed the economic viability of the Trans-Java Highway. Instead of consolidating the project into fewer segments, the government signed new concession agreements with the existing owners in 2006. Many of them have not been completed.

The only section of the Trans-Java Highway without a preexisting concession agreement was that connecting Solo to Kertosono via the intermediate town of Ngawi. The surrounding corridor contains densely populated areas and traffic consisting of heavy-duty vehicles transporting products such as oil palm, tea, and rubber. Though not on the Trans-Java

Highway itself, the city of Yogyakarta is one of the most popular tourist destinations in Indonesia and lies only 53 km from Solo. The completion of the Solo-Kertosono segment would support local social, economic, and tourism activities. It would also enhance regional development in central and eastern areas of Java.

Solo-Kertosono was touted as one of Indonesia's ten "model PPPs." It has become one of its 24 stalled road projects.

Sea Ports

With 18,307 islands,[135] Indonesia is the world's largest archipelagic state. Its territory includes the Malacca Strait, one of the world's busiest seaways.[136] Yet, Tanjung Priok, the main port of Jakarta, is the only Indonesian port for cargo in the strategic Malacca straits shipping lane. This port handles 70 percent of Indonesia's total exports and imports, but has undergone little change in its physical configuration from Dutch colonial times. Relative to other major ASEAN ports, its productivity has worsened markedly.[137]

Tanjung Priok has four container terminals, but their handling volume has surpassed their 5 million TEU (twenty-foot equivalent unit) capacity. Container traffic reached 5.8 million TEUs at the end of 2011, an increase of 23 percent from 2010.[138] This congestion, combined with other infrastructure bottlenecks, has made Indonesia's shipping costs the highest in the ASEAN region.

Indonesia's large seaports have been classified by region into four groups, and are managed by four state-owned enterprises, PT Pelabuhan

---

[135]Estimate for 2002 derived by Indonesia's National Insitute of Aeronautics and Space (LAPAN).

[136]US Navy Ports of Call: Indonesia, http://www.gettingaround.net/pages/poc-indonesia.php.

[137]The Study for Development of the Greater Jakarta Metropolitan Ports, 2003.

[138]*Jakarta Post*, January 9, 2012.

Indonesia (Pelindo) I, II, III, and IV, with non-overlapping jurisdictions. Tanjung Priok was previously under the jurisdiction of PT Pelindo II, which has recently renamed itself "Indonesian Port Corporation." Pelindo II operates in ten provinces across Indonesia, and manages twelve ports, including Tanjung Priok and Sunda Kelapa in North Jakarta, and Cirebon in West Java.

The Pelindos used to have a legislated monopoly in the main commercial ports and regulatory authority over private sector ports. The 2008 Shipping Law sought to remove the existing state monopoly in the port sector by opening it up to private sector participation. Whereas the Pelindos had played the role of owner, operator, and port authority, now they can only act as operators and have to lease facilities from the Government on the basis of long-term concession contracts. Legally, Pelindo II is now just the operator of Tanjung Priok, and it is required to hand over its existing assets to the Port Authority.[139] The role of the Port Authority is to oversee and administer commercial operations within each port by regulating, pricing, and supervising access to basic port infrastructure. The Port Authority is also responsible for designing and implementing the port master plan.[140] Furthermore, PT Pelindo II can no longer be appointed by the Government to develop ports, but must compete with private bidders for new projects.

It has been known for at least a decade that Indonesia needed a new terminal that could accommodate at least 6-7 million TEUs by 2015, or an additional capacity of 15 million TEUs by 2020.[141] The Kalibaru Terminal, also known as New Priok, is expected to increase port capacity by 1.9 million TEUs[142] and lower logistics costs from 17 percent to

---

[139]"Nation's Ports Risk Being Overwhelmed," *Jakarta Globe*, April 30, 2012.
[140]USAID (2008).
[141]Indonesia Infrastructure Call, http://www.apmterminals.com/aboutus. aspx?id=17551.
[142]"Pelindo II to take over Kalibaru Project," *The Jakarta Post*, February 2, 2012.

10 percent of production costs.[143] The first phase of the project has been budgeted at Rp 22,000 trillion. However, the tender process remained stalled for months until January 2012, when the Government cancelled the tender and directly awarded the project to Pelindo II.[144]

Energy[145]

Policy

When judged against the Government's stated objectives, energy policy in Indonesia is inefficient and inequitable. It is inefficient since higher national income and welfare could be achieved with the same inputs of energy and budget support. It is inequitable because the richest groups in society benefit the most from the controlled prices and quantitative restrictions on energy use.[146] Current energy policy subsidizes the better-off, encourages over-consumption, absorbs close to 20 percent of the government budget,[147] leads to fuel smuggling, exacerbates macro-

---

[143]"Trimming Logistics Costs: Pelindo II builds Three Ports Worth Rp 52.6 trillion," *The Jakarta Post*, June 27, 2012.

[144]Different explanations were provided by the Government to explain the abrupt cancellation of the tender. The main reason was that the tender process was too protracted and that if it proceeded, the port would only be ready in 2017. There was doubt that the tender process would meet the key goal of competition under the Shipping Law. The private participants had requested more time to conduct a feasibility study of the project, and might not have had adequate financing for the project. A number of companies that had passed the tender pre-qualification were thought to have minimal experience working on ports. Finally, the government announced that it could not afford to provide the Rp. 3.5 trillion needed for breakwater, channel dredging, and road building under the PPP scheme. By awarding the project to a state-owned enterprise, it was felt that the government will have its "hands off" the obligation to participate in financing.

[145]This section draws on Dapice (2012).

[146]Recent surveys of the Indonesian economy (World Bank 2012; OECD 2012) make both points.

[147]Gasoline and diesel prices in Indonesia are currently about fifty cents a liter, the lowest price in Asia, and only about half their cost at retail. Fuel subsidies over recent

economic instability, and encourages consumption of socially expensive liquid fuels.[148] It adds to the import bill, creates blackouts, and keeps tens of millions of Indonesians from gaining access to electricity. That is, current energy policy undermines inclusive growth and significantly lowers worker productivity undercutting Indonesia's ability to become and remain competitive. Energy policy in Indonesia is probably also ineffective, with outcomes that its supporters did not intend. The difficulty of proving ineffectiveness is that the stated goals of policy makers often misrepresent their intentions.

A specific example of Indonesia's inefficient, inequitable, and ineffective energy policy is electricity production, transmission, and distribution. There is a chronic shortage of supply, which is 35-45 percent less than the amount demanded—and the amount demanded is growing by approximately 9 to 11 percent per year. Rather than devote its budget to the expansion of power plants and transmission and distribution lines, the Government spends billions of dollars on subsidies designed to lower the price of electricity. This encourages consumption and ensures blackouts. The 2012 electricity subsidy is set at about Rp. 90 trillion, more than double the 2011 level, and represents over $40 for each Indonesian. Meanwhile, one-third of households lack connections and blackouts are common. The "crash" 10,000 megawatt (MW) program

---

years have cost $9-$10 billion per annum and energy subsidies are an estimated 24.1 percent of expenditure in the 2013 budget (OECD 2012, p.15). A plan to increase gasoline and diesel prices by one-third in 2012 was dropped due to political opposition. Not only do car owners, many of whom are the wealthiest Indonesians, enjoy these subsidies (there are roughly 10 million cars in Indonesia), but motorcycle users (more than 60 million) would also be hit by a fuel price increase. Their opposition was in spite of the fact that the advantage of cheap fuel is offset by higher travel times, congestion, and pollution.

[148]Diesel fuel is imported and its use is subsidized. An efficient short-term and sustainable long-term solution would be for the subsidy to be eliminated so that users are induced to shift to cheaper domestic substitutes such as liquefied petroleum gas.

is behind schedule.[149] Moreover, even if it were completed as originally planned, it would not resolve the underlying supply issue. The present policies are adversely affecting electricity consumers, industries that depend on a secure power supply, and unconnected households.[150] The most obvious beneficiaries are those who supply diesel fuel, which is imported and distributed in non-transparent and non-accountable ways.

Overview of Resources

Indonesia has large amounts of energy, but not much oil. It became a net oil importer in 2004, and the gap has been growing in spite of a modest contribution from biofuels. Oil is an expensive fuel, costing up to $1/ liter for gasoline, kerosene, and diesel. Coal is plentiful. There are significant supplies of natural gas and a large potential supply of geothermal and hydro power. Natural gas, which is cheaper than liquid fuels for the same amount of thermal energy, could be used instead of liquid fuels for many purposes.[151] Natural gas could replace diesel used in cars, trucks,

---

[149]The 10,000 MW program consists of 35 (primarily coal-fired) power plants, 10 on Java and Bali and 25 elsewhere. The crash program was responding to annual increases in power demand on Java-Bali of 6.7 percent. Sources: "PLN secures 65% of financing for first 10,000 MW program," *The Jakarta Globe*, January 31, 2009; World Bank Project appraisal AB5963, Project ID: P113078, World Bank (March 29, 2011).

[150]It is common for a "lifeline rate" to be given to households with low electricity consumption. Any future higher electricity rate could maintain this practice and ease the burden on the poor. In 2008, electricity costs for a median income family of four were Rp23000 a month, so a 10 percent increase would cost Rp2300 or about $0.25 a month. Electricity costs from diesel generators are about $0.35 per kwh or 4-5 times the price charged by PLN for smaller users. One kWh of electricity generated by diesel costs more than a month's extra cost for a 10 percent price hike for a median household.

[151]A barrel of crude oil has 42 gallons or 159 liters and 5.8 million BTU of energy and currently costs $100 to $120. The same thermal equivalent of natural gas costs $45 to $60 at a generous pipeline price of $8 to $10 per million BTU. With LNG, the equivalent price per barrel is $70-$87, with LNG export prices at $12 to $15 per million BTU. A ton of coal costs $100 to $120 and has 25 million BTU. This is $4-5 per million BTU.

and generators, as well as kerosene used for cooking.[152] But there is a shortage of natural gas on Java. Pipelines to Java have limited capacity, although existing capacity is not being fully utilized. Offshore and outer island gas fields are not developed. The construction of gas terminals to import gas is behind schedule and even when complete, they will be too small to cater to potential demand.[153]

Natural Gas: Gas fields have large potential reserves but are not adequately developed to meet domestic demand. Larger pipelines would have to be built from the fields north of Java, in Sumatra, or Kalimantan to Java, where the demand for gas is concentrated.[154] Electricity from gas-fired generators is clean and relatively cheap (eight to ten cents per kWh if pipeline gas is delivered at $10 per million BTU). These generators can be installed close to where electricity is needed. Industrial estates should be able to build generators to take care of their own factories and offices, and sell the surplus to PLN at negotiated prices. This could provide tens of thousands of MWs of additional power. The main barrier is a lack of coordinated policies, including the reluctance of PLN to invest heavily in power plants that, under the current tariff structure, would add to their losses. PLN's main expansion at present is in coal-fired generators on Java. These are the lowest cost option even though they exacerbate pollution.

Geothermal: There is an ample reserve of geothermal energy but it is currently under-developed, with less than 5 percent of the 28,000 MW potential now being tapped. The current policy is to buy geothermal power at prices up to 9.7 cents per kWh. For PLN, this is above the price charged to most consumers, but high enough to attract substantial

---

[152]Plans exist to switch some vehicles to natural gas. The consumption of kerosene has already declined, replaced by subsidized gas (in portable canisters).

[153]When completed, the floating storage and regasification unit will supply 200 million cu ft/day. Two large generators in northern Jakarta require twice that amount.

[154]Studies indicate that natural gas pipelines, even from Kalimantan, would be cheaper than using LNG.

investment – some larger projects have much lower costs. One issue creating delays is that since many geothermal fields are in forests, the Ministries of Energy and Forestry, as well as local authorities, have to agree to their development. Without administrative changes that facilitate cooperation and agreement, many geothermal projects will move slowly, if at all.[155] The Government's target for geothermal is 10,000 MW by 2014. Under present arrangements, this will not be met.[156]

Coal: Indonesia has large reserves of coal – 4.3 billion tons of proved reserves and perhaps thirty times as much yet to be determined. Most of this coal is sub-bituminous and lignite with low heat value. Indonesia is the second-largest coal exporter in the world, with 2011 exports of over 300 million tons and domestic use about one-fifth of that. Three large companies control 60 percent of national output, with the rest spread among dozens more.

There has been a domestic market obligation (DMO) for low-calorie coal producers. They have to sell about 20 percent (the amount varies by year) of their output to local users – mainly PLN – at a price well below their export price. The effect of this is roughly equivalent to a 10 percent sales tax. This DMO has reportedly led to abuses, where payments are made to avoid selling coal locally. In 2011, an alternative approach was proposed whereby exports of low-calorie coal would be prohibited. This would ban coal exports of roughly 130 million tons a year. At recent prices of $90 a ton, such a restriction would reduce export receipts by nearly $12 billion. The presumption is that by reducing the water content of coal and other treatments, low-calorie coal would be upgraded and sold for a higher price. There is also the possibility of an export tax

---

[155]Geothermal wells can cause small earth tremors, although if these are in forests they have few consequences. No major earthquake has been associated with these wells, but there may be damage to infrastructure if the wells are placed in built-up areas.

[156]This assessment has been reaffirmed by Nugroho (2013). He suggests a strategy for moving beyond the current barriers to geothermal development.

being levied on coal exporters.[157] This would reduce the domestic price by the amount of the tax and accomplish the goal of providing cheap coal to domestic users, particularly PLN.

It generally costs $35 to $45 a ton to produce coal and the selling price has recently been $90 to $100. A high export tax would reduce the profitability of investing in coal mine expansion. If the goal is to slow the rate of exploitation of reserves, reduce exports, and direct production to domestic use, the export tax is appropriate. A lower tax would reduce the disincentives but also result in a higher domestic coal price if the DMO were abandoned. Foreign investment in coal mining is already subdued due to the requirement that within ten years from the start of production, half of the shares of the mine or mining company must be held by Indonesians. Adding domestic processing and export taxes to the existing rules will further reduce the incentives for foreign investment in coal mining.[158]

Nuclear Energy: Indonesia has no nuclear power plants operating, but a 2006 Presidential Decree stated that 5 percent of electricity should come from nuclear power and renewable energy sources by 2025. The 2004 Asian tsunami and 2011 Fukushima reactor meltdowns have raised doubts. Critics point out that much of Indonesia is geologically active with volcanoes and earthquakes. Moreover, the place where nuclear energy makes economic sense – Java – is densely populated. One proposal is to build 22,000 MW of nuclear power on one of the lightly populated and geographically stable islands of Bangka-Belitung between Java and Sumatra. Moving the electricity to Java would be costly, as it would re-

---

[157]Chapter 4 discusses the restrictions being imposed by the GOI to promote "value added processing" of minerals, including coal. Export bans and heavy taxes on ore exports are already in place. One question policymakers need to ask and answer is why processers lack the incentive to add more value unless there is official interference.

[158]If the goal is to ensure domestic ownership of coal reserves with limited increases in output, this is a rational policy mix. It would also cater to concerns about local pollution or global warming if these were to have some weight in coal policy.

quire large capacity underwater transmission lines. To this point, there have only been preliminary explorations of this proposal.

Renewable Energy: The costs of solar energy have been dropping and are now only fifteen to twenty cents per kWh, with installations as small as fifty kilowatts.[159] This is not competitive with gas or geothermal, but is an option for sites not on the national grid or a regional grid. With diesel electricity costing thirty to forty cents per kWh, mini-grids with battery backup may be an economical way to extend electricity. The payment of "green subsidies" that lower the cost of capital or of solar cells would support modest electricity use by rural or village households. Currently, renewable energy accounts for 11 percent of total electricity capacity but only 5-6 percent of production. It comprises hydroelectricity (8 percent), geothermal (2 percent), with biofuels and solar making up the remainder.

Alternatives to solar are mini-hydro generators and biofuels. At present, biofuels cost as much as diesel and mini-hydro facilities have problems with low water flow in the dry season. Solar cells work even when it is cloudy, though not at night. If a larger local grid were possible, geothermal may be a better choice though a single site normally produces at least a few dozen megawatts. Solar, at current prices, is preferable for more dispersed households and villages where high costs are incurred extending the grid.

Resources versus Policy

Indonesia is not deficient in energy – natural resources are plentiful. However, the GOI has not devised and implemented policies that would create incentives to expand efficiently and effectively the capacity to use the country's broad combination of energy sources to support inclusive national development:

---

[159]These estimates come from www.solarbuzz.com, a commercial solar energy website that surveys the costs of solar systems. Its estimates assume a 5 percent cost of capital and no battery backup for non-residential systems. Using a higher cost of capital and adding batteries would result in higher costs.

- As in the case of transport, the public sector has not undertaken the investment that would ensure all Indonesians have basic access to reliable energy sources. This has kept their productivity low.
- Energy policy in Indonesia is still based on confusion between price and cost, with policy makers continuing the pretense that a low private price for fuel, mainly petrol and electricity, implies a low social cost. As examples throughout this study show, cheap fuel makes transport more congested and time-consuming not less, and cheap electricity keeps the supply unreliable and limited to the 65 percent of the population fortunate to be living near the existing grid. In this regard, current energy policies are non-inclusive. They also reduce Indonesia's capacity for further growth.

That is the downside. The upside is that Indonesia's energy policy is so convoluted and inefficient, and so many opportunities to reduce wasteful practices have been ignored, that were the policies to change, the country could take advantage of the efficiency gains for decades.

Indonesia's Soft Infrastructure Deficit: Transaction Costs and Productivity

Indonesia's capacity for rapid, inclusive growth is being undercut by high transaction costs that divert resources (including time and effort) from potentially more rewarding pursuits. The result is that productivity of all activities, including those being used to facilitate transactions, is lower and workers in general are less competitive than they might otherwise be. Although these costs are evident in many activities, e.g., wholesale and retail trade, business negotiations, dispute resolution, contracting, customs clearance, hiring and laying-off workers, among others, we focus on finance, money and banking, and financial management.

These examples demonstrate in stark terms key dimensions of inequality and lack of inclusiveness in Indonesia. The majority of Indonesians do not have access to formal financial arrangements because transactions costs are high in absolute terms and relative to incomes.[160] Moreover, even for those who do have access, financing costs remain high because the banks and other agencies will only lend under restricted conditions. These financing costs reflect the low level of confidence of both lenders and borrowers in Indonesia's financial system.

The low degree of confidence can be traced to the country's history of chronic inflation and financial instability. It persists in part because the general public doubts Bank Indonesia's capacity to manage transparently and even-handedly the financial system. The outcome is that many well-off Indonesians regularly bypass local financial institutions in favor of cheaper, more secure arrangements in Singapore and other efficiently managed offshore financial centers.

Most Indonesians cannot get bank credit. Those who can tend to obtain large loans (see below). This differential access contributes to the growth of bank credit at rates well above the real growth of national output.[161] The result is that Indonesia continues to experience chronic inflation at rates significantly above comparable international levels. As these higher rates of inflation feed through the economy, they interact with the stable nominal exchange rate, a goal specifically promoted by both the Ministry of Finance and Bank Indonesia, to progressively overvalue the real exchange rate.[162]

All of these factors – financial exclusion, low confidence, limited trust, a preference by large asset-holders for offshore banking, elevated

---

[160]The reverse holds as well: transactions costs are high, in part, because so few Indonesians have access to financial services.

[161]McCleod (2003) made an effort to correct the still pervasive view in Indonesia that changes in relative prices (e.g., an increase in fuel or food prices, or the sticker price of vehicles) are inflationary. Inflation, i.e., sustained increase in the general level of prices – particularly at the long term rate experienced in Indonesia – results from the rapid expansion of the monetary supply. An increase in relative prices (say of energy) without an accommodating increase in money supply is deflationary.

[162]Exchange rate stability is emphasized as a partial response to the major disruptions which occurred during *Krismon*. A progressively overvalued real exchange rate has the politically beneficial effect of enriching the new consumer class and maintaining urban tranquility.

rates of credit growth, high inflation, and a persistently overvalued real exchange rate – raise transaction costs and keep them high. Each of them is the exact opposite of what is required for financial development, a point widely demonstrated by decades of development research and experience. Taken together, these factors reflect the extreme shallowness of Indonesia's financial system, in both absolute and relative terms.[163]

For its per capita income, pattern of development, and the growth ambitions of its leaders, Indonesia has an exceptionally narrow financial system. The rural areas remain grossly under-served by financial services. The major banks concentrate their activity in the urban areas and the use of credit and effective demand for locally-denominated financial assets are both low. The ratios of money to GDP and domestic credit to GDP (shown in Figure 3.1), both common measures of financial depth, are low.[164] In 2010, the market capitalization of the Indonesian stock market was equivalent to 51 percent of GDP; the strength of creditors' legal rights on a scale of 0 to 10 (weak to strong) was 3.[165]

The shallow financial system helps account for the economy's inflationary bias. The growth of money (depicted in Figure 3.2) and credit

---

[163]One datum point tells much of the story. The share of domestic credit from banks in Indonesia in 2010 was 36.5 percent. Corresponding data for neighboring countries were: Philippines 49.2 percent; Malaysia 132.2 percent; Singapore 85.7 percent; India 71.1 percent; Bangladesh 65.9 percent; China 146.4 percent; and Thailand 135.5 percent (*WDI* 2012, Table 5.5, pp. 300-303).

[164]The money/GDP ratio of 0.38 in 2010 in Indonesia can be put in a broader context. In 1987, when South Korea's per capita income was $3000 (the same as Indonesia's in 2010), the ratio was 0.35. Corresponding data for Malaysia (1992) and Thailand (2006) were 1.02 and 1.09 respectively. The differences with respect to domestic credit to the private sector (one of the "formation factors" that underlie the money supply) stand out more starkly. For Indonesia, the ratio in 2010 was 0.29. Corresponding data for the other countries were 0.48, 0.95, and 1.09 respectively (Source: World Development Indicators online).

[165]*WDI* (2012, Tables 5.4 and 5.5) provides comparative data. In lower middle income countries, domestic credit provided by the banking system was 57.1 percent of GDP; stock market capitalization was 65.9 percent of GDP; and the legal rights index was 5.3. The last-mentioned datum is 10 in Singapore and Hong Kong.

feeds directly through to prices with little cushion from asset substitution.[166] The high velocity of these variables[167] lead to large and erratic changes in measures of inflation such as the CPI (shown in Figure 3.3) and GDP deflator.[168] More significant for Indonesia's international competitiveness, these rates of inflation have been well beyond those recorded by Indonesia's lower middle income comparators and its main competitors.[169]

Figure 3.1: Domestic Credit Provided by Banking Sector (% of GDP)

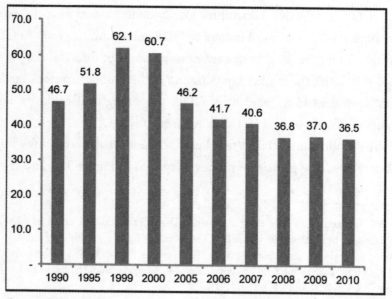

Source: World Bank, BPS

---

[166]Peiris *et al.* (2012, p.5).

[167]*WDI* (2012, Table 4.15, p.271) M2 grew by 24.3 percent per annum between 1990 and 2000; over the period 2000 to 2010, its annual growth rate was 12.7 percent.

[168]*WDI* 2012, Table 4.16, p. 275.

[169]*WDI* 2012, Table 4.16, pp.274-276.

Figure 3.2: Broad Money (% of GDP)

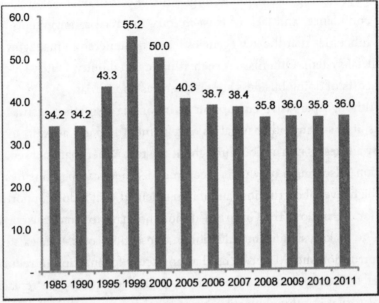

Source: BPS

Figure 3.3: CPI Inflation Rates (%)

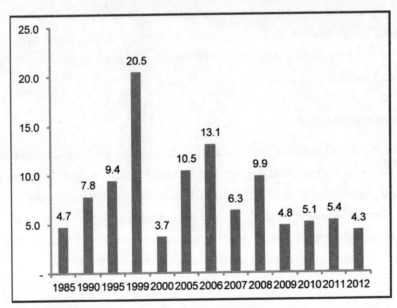

Source: BPS

The following discussion examines the effects of financial exclusion, low confidence, and lack of trust in local financial arrangements, and the difficulties that the key agencies have encountered in managing the financial system. Other issues such as policy credibility, Dutch Disease, and costs of doing business are discussed as appropriate.

Although pervasive corruption in Indonesia also raises transaction costs, it has many other negative development impacts as well, so this study addresses corruption throughout the text rather than in a separate section. Also, much of what is recommended here can be done despite the high level of corruption, and if implemented, will reduce opportunities for corruption. The Government does not have to "eradicate corruption" to make a significant reduction in transaction costs – the existence of corruption should not be used as an excuse for inaction in reducing other transaction costs. For example, policy initiatives like replacing regulatory discretion with rules-based regulation are not explicitly anti-corruption measures. Instead, they are attempts to reduce the cost of doing business by lowering the expense and uncertainty imposed by unpredictable and arbitrary government decisions. However, because these decisions are also often made by corrupt government officials, such reforms also have the effect of reducing opportunities for corruption (see Box 3.2).

Financial Exclusion

The quality of financial intermediation directly affects transaction costs. Policies and action that deepen the financial system reduce the real resources required to mediate economic interactions. Financial deepening is simultaneously the result of, and accompanied by, the emergence of increasingly sophisticated set of agencies/intermediaries that mobilize the surpluses of savers and transfer them to those who invest.

Box 3.2: Corruption and Growth

Corruption, broadly construed as the betrayal of public trust, degrades institutions, erodes public trust, sabotages due process, and undermines markets. Corruption does not "grease the wheels of commerce." If it did, the countries now at the bottom of Transparency International's rankings, such as Zimbabwe, Turkmenistan, North Korea, Sudan, and Afghanistan, would be experiencing high rates of sustained economic growth. Moreover, given the excesses of the Sukarno and Suharto regimes, many of which continue, Indonesia would already be a high income country – Indonesia is currently ranked 118.

Few Indonesians or foreigners with interests in Indonesia need reminding of the degree to which corruption intensifies privilege, aggravates inequality, perpetuates poverty, subverts markets, diverts public resources from their legitimate development purposes, and prevents the economy from growing rapidly, sustainably, and inclusively. They also do not need reminding how corruption raises transactions costs. Their everyday life is a regular reminder. A Google search "Indonesia, corruption" in May 2013 yielded 44,000,000 results in .57 seconds, well above the "hits per capita" produced by the same search for China, Vietnam, and the Philippines.

Democratization and press freedom have strengthened efforts to address corruption. Several laws passed over the last decade have boosted the authority and reach of the State Audit Authority (BPK). The Corruption Eradication Commission (KPK) was established under Law No. 30/2002. Upon taking office in 2004, President Yudhoyono gave his unqualified support to anti-corruption activities and numerous high level officials were subsequently prosecuted. In his second term, the President's enthusiasm for reducing corruption has diminished, especially as his close associates and party officials have been indicted. But despite antagonism from lawmakers, the efforts of the BPK and the KPK have earned the broad support of the general public.

At this point, there is little tangible evidence that corruption has been reduced in Indonesia; Transparency International ranking has not improved and the "costs of doing business" remain high.

Yet, perceptions have changed. During Suharto's tenure, there was a widespread resignation that little could be done about corruption. Nonetheless, since 1999, there has been a strong public demand for reform. The adoption of democratic procedures, the idea that accountability matters, and the increased access to information have been moving Indonesia beyond a system based on rule by law to one that is increasingly consistent with rule by law (Saich et al. 2010, pp. 122-125).

These changes are slowly taking hold and beginning to improve accountability, raise the level of trust within the society, and reduce the degree of official impunity. In the process, the changes are reducing transaction costs and strengthening the foundation for rapid, sustainable, and inclusive growth.

Over the last five decades, Indonesia has been through a number of phases of financial development and regression. One spectacularly successful program was the BRI (*Bank Rakyat Indonesia*) effort to help small farmers and rural producers gain access to loans during the agricultural-driven economic recovery of the late 1960s.[170] The success of this program spilled over to support the rapid expansion of manufacturing in the 1980s. With these changes, Indonesia experienced significant financial development.[171]

---

[170]Rosengard and Patten (1991); Cole and Duesenberry (1994); Cole and Slade (1993); Robinson (1997); Rosengard, *et al.* (2007).

[171]World Bank data (MetaData file) show that the ratio of net domestic credit to GDP was .01 in 1970. It rose to .08 in 1980 and was 0.47 in 1990.

That ended abruptly with *Krismon,* which followed a period of poorly regulated financial excess characterized by the ease with which the well-connected could acquire financial entities and then strip their assets, primarily through insider lending.[172] The financial meltdown was only one of the more obvious outcomes of an intensifying period of financial regression during which the growth of credit and finance became increasingly de-linked from real economic activity.[173] Indonesia has been recovering from *Krismon* ever since. The result shows up in three ways: borrowing costs are high, large numbers of Indonesians continue to have no access to formal financial institutions, and borrowing/lending remains highly restricted.

Borrowing costs have been high even for banks' best customers. The average annual rate banks charged to prime borrowers over the period 1986 to 2010 was 19.5 percent; with inflation averaging 10.5 percent over that period, the average real borrowing rate was 9 percent. There has been some moderation in borrowing costs over the last decade, with the nominal rate falling from 18.5 percent in 2000 to 13.3 percent in 2010 and, as shown in Figure 3.4, 12.4 percent in 2011.[174]

---

[172]Describing the impact of *Krismon* on Indonesia, Fane and McLeod (2002) stated: "...the main cause was that Indonesian banks flouted the prudential regulations on within-group lending and had far too little capital..."

[173]This is evident in the ratio of broad money to GDP. It was 0.08 in 1970, 0.13 in 1980, 0.34 in 1990, 0.5 in 1997 and 2000, and 0.36 in 2010. A similar pattern of disintermediation is evident in net domestic credit to the private sector. In 1993, it was 48 percent of GDP, increased to 61 percent of GDP in 1997, and then fell to 21 percent of GDP by 1999 (Source: World Bank MetaData file).

[174]World Bank MetaData file; *WDI* (2012, Table 4.15, p.271) By 2012, the lending rate had declined to 12% (IMF 2012, Box 3, p.12). Comparable rates in Singapore have been around 5 percent.

Figure 3.4: Nominal Prime Interest Rate (%)

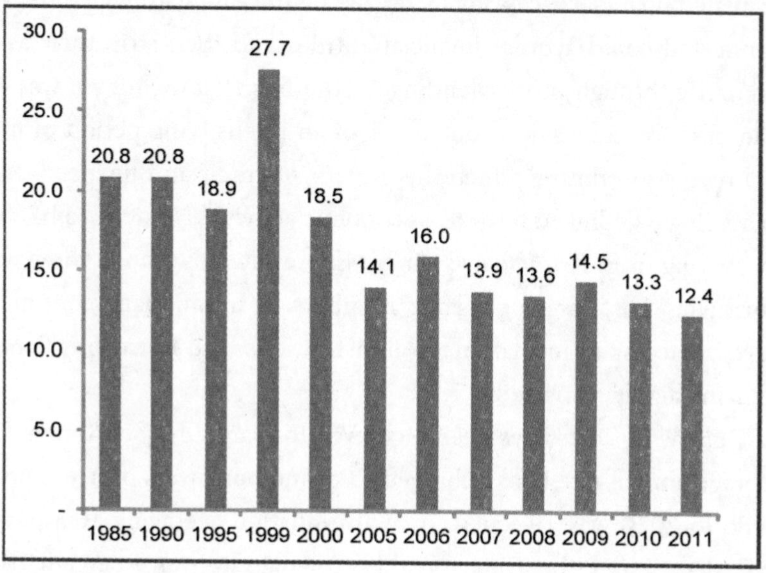

Source: BPS

Financial exclusion exacerbates inequality because it denies large numbers of Indonesians the opportunity to use credit to expand their productive capacities or more efficiently allocate their consumption over time. Producers and consumers use cash or, if they borrow, they typically pay significantly higher rates than those advertised in formal institutions and have access to credit for short periods. Each of these reduces efficiency which, in turn, lowers productivity and welfare.

An evident feature of financial exclusion, revealed by recent research, is that while there is a large nominal demand for credit and finance, there is no effective supply. Despite the overall soundness of the banking system,[175] many potentially productive borrowers cannot get loans (see Box 3.3.) In particular, small and medium enterprises (SMEs) are facing a credit crunch.[176] Access to microfinance services has also declined.

---

[175] World Bank/IMF (2010).
[176] Rosengard and Prasetyantoko (2011, p.273).

Indonesia is "…clearly under banked by standard measures of financial depth."[177] The World Bank household survey cited earlier accentuated the limited access by households to financial services. It showed that 40 percent of households did not borrow through financial organizations. Although some people chose not to borrow, many could not: "Access should not be confused with utilization, nor should all exclusion be deemed involuntary, but of the 40% who had no loans, only one-fifth said it was because they intentionally chose not to borrow. In contrast, 79% of households that did not save said it was because they had no money…"[178]

Box 3.3: Indonesia's Banking System

Indonesia's banking system has been through a number of convulsions over the past two decades. These include the dramatic deregulation and liberalization of the mid-1980s without accompanying changes in regulatory design or capacity, and the crash during the AFC a decade later. This reduced the number of banks from 239 in 1996 to 153 in 2000. The clean-up costs were the equivalent of 70 percent of the value of GDP in 1999.

The banking system is now liquid, solvent, and profitable, and despite the Bank Century debacle, was not directly damaged by Global Financial Crisis (GFC). The main impact on financial activity of the GFC was due to the slow-down in economic growth. Yet even with the restructuring, bank coverage remains limited, bank efficiency is low, and banking regulation and supervision are weak.

---

[177]Rosengard and Presetyantoko (2011).

[178]*Ibid*. Further evidence is provided by the World Bank Global Financial Inclusion Study 2012. As noted by the *Financial Times*, in 2010 "…only 20 percent of Indonesian adults—defined as age 15 or above—had saving accounts in any formal financial institutions, while only 9 percent went to banks or other financial firms to get loans." That is, close to 140 million adults did not have savings accounts in formal institutions (http://www.ft.com/cms/s/0/ced4782c-b8c9-11de-809b-00144feab49a.html#ixzz28MALOBBw).

Capital markets are undeveloped, with the banking sector dominating financial intermediation in Indonesia. Commercial banks hold 79 percent of total financial sector assets and bank credit is still only 44 percent of GDP. This is low relative to both ASEAN and BRIC countries. As noted in the text, roughly half of Indonesian households are estimated to lack access to formal financial services. This coverage could easily be higher. Banks are underleveraged, with a loan to deposit ratio at about 70 percent and loans making up just over half of total bank assets. There is little competition within the banking sector to encourage entry into underserved markets and spur the development of innovative products and delivery systems. The sector is dominated by a few banks: 4 banks account for 44 percent of total bank assets. Deposits are highly concentrated, with 0.1 percent of accounts totaling 46 percent of deposit value.

The Financial Services Authority (OJK), which is expected to be fully operational by the end of 2013, has yet to develop the technical capacity and political autonomy to conduct rigorous, independent bank regulation and supervision. In the meantime, Indonesia's efforts to re-regulate and consolidate the banking system after Krismon have had the unintended effect of concentrating credit risk and reducing access to financial services. Banks appear to be chasing the same customers in the same locations with the same conventional, comparably priced products. (Rosengard and Prasetyantoko 2011)

A number of banks, including BTPN (*Bank Tabungan Pensiunan Nasional*), Bank Mandiri, and Standard Chartered have been seeking to attract new customers through community lending and no-fee bank accounts.[179] This effort seeks to enable those who are currently un-banked

---

[179]Demopoulos (2009).

to begin formalizing their "saving habit." Although expanding rapidly at present, these programs will take a long time to redress the shallowness of the financial system and the under-banked nature of the country as a whole. Moreover, the real test is how readily the banks which mobilize the savings recycle them as loans to the local poor.[180]

For most individuals the inability, or continuing unwillingness, to use formal banking arrangements indicates that the transaction costs, particularly information costs, are too high relative to the tangible benefits (including convenience and timeliness) provided by mechanisms such as community-based fund pooling (*arisan*) and similar arrangements.[181] As a final cautionary point, the "voluntary" nature of financial exclusion should not be misinterpreted. The majority of Indonesians has not foresworn borrowing as part of an optimizing strategy.[182] If the financial system were deeper and if intermediation costs were lower, a significantly larger share of the population would borrow or lend than at present. The fragmentation of the financial system and high costs of financial transactions block this behavior to the overall detriment of broader growth and development.

Small borrowers, particularly MSMEs (micro, small and medium enterprises), tend to be cut out of the loan market since the banks make most of their loans to large enterprises and state-owned enterprises. Thus, although credit growth has been around 20 percent per annum over the last decade, the share for most banks of credit going to MSMEs was less than 20 percent of their lending.[183] This is due in part to increased concentration following the restructuring of the banking system in the wake of *Krismon*.

---

[180] A complaint our team heard in several regions (and discussed further below) was the financial resources mobilized by banks were regularly transferred to Jakarta rather than lent out locally.

[181] Zoetelief (1999); Mordoch (2007).

[182] Mordoch (2007, pp.16-17).

[183] Rosengard and Prasetyantoko (2011).

With fewer banks, there is less need now to compete and innovate.[184] That keeps transaction costs high.

Low Confidence and Lack of Trust

The low levels of confidence and lack of trust among asset-holders in Indonesia's financial system is evident from their behavior. An obvious indicator is that the financial system still has not recovered from *Krismon*.[185] Another is the degree to which asset-holders hedge themselves by making alternative financial arrangements. Some of the arrangements directly benefit other countries. When Indonesians hold US or Singapore dollars they generate seignorage for the monetary authorities of those countries.[186] By allowing locals to hold foreign currency accounts, Indonesia's monetary authorities provide a safety valve which reduces the chance that a black market in foreign exchange will re-emerge. This makes a virtue out of necessity, but it has two implications. First, it is an open admission by the monetary and fiscal authorities that they have limited confidence in their own capacities to deal with the shocks that will prompt the dumping of local currency. Second, the ability of asset holders to switch assets (an "exit" strategy) gives them few incentives to devote their own resources and effort (including "voice") to make the local financial system work more efficiently and inclusively.[187]

---

[184]Vallikappen and Meostafa (2013).

[185]Net domestic credit to GDP was 0.6 in 2000 and 0.36 in 2010 (World Bank Meta-Data file). Indonesia experienced far more disruption during *Krismon* (measured by the decline in real output, hyper-depreciation of the exchange rate, and bank losses) than any other country (McCleod and Fane 2002; McCleod 2003a; Hill 2012; Thee 2012).

[186]Seignorage accrues when there is a positive gap between real resources provided in exchange for fiat money and the real costs the monetary authority incurs issuing and maintaining the money. A common (though rough) measure of seignorage is the growth rate of base money, i.e., coin, bank vault cash, and currency with the public and commercial bank reserves at the central bank (Friedman 1971; Black 1989; McPherson 2000).

[187]These private incentives, however, do not let the Government or BI off the hook. An efficient financial system creates public goods/services and warrants public support and investment.

Although the rupiah is used in local trade and exchange, especially by those with low incomes, its holding costs are high due to the country's continuing history of chronic inflation.[188] One reflection of this cost is the high velocity of circulation (i.e., the ratio of GDP to money supply).[189]

The switch out of rupiah into other currencies and commodities adds to inflationary pressures. Asset owners respond to this loss of value by demanding a higher premium for holding rupiah-denominated assets. This puts upward pressure on the interest rate, explaining (at least in part) why interest rates in Indonesia are well above those in neighboring countries and much higher than rates in international financial centers such as Singapore and Hong Kong.[190] High interest rates constrain the opportunities for profitable investment, especially in long-term projects.[191]

Underlying these high costs is a general lack of trust in the medium and longer term pattern of financial development in Indonesia. Regular surveys undertaken by the World Bank highlight the costs of doing business in Indonesia both in absolute terms (e.g., the number of days and steps needed to start a business) and relative to the costs incurred in comparator countries. The World Bank's Doing Business Report focuses on issues such as starting a business, employing workers, obtaining credit, paying taxes,

---

[188]Following McCleod (2003), one of the major holding costs is the "decline in the value of money" associated with inflation. As shown in Figure 3.3, it has been high. From 1986 to 2010, CPI inflation in Indonesia averaged 10.5 percent per annum and from 1970 to 2010, it averaged 12.2 percent per annum.

[189]IMF (2012, Table 3, p.36).

[190]Palomba (2012). A relevant indicator is the 10-year government bond rate. In February 2012, it was 1.4 percent in Singapore, 1.2 percent in Hong Kong, and 3.8 percent in Indonesia (*Economist*, February 18, 2012, p.92). The Indonesian rate refers to dollar-denominated bonds. That is, the effective spread was higher than these nominal amounts show.

[191]This, in turn, helps explain why there has been so little private interest in investing in long-lived infrastructure projects – roads, ports, electricity generation – without special provisions that cover the costs of finance (among other risks).

permit and license fees, among others.[192] One dimension that is not directly reflected in the surveys is the degree of trust which locals have in the financial system. However, one measure is revealing: fewer than 12 percent of enterprises in Indonesia used banks to finance their operations.[193]

The limited attention given to trust in these business surveys is understandable. Trust is hard to measure[194] and some even see it as a non-issue. Business leaders, for example, tend to focus on the quality of short-term economic management, on the principle that if that deteriorates they can always scale back their investment. Others, particularly those who believe markets are efficient, expect that differing degrees of trust and confidence are already priced into asset values. They are correct to the extent that relevant asset markets exist and are competitive. But, the basic problem is that when trust is low, relevant markets often do not exist.

ficulties, the reactions of asset-holders reveal how little or how much trust/confidence they have in the financial system.[195] Several measures are relevant, such as the:

- premium on foreign exchange;
- discount on government or central bank bills relative to a recognized international asset;

---

[192]World Bank (2012); Athukorala and Hill (2010, Table 2.5, p. 19).

[193]WDI (2012, Tables 5.2 and 5.3) provide data on the costs of doing business.

[194]Trust, like confidence, is circular—societies based on trust/confidence tend to develop rapidly, and rapidly developing societies tend to have higher levels of trust/confidence. The paradigm in Acemoglu and Robinson (2012)—countries fail because of an oligarchy trap and countries with an oligarchy trap fail – is a recent widely-cited example. The challenge for Indonesia, which has low trust and (according to Jeffrey Winters) entrenched oligarchs, is how to begin creating the conditions that will enable trust to spread.

[195]Fukuyama (1995) argued that trust was an essential element in any society that reduces the social costs of interacting and transacting. Low trust societies have high transaction costs, some of which are so high they preclude the development of what in other countries are highly profitable markets (e.g., for long-term government debt or central bank bonds) and block the emergence of socially beneficial trade and exchange (e.g., insurance markets).

- difference between the prime lending rate and the "riskless" Treasury Bill or bond rate;
- share of wealth held in local financial assets relative to foreign alternatives;
- time-horizon of the average investment;
- willingness to hold financial as opposed to real assets;
- extent contracts are honored, reflected in the degree to which creditors expect to gain control of collateral in the event of default;[196]
- average length to maturity of bank or other loans;
- volatility of asset values to changes in financial market "news";
- degree to which borrowers can obtain loans on the financial merits of their project rather than their political and other connections; and
- time taken for the financial system to recover from a major shock.

Each of these indicators highlights particular weaknesses within Indonesia's financial system. Taken together they reaffirm that many, if not most, asset holders remain exceedingly skeptical of the capacities of Ministry of Finance and Bank Indonesia to meet their responsibilities.[197] Those concerns were reinforced during the Bank Century bailout. It has not helped confidence that the Financial Supervisory Agency (OJK), first proposed as an integrated supervisory body and mandated by Article 34 of Law 23/1999 to be established "not later than 31 December 2002," did not exist in 2011.[198] Despite the urgency to contain the losses and the promises

---

[196]In 2011 it took 40 procedures and an average of 570 days to enforce contracts in Indonesia (*WDI* 2012, Table 5.3). This was a marginally shorter time than for other lower middle income countries, but was significantly above that in Singapore (21, 150), South Korea (33, 230), Malaysia (42, 312), Vietnam (34, 295), and Thailand (36, 479).

[197]McCleod (2003); East Asian Analytical Unit (2000); IMF (2010).

[198]East Asia Analytical Unit (2000); Siregar and Williams (2004); Herwidayatimo (2002); FRBSF (2010); and Pradiytyo *et al.* (2011). Buehler (2012) indicated that the relevant legislation was passed in 2011 although, as McCleod (2011) noted, it was clear that BI was not going to relinquish its role as bank supervisor. As noted in Box 3.2, the agency is due to become fully operational by the end of 2013 (IMF 2012, p.21).

of meaningful reform made in the wake of *Krismon*, problems of influence-peddling, crony banking, insider deals, regulatory indulgence, and basic incapacity to appropriately supervise the financial system continue.

Since the principal feature of any financial asset is that its value depends on whether it is accepted rather than whether it is backed,[199] the above circumstances leave the GOI and Bank Indonesia with a binary choice. They can maintain their current policies, implicitly accepting that the financial system will remain shallow and that most Indonesians will be excluded and have minimal trust in its operational integrity and stability. Alternatively, they can actively modify their policies to begin creating the conditions that deepen the financial system and foster the sophistication needed to support rapid sustained inclusive growth.[200]

Confusion about Bank Indonesia's Role

The contribution of Bank Indonesia (BI) to Indonesia's development has been undermined in two ways. The first is due to BI's ineffective handling of inflation targeting. This derives from the convenient misinterpretation by BI principals of the responsibilities of an independent central bank. The second is the adverse effects of the way in which the one-size-fits-all monetary and exchange rate policy is managed.

Since New Zealand first legalized the pursuit of a specific inflation rate as the sole objective of its central bank, numerous other countries have become "inflation nutters" (as Bank of England Governor Mervyn King's referred to them only half in jest). BI, which formally adopted inflation targeting in 2005, was late on the scene. Most major central banks (the Federal Reserve, the Bank of England, the ECB, and the Bank of Japan)

---

[199]Duesenberry (1964).

[200]The latter is consistent with the GOI's goals of having Indonesia among the ten largest economies in the world by 2030 and among the top six by 2050 (BAPPENAS 2011, Preface by Dr. H. Susilo Bambang Yudhoyono). None of this can materialize with a shallow financial system.

have inflation as a target, although they modify it in numerous, often idio-syncratic, ways.[201]

The GOI granted BI "independence" in the aftermath of *Krismon*. While this action was widely advocated by prominent academics and international agencies, especially the World Bank, many of its potential advantages were over-played. The presumption was that an "indepen-dent" agency (such as the central bank) would be free of political in-terference and have the discretion to resolve (or work around) many of the institutional deficiencies of the financial system. Missed in all this strategizing was the fact that the bank being granted independence may not have the necessary capacities to fulfill its role.

The rationale for GOI granting BI "independence" is contained in the Introduction to the enabling legislation: "…in order to assure the accom-plishment of maintaining the stability of the rupiah value, it is necessary to have an independent Central Bank." Article 4, Point 2 states "Bank Indonesia is an independent state institution, which is free from any interferences of the Government and/or any other parties, except for matters explicitly prescribed in this Act."[202] This point was reinforced in Article 9, Points 1 and 2, which assert: "Other parties shall not interfere with the implementation of the tasks of Bank Indonesia as referred to in Article 8" and "Bank Indonesia shall refuse and or ignore any form of in-terferences conducted by any parties in the implementation of its tasks."

---

[201]The Bank of England, for instance, describes its "monetary policy framework" as follows: "A target of 2% does not mean that inflation will be held at this rate con-stantly. That would be neither possible nor desirable. Interest rates would be changing all the time, and by large amounts, causing unnecessary uncertainty and volatility in the economy. Even then it would not be possible to keep inflation at 2% in each and every month. Instead, the MPC's [Monetary Policy Committee] aim is to set interest rates so that inflation can be brought back to target within a reasonable time period without creating undue instability in the system" (www.bankofengland.co.uk/monetarypolicy accessed February 4, 2013).

[202]McCleod (2003) pointed out that BI largely wrote Act No. 23/1999 on Bank Indonesia.

These points were "elucidated" in subsequent legislation (Law No. 3/2004) giving BI independence, autonomy, and complete discretion to resist any outside influence.[203]

This insulation from outside "interference" is unfortunate. Based on BI's published material and actions, its principals and staff could benefit from some. If they were to take note, they could learn that, as an institution, BI is "independent" within but not of the Government of Indonesia.[204] At present, BI's principals and staff have interpreted their independence as giving them the authority to proceed without hindrance except as required by *their* interpretation of the Act. The implication is that no one – well-meaning government officials, concerned citizens, academics, or others – has any right to "interfere" as BI officials define the term.

It would be to Indonesia's benefit if some constructive outside "interference" could modify BI's views and practices.[205] What might that be? A fruitful start would be to exercise more care in describing what the Bank is meant to do and how it means to do it. Referring to its "Objectives and Tasks of Bank Indonesia," the BI website asserts: "In its capacity as central bank, Bank Indonesia has one single objective of achieving and maintaining stability of the Rupiah value." It explains:

"The stability of the value of the Rupiah comprises two as-

---

[203]As interpreted by its principals, the Bank is "…an independent state institution, …[which]… is fully autonomous in formulating and implementing each of its tasks and authority as stipulated in the Act. External parties are strictly prohibited from interfering with Bank Indonesia's implementation of its tasks, and Bank Indonesia has the duty to refuse or disregard any attempt of interference in any form by any party." [Source: www.bi.go.id/web/en/] This interpretation is consistent with Article 4, point 2 and Article 9 of the Bank Indonesia Act (No. 23, May 19, 1999).

[204]This point was made by Robert V. Roosa who, as Under Secretary to the US Treasury, was testifying before Congress. (This anecdote was recounted by Professor James S. Duesenberry.)

[205]BI is fulfilling its legal mandate to operate transparently and accountably by publicizing the outcome of its policy deliberations. Notwithstanding this welcome example of official transparency, academic analysis indicates that the BI's policy statements are regularly misunderstood or misinterpreted (Sahminan 2008).

pects, one is stability of Rupiah value against goods and services and the other is the stability of the exchange rate of the Rupiah against other currencies. The first aspect is as reflected by the rate of inflation and the second aspect is as reflected by the development of Rupiah exchange rate against other currencies."

The website describes the operation of its Inflation Targeting Framework (ITF) which involves the "...setting of the policy rate (BI Rate) with the expectation of influencing money market rates...[and]...ultimately...output and inflation." The website describes the expected policy transmission mechanism.

Visitors to the website and those who read the linked Acts and quarterly "Monetary Policy Response" will recognize that BI has not come to grips with its self-inflicted policy dilemma. Of several, one example will illustrate. The "Monetary Policy Response Quarter III 2011" asserts: "Going forward, Bank Indonesia is determined to continue maintaining the stability of the Rupiah exchange rate that is needed to secure macroeconomic stability."[206] This relationship is back-to-front. It is macroeconomic stability that will limit movements in the exchange rate, not the other way round.[207]

A further outside suggestion that BI principals and staff could usefully heed is matching instruments with targets.[208] At present, BI has

---

[206]Thee and Negara (2010) highlight the inconsistency in BI's attempts to keep inflation low (which requires an increase in the Bank Rate to restrict the growth of credit) while simultaneously attempting to prevent the exchange rate from appreciating.

[207]History has proof. Prior to their abandonment in 1972, fixed exchange rates did not "secure" macroeconomic stability. Closer to the present, BI officials could fruitfully note the activities of other major central banks (the Federal Reserve, ECB, Bank of Japan, Bank of Canada, Bank of England), none of which seek to stabilize the exchange rate to promote macroeconomic stability.

[208]There is a detailed literature in economics, beginning with contributions by Jan Tinbergen and Lawrence Klein and elaborated later by Robert Mundell and others, which emphasizes the importance of matching instruments to targets (Tinbergen 1952; Mundell 1962; Klein 1971).

two targets (low inflation and a stable exchange rate) and only one instrument (the BI Rate). BI's approach has itself and by extension the whole country, in a bind.[209] Worse, because BI is "independent" there is nothing that anyone can do to rectify the situation, except those who might change the relevant Act.[210]

The bind is the following. BI has specific inflation targets: 5 percent (±1 percent) in 2011 and 4.5 percent (±1 percent) in 2012.[211] If it achieves this target, Indonesia will be inflating at rates above those of its principal trading partners.[212] Under these circumstances, a stable rupiah value (shown in Figure 3.5), an explicit BI goal, progressively revalues the real exchange rate on a bilateral and effective basis.[213] This is what the aggregate data have affirmed since BI formally adopted inflation targeting in 2005.[214] Using exchange rate and consumer price data from the World Bank's World Development Indicators for China, the United States, Japan, Malaysia, Singapore, and Korea, over the period 2005 to 2011 the rupiah appreciated in real terms against these respective cur-

---

[209]That bind is further complicated by the suggestion in the ITF (BI Indonesia 2008) that BI "coordinates" with other policy objectives of other parts of the government. Doing this would add more targets.

[210]The problem is deeper. Changing the Act may not suffice because it would depend on who writes the amendments and how BI principals and its officials interpret them.

[211]"Monetary Policy Response Quarter III 2011"17/10/2011 at www.bi.go.id/web/en (accessed August 16, 2012). The latter target was reaffirmed for 2013 in "Monetary Policy Response Quarter I 2012" 25/04/2012.

[212]The recent past is a relevant guide. Over the period 2005 to 2012, while the increase in the CPI for Indonesia was 61.8 percent, the respective increases in China, the US, Japan, Hong Kong, Malaysia, Singapore, and Korea were 27.7, 18.5, -0.8, 21.8, 19.9, 26.4, and 24.2 percent.

[213]Chinn (2006). The performance of BI in stabilizing the rupiah, at best, has been problematic. Based on IMF data (IMF 2012, Table 1, p.34), the change in the Rp/US$ exchange rate was +6.9 percent in 2009 (i.e., a depreciation), 12.8 percent in 2010 (i.e., an appreciation), -3.8 percent in 2011, and +7.2 percent in 2012. Over the period 2008 to 2012, the rupiah appreciated 10.8 percent against the US dollar.

[214]The trend discussed below is evident from 2000 onwards, i.e., the whole era of BI independence.

rencies by 28.3, 32.1, 41.5, 30.7, 29.6, and 28.9 percent.[215] These data suggest that the apparent "moderation" in the rate of inflation (Figure 3.3) has been achieved at the expense of declining international competitiveness, further underscoring the dynamic damage that BI "independence" involves.

Figure 3.5: Nominal Exchange Rate Against USD

Exchange Rate against USD

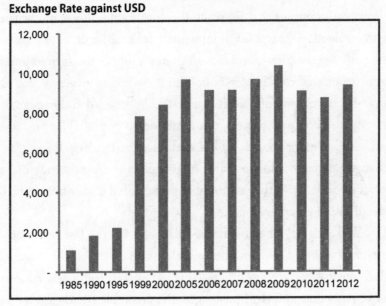

Source: BPS

The resulting pressures on the Indonesian economy have shown up in several ways. By inappropriately targeting exchange rate stability Indo-

---

[215]BI is not the only agency confounded over the exchange rate. Both the EIU and the IMF (2012 Article IV) have projections to 2017 showing that Indonesia will continue growing at rates significantly above 6 percent per annum while the real exchange rate continues to appreciate (given the assumed stability of the exchange rate and the projected increase in Indonesian prices). EIU (January 2013, p.7) and IMF (2012, Table 6, p.39; Table II.I, p. 45).

nesia, like Ghana, Zambia, Angola, Nigeria, Russia, and other resource-dependent developing countries, has experienced Dutch Disease (a point considered further in Box 3.4). The systematic increase in the prices of non-tradables relative to tradables (or the appreciation of the real exchange rate) has been hollowing out the country's manufacturing capacity, undercutting staple food production, and because of the slow growth in high productivity employment, making it increasingly difficult for labor to transfer out of low productivity activities (a point examined in Annex 2).

Practical examples that illustrate the compound effects of exchange rate overvaluation (the point of immediate interest here), high transport costs (discussed earlier), and lack of public support for agricultural research (examined in Chapter Four) are provided in Annex 4 and Box 3.5. These developments have systematically reduced Indonesia's productivity and competitiveness, undermining its potential for sustained, rapid, and inclusive growth. These examples, particularly the effects of exchange rate over-valuation, also help explain the persistence of high rates of informality in the economy (a point noted earlier but discussed in detail in the Chapter Four).

These trends have been counter-balanced over the last few years by the expansive world demand for natural resources – coal, copper, cocoa, coffee, and rubber among others. This has spared Indonesia from balance of payments and debt problems. The favorable trends are unlikely to last, particularly in view of the gap that has emerged in the growth of imports relative to exports.[216]

The above data demonstrate in stark terms BI's general lack of success in containing inflation at rates consistent with international performance. One outcome is that BI has a serious credibility problem (discussed in more detail in Annex 5). Given its track record, few people reasonably

---

[216]*WDI* (2012, Table 6.1) shows that the volume and value of exports over the period 2000-2010 grew by 0.8 and 11 percent respectively. Corresponding data for imports were 6.5 and 14.4 percent.

expect BI to meet its inflation target. This induces behavior, such as the increased velocity of circulation noted earlier and flight to foreign currency that makes it even more difficult for the BI to meet its target. Moreover, BI has supported its attempts to reduce inflation by large sales of foreign exchange.[217] This has insulated the economy from exchange rate movements, which under normal circumstances would have flowed through to domestic prices.

The second issue noted earlier, namely the adverse effects of the one-size-fits-all monetary and exchange rate policy cannot be fully or fairly attributed to BI alone. Central banks across the globe that rely on open market operations to influence their financial sectors have limited capacity to run differentiated monetary policies. Arbitrage by local and foreign asset-holders would quickly undermine any attempt to sustain differentiated policy rates or the purchase and sale of foreign exchange at different rates across regions. But what central banks (including BI) can do and, moreover, should be expected to do, is to cooperate with the fiscal authorities and other relevant agencies to moderate the most glaring disparities in economic opportunities across regions created by the one-size-fits-all monetary and exchange rate policies. Why does this matter?

Box 3.4: Dutch Disease

Opinions differ whether Indonesia has been experiencing Dutch Disease. Some observers note that recent economic policies have regenerated the former colonial economy that was driven largely by resource extraction. Others have argued that there is no Dutch Disease and that the real exchange rate is broadly consistent with underlying fundamentals.

---

[217]Bland (2012); Unditu, Norgay, and Siehaan (2012); Vallikappen and Moestafa (2013).

Although differences in viewpoint can be traced to the data used and the time period considered, the issue is not about scoring debating points but how to promote rapid, sustained, and inclusive growth. That is, the issue is whether the combined effects of fiscal, monetary, and debt management policies generate values for the real exchange rate that sustainably boost Indonesia's productivity and competitiveness.

There are many indications that this has not been the case over the past decade. Natural resource exports have dominated Indonesia's trade, the country's relative contribution to manufactured value chains in Asia and throughout the world has declined, manufacturing employment has "stabilized" at levels reached in the 1990s, and the contribution of manufacturing to GDP has fallen from 28 to 24 percent. The Government is

imposing taxes and restrictions to force producers to add value to their natural resources because local market prices, when converted at the current exchange rate, do not provide them with the incentive to do so voluntarily. Other changes, such as the expansion of the "new consumer class" and its growing dependence on imports, have left Indonesia consuming relatively fewer local manufactures. The major part of new foreign direct investment has been in natural resources rather than manufacturing or services. Recent rates of growth in Batam, a special economic zone designed to operate as an export platform, barely exceeds that of the rest of the economy, despite its considerable locational, institutional, and logistical advantages. Even with import restrictions on a variety of products, key agricultural staple commodities are being imported in larger amounts. The expansion of natural resource exports has done nothing substantive to more closely integrate the economy. Finally, the rupiah has appreciated by roughly 40 percent in real terms against the dong and the yuan over the last decade.

These trends reflect an economy that has become habituated to natural resource exploitation, resulting in shifts in the structure of the economy that undercut the competitiveness of tradables, particularly manufacturing and small-scale agriculture. In the process, the underlying rate of growth of output has been de-linked from increases in the value of local incomes (expressed in dollar terms). To illustrate, over the decade 2000 to 2010, the growth rate of per capita real income (measured in local currency units) averaged 4 percent, whereas the growth rate in the US dollar value of income per capita averaged 14.3 percent. Over the longer term, real per capita income and income expressed in foreign currency terms can only diverge to the degree to which Indonesian labor productivity growth exceeds that of its main competitors. That has clearly not been the case in Indonesia over the last decade.

These trends all reflect an adverse shift in Indonesia's ability to compete in world markets. Taken together, they are evidence of Dutch Disease. Remedying that situation will require a change in the fiscal and monetary policy stances of the Ministry of Finance and Bank Indonesia. That change

would involve measures to devalue the exchange rate so that it reflects differentials in Indonesia's productivity consistent with its high rate of inflation relative to trading partners, as well as the additional costs imposed by encroaching government intervention, regulations, weak infrastructure, high financing costs, and rising formal sector wages.

For a more detailed discussion of Dutch Disease in Indonesia, see: (Basri and Hill 2008); (Basri 2010); (Saich et al. 2010); (Basri and Papanek 2012); (IMF 2011); (OECD 2012); (Nasution 2012, 2013).

Box 3.5: Garlic, Salt, and Oranges - A Taste of Declining International Competitiveness

Once self-sufficient in garlic, salt, and honey oranges, Indonesia now imports these commodities. The issues of garlic (examined in Annex 4), salt, and honey oranges are indicative of the problems for local producers created by the high costs of transport, the limited and declining local support for agricultural research, and the progressive overvaluation of the exchange rate.

While diminished competitiveness in garlic and oranges has been noted, the trends in salt imports have elicited stronger reactions. Former president Megawati described the situation as "incomprehensible" and members of the local media labeled the situation a "shameful paradox." (Sihite and Sihaloho 2012) Superficially, Indonesia has the appropriate conditions for salt production—long, shallow shorelines, hot weather, and local salt farms. Nonetheless, salt imports, primarily from Australia, Germany, India, Singapore, and New Zealand, have been around 1.5 million tons per year. BPS data show that for 2011, 2.8 million tons of salt were imported at a cost of $146.5 million. (Hitipeuw 2012)

There are four issues behind these findings. First, Indonesia's 60,000 hectares of salt farms supplies only 55 percent of local consumption. (Baskoro 2012); (Jakarta Globe 2012) Second, the salt farms are scattered across Indonesia and transporting salt (a high volume, low value commodity) is expensive. Third, local salt does not reach the standards now being demanded by the "new consumer class." Fourth, as emphasized elsewhere in this chapter, the current value of the rupiah subsidizes imports and discourages domestic production.

Officials have expressed concern about Indonesia's growing import dependence for these (and numerous other) commodities. Appropriately interpreted, these trends are a useful guide for future policy:

- when local commodities cannot be transported to market more cheaply than the commodities can be imported, local infrastructure needs to be improved in ways that reduce logistics costs;

- when technological advance abroad outstrips the techniques available locally, additional local research to improve quality would be beneficial; and

- when a large number of local commodities cannot compete with imports on the basis of price, monetary and fiscal policies that are over-valuing the local real exchange rate need to be re-examined and modified.

A basic theme of this study is that Indonesia has the potential to achieve rapid, inclusive growth for the next several decades through policies and programs that sustainably integrate and extend the country's domestic market, as well as re-connect a unified and vibrant domestic market with global value chains. A sub-theme is that many of the current actions and activities by the Government and its official agencies regularly undercut that potential.

One of these is the practice of managing the Indonesian economy as if it were an integrated entity that conveniently looks and behaves much like the Jakarta greater metropolitan area. The implication is that while BI cannot avoid a one-size-fits-all approach, its monetary policies need to be appropriate to the whole economy, especially in view of the limited degree to which the domestic market is extended, its low level of regional integration, and the fragmentation of money and financial markets. Indeed, the surest means by which BI and other agencies, such as the Ministry of Finance, can block extension of the domestic market and hinder further integration of the national economy is to continue their current practice of pretending that Indonesia as a whole is a unitary monetary and exchange rate entity that behaves and responds like the country's richest region.

The problems of operating a one-size-fits-all are not unique to Indonesia. The recent difficulties countries within the Euro region are having with debt, financial fragility, and fiscal imbalance highlight some of the difficulties.[218] The studies of these circumstances, including those which relate to a coherent "optimal currency area" such as the United States, show that monetary policy has heterogeneous regional impacts.[219]

There are several reasons for this heterogeneity:

- Bank deposits are significantly more mobile across regions than bank credits, largely on account of differential (asymmetric) access to information by lenders.[220]
- Structural differences in output, employment, education, infrastructure, and "neighborhood" effects (such as interaction with other countries) explain some other impacts. Recent research has shown that many of the same issues apply to Indonesia.[221]

These effects have been accentuated by the management (and manipulation) of the exchange rate. Indeed, economic historians have noted that a one-size-fits-all exchange rate policy has been a source of regional concern (and even tension) from Sukarno's time.[222]

---

[218]Wynne and Koech (2012); Malkin and Nechio (2012). Both of these studies applied the Taylor Rule on a regional basis. Their analyses highlighted the different regional impacts – none of the Taylor Rules specifically constructed for the regions matched the overall Rule being used by either the Fed or the ECB. Given its closer degree of financial integration, the discrepancies were less in the US than in Europe.

[219]Crone (2012).

[220]During our team's visit to South Sulawesi, officials in Makassar noted that the region experienced a regular drain of finance to the Jakarta area in particular, but to other regions as well. One reason offered was that the banks, most of which had headquarters in Jakarta, did not make the effort to learn about the potential of local customers.

[221]Ridhwan et.al (2011); "...the output effects of the monetary policy actions tend to vary substantially across Indonesia's regions in terms of both magnitude and timing" (Ridhwan 2011, p.177). See also Ridhwan et al. (2011). Georgopoulos (2010) found similar regional impacts in Canada.

[222]Economic historians have noted that the general over-valuation of the exchange rate (and operation of multiple exchange rate system) that was administered centrally

The one-size-fits-all monetary and exchange rate policies in Indonesia reinforce differences in economic prospects and growth rates across regions. *Krismon* provided a natural experiment. At the same time as the economy of much of Java was imploding, economic activity in Batam, Riau, Kalimantan, and South Sulawesi was exceptionally robust, in large part due to the export stimulus provided by the sharply depreciated exchange rate. That is, the devalued currency boosted growth in some regions outside Java, while it was simultaneously undercutting economic activity in the Jakarta region, where the over-leveraged and deeply dollar-indebted financial entities were located. The data in Figures 3.6 and 3.7 confirm the differential performance both for regional growth and for the expansion of manufacturing.

Figure 3.6: Share of Manufacturing Output (% by Region)

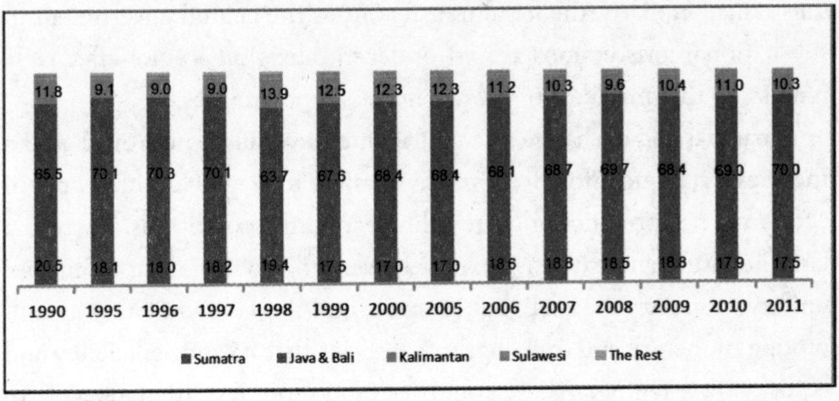

Source: BPS

during the Sukarno regime was a source of regional friction, particularly among the resource-rich regions (Feith 1962; Dick 2002, Ch. 6, pp.179-186; Ricklefs 2003).

**Figure 3.7: Share of Manufacturing Output –
Zoom in on the AFC (% by Region)**

Share of Regional Output (%)	1990	1995	1996	1997	1998	1999	2000
Sumatra	20.5	18.1	18.0	18.2	19.4	17.5	17.0
Java & Bali	65.5	70.1	70.3	70.1	63.7	67.6	68.4
Kalimantan	11.8	9.1	9.0	9.0	13.9	12.5	12.3
Sulawesi	1.4	1.8	1.7	1.7	2.0	1.7	1.8
The Rest	0.9	1.0	1.0	1.1	1.0	0.7	0.5

Source: BPS

These differential regional effects show up in numerous indicators. The large regional income gaps were noted earlier. These gaps have been moderated to the extent that factors of production (labor and capital) move across regions. As described in Chapter 4, relatively small numbers of workers have been moving to Kalimantan, Riau, and Batam in response to the rising demand for labor. The overall economic impact has been limited because the migrant workers generally lack the necessary skills. Similarly, the fiscal transfers from the central government to sub-national jurisdictions as part of decentralization are not effectively redressing the problems of low economic opportunities.

Financial and exchange rate management would be improved across Indonesia if some effort were made to allow for regional differences in economic performance and prevailing economic conditions. There is a large literature and extensive experience among countries that comprise unitary monetary areas (Brazil, Canada, and the United States) in promoting monetary and exchange rate policies that balance efficiency and equity across regions. These countries (and more recently China) have done what the World Bank suggested in its economic geography framework (referred to in Chapter 2). A key proposition was that governments and their agencies needed to ensure that resources from regions with high economic density were constructively redistributed to those with low economic density.[223] Current arrangements in Indonesia have the reverse effect: as noted in Chapter 1, they favor rich regions.

---

[223]World Bank (2009, Ch. 8).

How might BI respond? It is in a bind. It has only one instrument, the Bank Rate, and two targets, one for inflation and one to meet the indeterminate goal of stabilizing the exchange rate. To begin the process of improving its macroeconomic management, BI needs to avoid all manipulation of the exchange rate. The short-term impact would be a sharp depreciation of the exchange rate, particularly when asset holders begin to realize the pressures that have been mounting on the balance of payments. A depreciated exchange rate would improve the profitability of export-oriented industries, scale back the consumption of the new consumer class through higher import prices, and enable Indonesia's producers to offset some of the competitive disadvantages associated with high logistics and transaction costs. It would also boost regional activity helping to extend the domestic market. A further effect is that it would improve BI's performance. Its efforts to reduce inflation (through the instruments it can influence) will not be compromised by the exchange rate and other distractions. Continued over time, improvements in BIs performance will raise the degree of trust among the general public in BI to manage better the financial system.

The present low level of confidence and trust in the financial system poses a major credibility problem for both BI and the Government. As explained in Annex 5, it will not be easy to overcome. Re-establishing credibility will require major improvements in capacity and governance. A Harvard Kennedy School prequel to this study examined the challenges and opportunities of promoting institutional reform and improving governance, and the conclusions derived there still apply.[224] One matter that deserves immediate attention is for the Government to revisit the nature of independence which BI has conferred upon itself.

---

[224]Saich *et al.* (2010, esp. Ch. 4).

Lessons and Policy Prescriptions

The lack of infrastructure undercuts Indonesia's development potential, reduces productivity and competitiveness, and lowers standards of living. It is major impediment to the quest for rapid, inclusive growth. Indonesia's infrastructure deficiencies are critical and policy makers should not allow them to worsen.

Public sector capacities should be fully exploited so that all available public resources are effectively deployed. This is obvious in the case of line ministries, perhaps because their budgets are allocated annually from a central pool of public resources. But Indonesia also has 141 state corporations, two of which are Jasa Marga and Pelindo II. Collectively, these state-owned-enterprises have an operational budget of Rp 1,100 trillion per year and control assets worth Rp 2,500 trillion (around US$280 billion), an amount equivalent to 40 percent of the country's GDP. The large pool of financial and technical resources available to these corporations could have a major impact on Indonesia's infrastructure development. The recent trend of promoting "corporatization" of state-owned entities makes sense in terms of efficiency and accountability. But that should not dominate the role of these agencies. State-owned-enterprises need to be used proactively by the Government to promote development.

PPPs are useful in come contexts, but not every project is suitable as a PPP. For example, the Solo-Kertosono project is so closely linked to other segments of the Trans-Java highway that segmenting it geographically and relative to the risks involved is practically impossible. The fact that the developers of other segments of the Trans-Java highway have been stalling, including even Jasa Marga, is not surprising since early movers will not start generating sufficient revenue until all the segments have been completed and traffic can flow smoothly. The challenge of land acquisition, an issue the Government has been addressing, is an additional complexity in toll road projects that has blocked progress of Solo-Kertosono and many other road projects. But it is not cost that is crippling the development of infrastructure projects; rather, it is the inherent uncertainty and political sensitivity of the process. The exaggerated emphasis on PPPs and the reluctance to spend directly from the budget have stalled infrastructure development. Coercing projects to look like PPPs without maintaining the value drivers of a PPP is simply adding to the cost of projects and delaying their implementation. To be suitable for a PPP, all of the land required for an infrastructure project needs to be acquired before the project is bid out.

It is important to attract strong and competent private players who have experience with construction and the full life-cycle of managing a project. It is they who are capable of bringing about the efficiency gains and innovation that are the primary value drivers of a PPP. In addition to engineering capacity, these players need to have the skills to handle risks and be of an appropriate size to bear them when necessary.

A further point is that state-owned enterprises are not private firms. In Indonesia, firms such as Jasa Marga and the Pelindos were both builders and operators and, effectively, their own regulators. They understand the sector, possess the requisite expertise, and also have access to explicit and implicit resources of the Government. Nonetheless, in the new corporatized model which the Government has been promoting, they are being allowed to bid against private firms in tenders for PPP projects. This distorts the playing field and deters serious private bidders.

The volume of private financing required for infrastructure development is large.[225] Banks have remained the primary source of infrastructure funds in Indonesia. But state-owned banks dominate the banking sector, and any risks transferred to state-owned banks are eventually borne by the state. Furthermore, banks have been wary of lending to nascent private developers of roads and other infrastructure.

---

[225]In a report for Morgan Stanley, Tan (2011, pp.6-7) estimated that for next five years infrastructure spending will be $250 billion, the majority of which will be from the private sector.

Indonesia has numerous energy alternatives. Its policies do not efficiently exploit their potential. The country could develop tens of thousands of megawatts of geothermal, natural gas, hydro and even solar electricity for less than the present cost of producing electricity using diesel fuel. Indonesia could also significantly improve productivity if it were to switch major parts of its transportation system from liquid fuel to natural gas. Since liquid fuels are heavily subsidized, consumers have no incentive to make that change. Furthermore, since so much of the government's budget is pre-empted by fuel subsidies, the investment funds to speed the conversion are not available. As solar prices fall and as battery technology improves, more rural households will be able to switch from diesel to solar electricity without subsidies. The extension of power to households that are currently not connected could be accelerated by special loan programs to expand the use of renewable energy. This would further integrate the domestic economy and foster inclusiveness in the process.

Lowering the costs of financial intermediation will also play a significant role in reducing transaction costs and broadening the opportunity for those with low incomes to raise their productivity. By eliminating regulations that restrict competition and favor large banks, Indonesia has the opportunity to promote a more inclusive, deeper, and stable financial system. This could be supported by explicit measures to encourage the spread of innovative banking practices and rural finance.

A major improvement would occur if the management of the monetary system by BI were made consistent with the objectives of promoting rapid sustained inclusive growth. BI's demonstrated inability to target inflation in ways that reduce its rate to comparable international levels without manipulating the exchange rate has been undermining Indonesia's growth. It would be useful to revisit how BI interprets its responsibilities as an "independent" central bank. In this regard, the differential impact of BI's current one-size-fits all approach to monetary and exchange rate management in which the operating presumption is that all of Indonesia looks and behaves in financial terms like the Jakarta region also needs to be reassessed. On both counts, the distortions generated raise transaction costs, forcing asset-holders to either curtail their economic activities or seek alternative accommodation abroad. In the process, Indonesia's productivity is diminished and improvements in competitiveness are held back.

Indonesia has substantial room to improve productivity and competitiveness through constructive changes in policies related to infrastructure, energy, and financial intermediation. Current policies are wasting resources. Reducing inefficiency and expanding appropriate institutional arrangements in all three areas will boost incomes, promote inclusion, diminish inequality, and move Indonesia closer to achieving rapid sustained inclusive growth.

CHAPTER FOUR

Developing and Utilizing Human Resources: Promoting Productive Employment and Livelihoods

If you want one year of prosperity, grow grain.
If you want ten years of prosperity, grow trees.
If you want one hundred years of prosperity, grow people.
CHINESE PROVERB

Investments that improve hard and soft infrastructure will lower logistics and transaction costs and raise productivity. Because these costs are so high, the potential gains for Indonesia are huge. The same applies for productive work, the topic discussed in this chapter. Productivity and earnings are currently so low among such a large number of Indonesian workers that policies and programs that boost output and incomes will stimulate and support inclusive growth for decades to come.

There are a number of potential paths. Investment in hard and soft infrastructure will raise productive work directly as facilities expand and institutions improve, and indirectly as entrepreneurship and enterprise increase in response to the removal of restrictions. For example, one restriction that currently undermines productive work is legislated discrimination in favor of select groups of workers. This forces the majority of workers (the "outsiders") to cope through whatever informal means they can devise.

Another barrier is Indonesia's chronically under-developed human capital. Despite impressive gains in primary and secondary education over the last three decades, higher level capacities, reflected in knowledge, skills and aptitudes, are inadequate to take advantage of existing and emerging development opportunities.

A third barrier to the rapid expansion of productive work is the lack of inclusive growth. The boom in natural resources has substantially increased output. However, due to the capital intensive nature of much of the natural resource production and processing, the resultant growth is having only a modest impact on employment. As noted in Chapter One, Indonesia is now on a development trajectory of essentially jobless growth.

The chapter begins by explaining the connections between productive work and rapid, inclusive growth. The main challenge revolves around mechanisms and inducements that support workers' efforts to raise their productivity and incomes, and how the Government can facilitate those efforts. One way forward is for the Government to actively support workers to create the capacities that help them raise their productivity. This will require policies and programs that help move economic activity progressively beyond the hooking and crooking, and digging, trucking, barging, and dumping associated with exploiting natural resources, to endeavors that increasingly build upon knowledge and knowledge-based services. To do this, Indonesia will need to enhance the quality of its higher education (HE), and take advantage of the educational and knowledge-generating capacities of inclusive growth itself.

Productive Work, Employment, Livelihoods, and Economic Growth

Productive work adds value. A *productive* worker's value product (the quantity of output multiplied by its price) exceeds his/her direct and indirect costs (wages, benefits, supervision, associated facilities, and equipment). If all new jobs in Indonesia were the result of the increased demand for labor in organized, structured, formal settings, the discussion could be confined to this category alone. That is not possible since the majority of employment growth occurs in the non-organized, non-structured, informal sector.[226]

Over recent decades, more than six out of every ten new jobs have been located (or "generated") in the informal sector, a point highlighted in Box 4.1. That trend continues. To illustrate, in February 2011, the population aged 15 years and over was 170.7 million.[227] In this cohort, 119.4 million were economically active; of these, 111.3 million were working with 8.1 million classified as unemployed. Among those who were working, 34.2 million were occupied less than full time – 18.5 million were part-time workers and 15.7 million were identified as underemployed. These data indicate the potential gains available if productivity could be increased. Based on the "time available" and "willingness" to work criteria, there is plenty of scope to increase output. Whether there is "surplus" labor rather than labor which is poorly organized and motivated is taken up later.

---

[226]Jose Castillo noted that "informal is a deliberately ambiguous term. It encompasses activities that are 'casual' or lack 'precise form', or lie 'outside of what is prescribed'" (Brillembourg 2006). Informal activities are also identified by their practices (social, economic) and nature (spatial spread, timing, cooperative nature). These dimensions usefully shift discussions of informality beyond the conventionally implied notions of extra-legal, marginalized, or unproductive features of the activities typically used in standard statistical agency designations. Bacchetta, Ernst and Bustamante (2009) examine some of these distinctions.

[227]BPS "Trends of the Selected Socio-Economic Indicators of Indonesia," August 2011, Table 2.17, p.23; BPS *Strategic Data* 2011, Table 5.1, p.37.

The population aged 15 years and above by sector is shown in Figure 4.1 below. There has been some structural change with the share of agricultural declining. But, as discussed more broadly in the study, this change, combined with other shifts, has been inadequate to significantly change the balance between informal and formal sector employment.

The data in Figure 4.2 explain why this study emphasizes productive work (i.e., employment and livelihood-related activities) and avoids focusing on the formal/informal nature of activities. No doubt the Government, in its pursuit of upper middle income status for Indonesia, would prefer that all future employment be created in the formal sector. That will not happen. The policy challenge is to expand productive work irrespective of where it is located or however it is designated. That will happen when all work throughout the country generates earnings that exceed each worker's reservation wage.[228]

---

[228]The "reservation wage" is the income/earnings that induce a worker to (voluntarily) supply his/her labor for a particular activity. It is related to the worker's skills, preferences, personal circumstances, location, and access to complementary productive inputs.

Box 4.1: Informal Work

There are several sources – BPS, International Labour Office, World Bank among others – which show that informal employment in Indonesia exceeds 65 percent of the work force.

For example, the Decent Work Country Profile (ILO 2011, Table 2, pp.10-12) reported that in 1996 informal workers comprised 64.3 percent of the labor force. In 2010, the share was 66.9 percent.

The share was even greater for women. There were 59.7 percent of males in informal employment in 1996 and 64.8 percent in 2010. Corresponding data for females were 71.7 percent and 70.4 percent, respectively.

Calculations derived from the Indonesian Family Life Survey (IFLS) for the period 1993 to 2007 show that informal workers have the following occupational breakdown: agriculture 33 percent; manufacturing 13 percent; wholesale trade 17 percent; personal services 16 percent; and 21percent in other occupations. Figure 4.2 show these data over time.

BPS data indicate that own-account workers increased from 21.8 percent in 1996 to 24.4 percent of total employment in 1999, partly as a result of Krismon. By 2010, that share had fallen to 19.4 percent.

The BPS data, however, also reveal a gradual rise in casual employment, defined as persons who work at their own risk without the assistance of their family members or employees. Most of these workers were in non-agricultural activities. The share of casual employees in agriculture increased from 4.0 percent in 2001 to 5.4 percent in 2010. The corresponding data for non- agriculture were 2.7 percent to 4.7 percent, respectively.

Figure 4.1: Population 15 Years of Age and Over by Main Industry (% Pop)

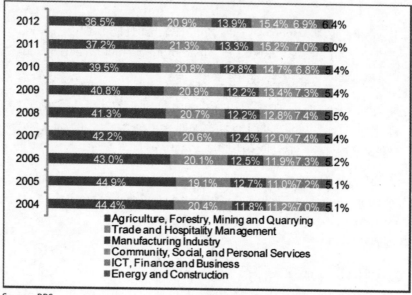

Source: BPS

**Figure 4.2: Population 15 Years of Age and Over
by Main Employment Status (% Pop)**

Source: BPS

Productive work of all types and labor at all skill levels are central to the task of promoting rapid, sustained, and inclusive growth. For their productive services, workers receive income. Workers are also consumers and their expenditure (or absorption) comprises a major component of aggregate demand. Workers are investors as well, obtaining resources for this purpose from others (through borrowing) or their own savings (i.e., income they do not consume). Moreover, workers are the largest group in society for whom economic development is intended, and to whom the benefits of inclusive growth will accrue. Finally, workers' skills, including managerial and entrepreneurial capacities, are major components of the economy's human capital stock.

When viewed in this way, workers – their absolute number, economic behavior, and productivity—are integral to the economy's circular flows of output, expenditure, and income.

As voters or members of particular groups (labor unions, employer associations, cooperatives, or other pressure groups), workers have the potential for independent social and political action, something that is not directly available to other economic resources—land, capital, information.[229]

Workers' actions (or lack of action) can have profound consequences for an economy's growth and development. History has many examples. Countries with a large stock of human capital and workers who could be readily used (as in Germany, Belgium, and Japan) recovered quickly once complementary factors such as physical capital, recurrent inputs, and finance became available. Countries with low levels of human capital (such as Mozambique, Ethiopia, and Haiti) have made limited sustained headway even when they have had access to extravagant flows of foreign aid and complementary inputs (foreign exchange, finance, and capital equipment).

---

[229]These entities are represented by other workers, typically designated as owners, directors, or "capitalists."

It is often too easy for the political and business elites (workers themselves) to overlook the need to emphasize the instrumental role of productive work as they "run" the country and/or make their fortunes pumping oil or gas, digging and exporting coal, or producing palm oil. The short-term gains in growth and wealth, combined with the monopoly rent of an "easy life" available from natural resource extraction, have been too tempting and too lucrative when compared to the much harder tasks of educating the population, electrifying the country to boost overall productivity and welfare, more closely integrating the regions, and creating public amenities that improve social welfare.[230] Indonesia is not alone in having leaders who concentrate on short-term gains. The reality is that long term development broadly conceived, especially rapid, inclusive growth, is often too difficult for most governments to foster and sustain.[231]

Box 4.2: Labor Productivity and Long-Term Growth and Development

Modern economists reject the notion that labor is the only source of value, a point that was central to the theories of Ricardo and Marx.

Over recent decades, however, economists from different branches of the discipline have argued that labor productivity is fundamentally all that matters for long-term economic growth.

---

[230]This view is wide spread. The Economic Intelligence Unit's website for Indonesia noted: "There are signs that the president, Susilo Bambang Yudhoyono, is losing influence in the last years of his term. Hopes for new policy initiatives are fading, as conservatives have faced down reformers within the ruling coalition." (EIU January 14, 2013).

[231]The small number of "high-growth performers" identified by The Growth Commission (World Bank 2008; Brady and Spence 2010) is evidence of the incapacity of the "low-growth performers" to take the necessary measures to improve their performance.

The point has been made in several ways.

During the 1960s, when there were concerted attempts to under-stand the "residual" in economic growth, i.e., growth that was not explained by measured inputs of physical capital and labor, attention began to focus on the notion of human capital. (Schultz 1962, 1963) Harry Johnson specifically argued that economic development could be interpreted as a "generalized process of capital accumulation" where capital was broadly defined to include human, physical and social capi-tal. (H.G. Johnson, 1964) Subsequent studies by Denison and others demonstrated that this broader definition of capital helped account for a larger share of the contribution to growth of labor, particularly labor skills, worker participation, and their knowledge. (Denison 1962, 1967)

This point was later reinforced by Michael Kremer, who enquired why it was that humans have made much dramatic advances over recent millennia when there was no evidence that individuals have become intrinsically more intelligent over time. (Kremer 1973) His answer was, through organization and effective administration, they had combined their labor in ways that systemically brought their skills and knowledge to bear on a progressively broader range of problems. In effect, by combining their labor skills, humans gained the knowledge and apti-tudes with made them more productive.

D.Gale Johnson provided a different perspective. (Johnson 2000) He noted that natural resources – oceans, forests, lakes, minerals, the at-mosphere, the structure and position of the continents – have been fixed over the brief geological era relevant to human history. With these resources already given, he concluded that the only variable that could account for the sustained rise in standards of living over time was the increased capacity of human labor to use these resources productively.

Drawing on recent historical experience, Paul Krugman argued that, not-withstanding cross-country differences in natural resource endowments, the feature which distinguished countries that grew rapidly (and sustainably) from those which did not has been, and remains, differences in labor productivity: "Productivity isn't everything, but in the long run it is almost everything. A country's ability to improve its standard of living over time depends almost entirely on its ability to raise its output per worker." (Krugman 1990, p. 9)

Societies that became and remained rich discovered ways of generating sustained improvements in labor productivity. Poor societies had not and, as yet, have not discovered how to do so. History has numerous examples of many countries – Egypt, Greece, Rome, Thrace, Spain, and China -- that were once rich but could not sustain the conditions that would have allowed them to remain that way. A contemporary example is Argentina. One of the ten richest countries in the world at the time of WWI, by 2010 Argentina's per capita income was 85th in the world (WDI 2012, Table 1.1).

While the GOI's inattention to the long-term elements that will promote sustained inclusive growth may reflect incapacity or negligence, it cannot be the result of lack of knowledge. There is now ample evidence that labor productivity (or in terms being discussed here, productive work) is "almost" all that matters for long term economic growth and development. This point has been reaffirmed by a variety of research, briefly reviewed in Box 4.2.

It confirms an earlier point that, if the GOI wishes to promote rapid, sustained, and inclusive growth, it will need to re-orient its present support away from particular social groups (i.e., users of fuel and electricity, steel producers, and targeted import restrictions) to the broad-based activities that raise labor productivity and improve competitiveness (i.e., integrating and extending the domestic market). The long run is a sequence of short-runs and all growth trajectories are path dependent.

Deficiencies or excesses at one point on the time path have subsequent repercussions (or knock-on effects).

For evidence, Indonesia need only consider the opportunities lost because of short-term decisions in previous years not to complete the trans-Java highway, or expand the port of Tanjung Priok, or engage in additional oil and gas exploration, or subsidize inter-island transport, or better supervise the financial system, or slow down the proliferation of districts, or reduce subsidies on petrol, or raise electricity tariffs, and numerous others. Each of these decisions *not to act* responded to short-term exigencies. Collectively, they now both determine and constrain the direction and rate at which the economy can progress.

The link from rising labor productivity to improving standards of living, derived from productive employment and remunerative livelihoods, is central to promoting rapid, sustained, and inclusive growth. The challenges associated with strengthening this link are formidable. Data from the last three decades, the longest period for which coherent series exist, show that labor productivity in Indonesia has risen in spurts but at a relatively low rate,[232] especially when compared to other lower middle income countries and to most of Indonesia's Asian neighbors.

The following section examines how that might change. The focus is on direct actions that expand the opportunities for productive work. They include reducing food insecurity, expanding manufacturing employment, modifying labor regulations, increasing labor migration, raising the productivity of informal work, and upgrading of the skills and capacities of all workers.

---

[232]The World Bank's MetaData base shows that between 1980 and 2010 real output per worker in Indonesia rose by an average of 4.3 percent per annum (see: IND_Country_MetaData_en_EXCEL.xls). In the absence of a breakdown of rural and urban labor force growth for the whole period, we derive agricultural GDP per capita using estimates of the rural population. This increased by 4.8 percent per annum, while non-agricultural GDP per capita (using urban population as the denominator) increased by 1.7 percent per annum. The implications for long-term growth are examined further in McPherson and Vas (2012).

Boosting Productive Work in Indonesia

Creating the conditions that increase the productivity of all occupations, formal and informal, will not be easy. Many, if not most informal workers gain their livelihoods from combinations of activities – on-farm, off-farm, and various activities that relate to fabrication, processing, distribution, and service activities. This limits the potential for improving productivity.[233] Based on local and international experience, raising the productivity of multi-part occupations has been especially difficult.

The challenges of adapting to a growing setting of fragmented jobs and part-time work has recently been examined in the *World of Work Report* 2012.[234] Several factors affect the productivity of joint-work: the proximity of one job to the other and commuting times; the respective skill requirements; the timing of each job (productivity in seasonal non-overlapping activities can be increased more readily than in contemporaneous part-time jobs); how efficiently each task is organized and managed; and the quality of co-workers. Workers have to boost their skills in several tasks and efficiently combine their activities so that overall productivity (output per work day or hour) can rise.

These circumstances direct attention to livelihood generation. The activities involved tend to be more fluid and less structured than regular employment, making them less easy to identify and measure. That, however, does not make them less relevant or significant, particularly for the people involved. But it does compound the problems of devising appropriate policies.

Policy makers will find it constructive to start from the premise that most people would prefer to work to live rather than the reverse, even if

---

[233] Acccording to Bacchetta, Ernst, and Bustamante (2009, p.27) this trend is common to many developing countries and is independent of the effects of globalization (trade, finance, investment flows). The ILO study of decent work (ILO 2011) has similar observations regarding work fragmentation and part-time employment.
[234] ILO (2012).

life's misfortunes force the latter on many of them. This means that the calculus of employment "creation" remains the same whether the work is formal or informal – employment policies should focus on enhancing the demand for labor (or input of labor) that is derived from the expected returns from productive work. The same logic applies to self-employment. No one will regularly and continually toil in an occupation that takes more effort than the value of the in-kind or monetary return.

This perspective is needed to move policy makers beyond the convenient rationalization that those who do not find a productive job will "find work" through some (often family-related) work-sharing arrangements. This is commonly referred to in Indonesia as the notion of "involution," or "change without progress," and it deeply influences views of informal employment, as well as of agricultural employment (from whence the concept was first formulated).

Reducing Food Insecurity

Inclusive growth is a mirage when a large share of the population remains food insecure, and Indonesia is presently chronically food insecure when viewed from both supply and access.[235] Roughly 110 million Indonesians, or around 46 percent of the population, subsist on less than the international benchmark of $2 per day. Research reveals that income poverty, as represented by this $2 benchmark, poses greater risks of insecurity and vulnerability for the poor than consumption poverty.[236] Malnourished adults cannot work productively, and under-nourished children will not grow up to be healthy, productive future workers.

Food insecurity is a serious problem in Indonesia. The number of under-five children who are malnourished is large, despite the expansion of Government support through food distribution and cash transfers.

---

[235]FAO (2006).
[236]Meyer and Sullivan (2012).

Existing policies, including RASKIN and cash transfers, will not materially or rapidly modify this situation. Using an expression popularized in 1990s, these are "hand-outs, not hand-ups." Welfare is essential for the destitute and those who cannot help themselves, but productive work is the only sustainable means of raising living standards for the remainder. Food insecurity results from poverty and rising inequality. It is perhaps the most obvious indication that growth is non-inclusive. Reducing food insecurity requires activities that simultaneously increase the overall supply of food and ensure that everyone has access to the food.

The Government has numerous ways of addressing food insecurity. One is to boost investment in relevant infrastructure such as roads, bridges, storage, irrigation, wharves, and ports. This will have both direct and indirect effects on the capacity to produce and deliver additional food to where it can be effectively used. It will also increase productive work, particularly in rural areas, thereby enabling families to gain access to food. These initiatives could be easily supported if the Government reallocated the budget from expenditures that do not support farmers, and used the freed-up resources in ways that do. For example, fertilizer subsidies, which are paid to fertilizer producers, do not help farmers,[237] while government neglect of agricultural research, relative to past expenditures and in relation to comparator and competitor countries, has undermined the dynamism of the food sector in particular and agriculture more generally.[238]

---

[237] Osorio et al. (2011, p.4-6) Over recent years, the Government has been spending more than four times as much on fertilizer subsidies as on irrigation expansion and rehabilitation. Studies of the incidence of the subsidies show that they are highly regressive, with the largest farmers capturing most of the benefits. Furthermore, more and 90 percent of farmers pay more than the "maximum" (subsidized) price for fertilizer.

[238] Warr (2011, Figure 6; 2012); Oberman et al. (2012, p.47); Blanco Armas et al. (2010, 2012) Their data suggest that Indonesia has largely abandoned public support for agricultural research and extension. The expenditure per capita and budget share are among the lowest for any large agricultural country, especially in Asia. In effect, Indonesia is free-riding on the international agricultural research community.

The Government could further diminish food insecurity, especially among small-scale farmers, by removing or sharply modifying counter-productive restrictions on agricultural activity. Some of these restrictions include the inter-island shipment of livestock, currently confined to large licensed operators, the ban on rattan exports, and the export tax on cocoa and other agricultural commodities. The last two have been designed to encourage domestic value-added. In practice, they discourage domestic production and encourage smuggling, neither of which sustainably enhances rural incomes or welfare. The Government could also support agriculture by ensuring that mining companies rehabilitate the areas ravaged by their operations.[239]

Other actions which would help are noted throughout the study. Perhaps the most important would be a shift in attitude. This would involve recognition by the Government of the need to move beyond stop-gap measures – of food distribution and cash transfers – that do not address the basic problems of low food consumption and inadequate income (purchasing power). This shift in attitude should not be politically difficult since it is fully consistent with Government's expressed desire for achieving rapid inclusive growth. It might be administratively hard though.

The above activities, if implemented, will significantly increase both the demand for and supply of food, as well as other agricultural products. It is difficult to project the outcome on the real cost of food, measured as the share of income spent on food, especially in the short and medium terms. The long-run impact, however, is easy to predict: the real cost of food will decline.

---

[239]Several large foreign-owned mining companies have been replacing the over-burden removed during mining operations. Farmers resettled on this land have obtained markedly higher yields for maize, rice, and fruits than previously. Fish farming has expanded in some areas. Our team visited a number of sites in East Kalimantan where restoration activity is well advanced. We also saw mining areas which had been abandoned, mostly by small miners, where no recovery effort had been made.

Several scholars, however, have analyzed food budgets and consumer surveys in Indonesia and concluded that higher food prices will undermine food security.[240] This conclusion directly contradicts decades of experience showing that the best antidote to high food prices is high food prices.[241] This is especially true when most of the poor live in rural areas.

Their conclusion derives from evidence that higher food prices impose a welfare loss on food consumers, and that many small farmers in Indonesia are net food consumers. The implication is that any increase in income farmers derive from selling food products will be more than offset by the higher expenditures they will incur when they purchase food. Although this is a valid static argument, it is mistaken when viewed in dynamic terms.

This can be verified by running the logic in reverse. Suppose that in order to improve the net welfare of farmers who are net food consumers, the government lowered the price of food. This will temporarily add to the farmers' welfare as long as the food prices were adequate to induce them to continue their current levels of production. However, lower food prices discourage investment. With lower investment, production will fall and food shortages will lead to higher prices.[242] To prevent

---

[240]Warr (2011); Setyoko, Trewin and Vanzetti (2012).

[241]The maxim holds. Despite the panic in 2008 – complete with import restrictions and frenzied buying – food prices began to fall as agricultural supply expanded. The World Bank food price index (2005=100) was 159 in 2008 and 142 in 2009 and 170 in 2010 (WDI 2012, Table 6.5, p.349; World Bank Pink Sheet February 2013). Prices fell dramatically after the 1973 food shock and barely budged for two decades. That, in turn, put pressure on supplies, which aggravated the recent price spikes. (Some context: food prices were higher in 1970, and particularly in 1973, than in any subsequent year up to 2009. Real prices finally rose above 1970s levels only in 2010.) Recent data from the Food and Agricultural Organization (FAO) and US Department of Agriculture show that world cereal production in 2012 was 2.3 billion tons, just below the record reached in 2011 (FAO 2011). Due to this supply response, food prices are falling (USDA March 8, 2013; Bloomberg March 28, 2013).

[242]A shift from CIF to FOB prices will lower food prices; a move in the opposite direction will raise them.

that, the Government would need to increasingly subsidize imports to compensate for shortfalls in domestic supply. Neither of these options is sustainable.

Further evidence is provided by Indonesia's experience. During the early years of the New Order regime, major attention was given to expanding the supply of food to improve national food security. This was done by raising food prices, expanding rural infrastructure, promoting adaptive agricultural research, improving access to rural credit, and revamping marketing arrangements. All of these actions increased the net price that farmers received for their output. Their responses were dramatic. Indonesia was transformed from being the largest importer of rice in the world to self-sufficiency within a decade. The welfare of farmers, including those who were net food consumers, improved as employment opportunities rose even for the landless.

Major additional efforts to boost agricultural output in Indonesia need to be made. It will help reduce rural poverty. It will also enable Indonesia to take advantage of the expanding world demand for agricultural products.[243]

Since *Krismon*, poverty has become increasingly concentrated in the agricultural sector and rural areas. This is the result of the sharp decline in the contribution of agriculture to GDP, combined with lagging adjustment of the rural labor force. The rural-urban income gap, which had been closing during the 1980s and 1990s, has widened over recent years. Creating "pathways out of [this] poverty" will require broad-based rural development.[244]

One constructive pathway will be to boost production to cater to the increase in global demand for food, fiber, bio-fuel, industrial feedstock,

---

[243]The recent McKinsey Report on Indonesia (Oberman *et al*. 2012, Section 3.2) emphasized the country's agricultural potential.

[244]The World Development Report 2008 "Agriculture for Development" (World Bank 2007, Ch.3) emphasizes three main pathways – increased farmer productivity, higher output from off-farm activities through entrepreneurship, and migration to higher paying urban jobs. Each of these is relevant to Indonesia.

and animal feed requirements. Countries with large populations such as China, India, Vietnam, Bangladesh, and India are already at, or fast approaching, their arable land frontiers. Part of the upward momentum in world food prices has been the increased demand by these countries, combined with the limited supply response thus far from major agricultural producers, although that response has recently accelerated.

Indonesia is one of a small group of developing countries (which includes Brazil and the Democratic Republic of Congo) that have the capacity for the large-scale expansion of water- and land-intensive agricultural production. One dimension of Indonesia's future efforts to exploit its dynamic comparative advantage will be to bring this land into production and raise its productivity (see Box 4.3).

Box 4.3: Agricultural Workers and Output on Java and Outer Islands, 2007-2011

The number of workers in agriculture (including food, non-food, livestock, forestry and fisheries) in Indonesia fell slightly from 41.2 million in 2007 to 39.3 million in 2011, a drop of 4.6 percent. At the same time, the real output of agriculture grew from Rp. 271.6 trillion (in 2000 constant prices) to 313.9 trillion, an increase of 15.6 percent. Agricultural output per agricultural worker rose from Rp 6.59 million to Rp 7.99 million, a 21 percent real increase.

Is this evidence of large amounts of surplus labor?

One way to look to answer this is to compare Java and other regions with output:

	Ag. Workers (millions)		Ag. Output (Rp trillion in 2000 prices)		Ag Output/Ag Worker		
	2007	2011	2007	2011	2007	2011	Change
Java	20.1	17.7	124.8	140.9	6.2	8.0	+28%
Non-Java	21.1	21.6	146.8	173.9	7.0	8.0	+16%

The increase in output per worker indicates that there was some plot consolidation, mechanization, and/or shift to higher value crops in Java. It is not evidence of "surplus" labor in the classical sense of zero or very low marginal product below the wage rate. The reason to suspect it was not "surplus" is that Java has productivity equal to that of the Outer Islands where highly productive tree crops predominate. Even in 2007, labor productivity on Java was about 90 percent of the Outer Islands level.

Rapid adjustment indicates an active labor market that fosters labor mobility. Indeed, the majority of labor in Java works outside of agriculture. Those in agriculture often work part-time with other jobs. The overall share of agricultural workers in the labor force is falling, yet output is rising. In the Outer Islands, the pattern of growing numbers in agriculture with growing output and growing productivity is the direct opposite of surplus labor.

To some degree, this is already underway through the production of oil palm, rubber, cocoa, and other commodities. Figure 4.3 shows that the share of arable land has risen over recent years and the contribution of agriculture to GDP, while low in relation to the share of labor in agriculture (Figure 4.4), has been rising. These changes will result in a combination of higher employment and increasing labor productivity within agriculture, which will raise agricultural incomes and contribute to inclusive growth. Much more will be needed though, if Indonesia is to respond appropriately over coming decades to the rising food and fiber demands of its Asian neighbors, as well as meet increased local demand for higher quality food.

Figure 4.3: Arable Land and Agricultural Output

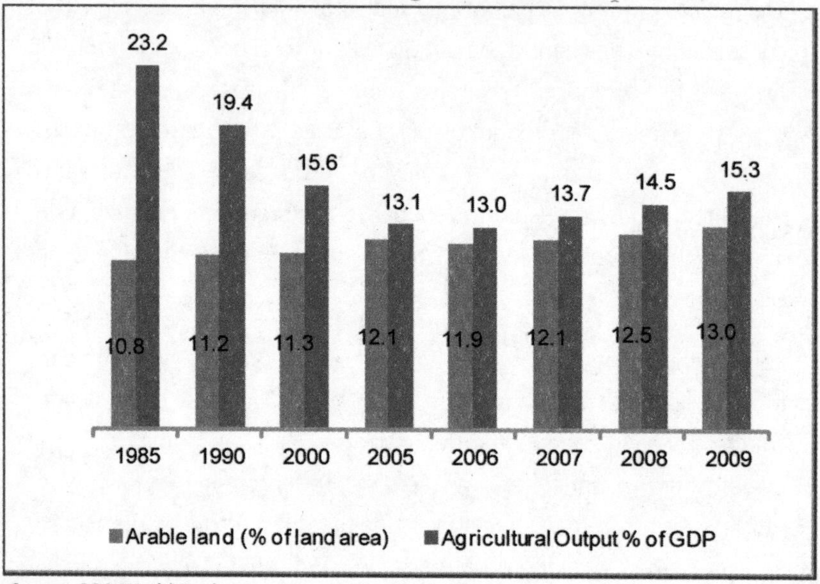

Source: BPS, World Bank

A potential difficulty will be the adverse demographic shift in the sector. The average age of farmers has been increasing, largely because agricultural work is unattractive to younger workers. Data from the Ministry of Agriculture show that in 2011, almost 80 percent of the country's farmers were 45 years or older. This is a sharp increase from three years earlier, when the average age of the same cohort was 40 years.[245] The growth of agricultural output over the decade 2000-2010 averaged 3.5 percent per annum, stimulated by the rapid growth of key agricultural exports – palm oil, rubber, cocoa, coffee, and several other commodities. This rate of expansion will be difficult to maintain given the exceedingly weak agricultural research system and declining public support for research on agriculture.[246] The

---

[245]www.gbgindonesia.com/en/agriculture/article/2011/agriculture_overview_of_indonesia.php.

[246]Our team visited numerous agricultural production areas and IPB in Bogor. The few officials who took note of trends and levels of agricultural research support were pessimistic. Most new ideas related to agriculture come from abroad, although declining

irony of the latter development is that there is a need for a major expansion in agricultural research precisely to respond to the knowledge and technical problems which confront the aging agricultural labor force.[247]

Figure 4.4: Employment in Agriculture (% of total) vs. Agriculture Output (% GDP)

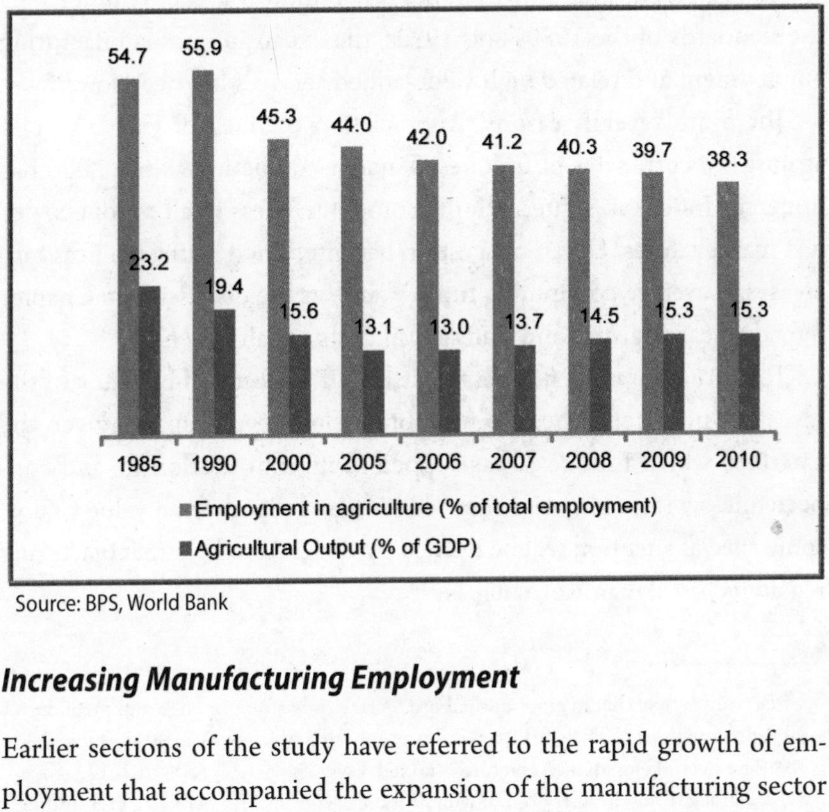

Source: BPS, World Bank

Increasing Manufacturing Employment

Earlier sections of the study have referred to the rapid growth of employment that accompanied the expansion of the manufacturing sector

---

research capacity in Indonesia is making international collaboration difficult. Palm oil research continues as this is being funded privately.

[247]Aging farming populations are common across Asia. It is difficult enough generating applicable technologies and techniques for young, vigorous, well-educated farmers. It becomes highly problematic for older farmers who have less education (though plenty of experience) and who, due to habit, circumstance, and risk aversion are less adaptable. It is worth noting in passing that Indonesia is unlike many other Asian countries in that it has not experienced much feminization of agriculture (Agarwal 2011).

from the mid-1980s onwards. During this period, a major source of growth was the transfer of large amounts of labor out of low productivity agricultural and rural activities to higher productivity jobs in the expanding urban-based manufacturing sector.

Over the last decade, the brisk pace of urbanization, with 60 percent of the population now classified as urban, has not been associated with commensurate output growth in the urban-industrial sector. Indeed, by the standards of the 1980s and 1990s, the expansion of manufacturing employment and related high value-added services has been low.[248]

There are several reasons. Appreciation of the real exchange rate against the currencies of Indonesia's major competitors since 2000 has undercut Indonesia's international competitiveness in all products, not just manufactures. Urban congestion has intensified, with significant increases in average commuting times[249] and, as the discussion in Chapter 3 made clear, logistics and transaction costs are already high.

This situation need not persist. It would be rectified by many of the measures noted elsewhere to promote inclusive growth. Yet, given the extent to which Indonesia has slipped in its contribution to, and connectedness with international production and distribution value chains, some special attention will be needed by the GOI to help manufacturing regain its lost dynamism, such as:[250]

---

[248]BPS data show that average annual production growth in for large and medium establishments from 2005 to 2011 was 2.7 percent (BPS *Strategic Data* 2011, Table 5.2, p.38). The overall employment picture is mixed. Over the period 2004 to 2012 (August) "Manufacturing Industry" employment increased from 11.8 percent (11.1 million workers) to 13.9 percent of total employment (15.4 million). The "manufacturing component" fared less well. In 2004, its share of total employment was 4.6 percent; by 2009, it had fallen to 4.2 percent (BPS online "Total Workers by Sub-Sector" and "Population 15 Years of Age and Over Worked by Main Industry 2004-2012").

[249]ILO (2011, Table 11) provides evidence on comparative commuting time in major centers in Indonesia.

[250]To illustrate, per capita manufactured exports from China in 2000 were $195; by 2010, they were $1180. Corresponding data for Indonesia were $311 and $657, respectively (*WDI* 2012, Table 4.4). Comparisons with Thailand, Vietnam, and Singapore indicate a similar, though less dramatic, trend.

- **promoting value-added exports** via an appropriately valued exchange rate rather than by selective and counterproductive protectionist measures; and
- **dismantling employment regulations** that have raised the costs and reduced the incentives for formal, large-scale employers to expand labor-intensive activities.

Promoting Value-Added Exports: Over recent years, the need to promote value added exports has been stressed at the highest level of Government.[251] To support this goal, the GOI has been erecting an elaborate system of export taxes and controls to require Indonesian firms to undertake more local processing so as to "add more value." There is a parallel program underway to promote import substitution.[252] A report that examined the government's drive to add value to exports noted:

"These policies are in line with common perceptions that Indonesian industries should produce goods with higher added value. Restrictions on the exports of raw rattan and mining products, the export tax on crude palm oil and incentive schemes to in-

---

[251]The trade minister, Gita Wirjawan, was quoted: "I am not against exports. I am much in favor of exporting goods that have value added" (Yulisman and Haswidi 2012).

[252]Anas (2012) noted: "… there are new regulations on horticultural imports. Horticulture can only enter Indonesia at select ports, which excludes the busiest port of Tanjung Priok in Jakarta. New regulations also state that only registered importers can deal with horticulture imports. To become a registered horticulture importer a firm must get a recommendation from the designated directorate general at the Ministry of Agriculture. Second, in May 2012 the government passed a new regulation on imports of finished goods. Unlike in the old legislation, a general importer is now only allowed to import goods that fall under one heading, and an importing producer is now only allowed to import finished goods for market testing and as complementary goods….The third new policy is the regulation of exports of 65 mining commodities including nickel, tin, gold, copper, silver, lead, zinc, chromium, platinum, bauxite, iron ore and manganese. These commodities will be subject to a 20 per cent export tax. Also, to be legally eligible to export these 65 commodities miners are required to be registered exporters and all exportation needs to be verified by surveyors."

crease domestic production all point to the same intention. Such obsession with increasing domestic added value is not limited to raw material production, but also involves manufacturing products. The fact that almost 70 percent of industrial goods imported are parts and components has raised concern about the country's dependence on imports."[253]

In addition to ignoring Indonesia's own history and extensive international experience regarding the negative effects of protection, the GOI's goals are misleading at best and confused at worst. Since exports, by definition, add value, the issue cannot be about adding value through this means. Moreover, since a major reason why many policymakers believe Indonesia was spared the ravages of the Global Economic Crisis was due to its diminished dependence on trade, the issue cannot be about increasing the contribution of exports to GDP. The principal concern about adding value to exports should relate to reducing the resource cost (time, labor input, capital contribution, finance charges) of producing a given level of exports. That is, the concern should be about increasing the productivity of exporters. However, if this is the Government's intention, its export taxes and increased restrictions on trade are the exact opposite of how to proceed.

The fundamental problem is that the Government's push for "value added exports" misconstrues the nature of economic inter-dependence. Because of inter-dependence, which in practice is reflected through inter-sectoral linkages, questions of whether value is being added or subtracted can only be answered by examining the direct and indirect costs of production. Value added in any economy comprises the gross value of all sales (or purchases) less the value (both market-based and imputed) of the goods and services that are directly and indirectly used

---

[253]Damuri (2012).

up or transformed in the production process. Imports are subtracted since they represent value-added (i.e., the exports) of other countries.[254] A well-known result in economics is that because of inter-sector linkages, the nominal impact of taxes and regulations (the items/activities on which taxes are levied or to which regulations apply) regularly differs significantly from their incidence (where they are borne). Because of this "shifting," there is no guarantee that, on a net basis, Government interventions ensure that value, in fact, is added. Value can readily diminish due to inefficiencies (i.e., higher costs) generated throughout the production/distribution chain.

Whether this occurs can only be determined on a case-by-case basis using computations derived from the relevant inter-sector sales and purchases of productive inputs. In one instance, however, the answer is relatively clear. The recent prohibition on rattan exports has undercut the employment and livelihoods of thousands of rattan producers who formerly gathered and processed the roughly 650,000 tons of raw rattan that used to be exported. An offset to this loss of jobs among rattan producers was the increase in jobs for the few local firms that used 15,000 tons of rattan to produce exportable furniture products. So far, the evidence is that restrictions have substantially subtracted value through the net loss of jobs.[255]

This example and the importance of case-by-case calculations to guide policy suggest the need for caution. This is especially true with respect to manufacturing production and distribution value chains or international production networks that take advantage of the international division of labor. These value chains have emerged because none

---

[254]The impact is determined by studying the inter-industry deliveries and purchases using input-output analysis. In principle, these provide measures of the rate of effective protection and domestic resource cost of producing the goods subject to the restrictions (Corden 1966; Bruno 1972; Marks and Rahardja 2012).

[255]The ban on rattan exports has created significant hardship locally (Abdussalam 2011; Simanjuntak 2012; Yulisman and Haswidi 2012).

of the products can be efficiently produced within a single country.[256] Accordingly, all products within these chains have some direct and indirect imported content. Restrictions that seek to add value in these cases result in the participating country losing its market share, something that Indonesia has experienced over the last decade.[257]

There is plenty of international and local evidence confirming that trade restrictions do not sustainably boost exports. That same evidence indicates that incentives boost exports and net value-added. Switching from restrictions to incentives and inducements would enable the GOI to back away from its strategically inept and counterproductive program of import substitution.[258]

The ineptitude is evident at two levels. The import substitution program is so obvious that it has provoked a backlash in the international press[259] and from Indonesia's major trading partners. Both the United States and

---

[256]Damuri (2012).

[257]Discussions by our team with foreign trade representatives and industrialists indicated that much of the recent manufacturing investment from their countries in Indonesia has been strategic. These include shoe manufacturers locating facilities in several Asian countries to ensure different sources of supply for their global operations; others have moved facilities from flood-prone areas; or, in the case of vehicles, manufacturers have expanded their facilities to take advantage of local demand rather than to use Indonesia as an export platform. There were few examples of new investment that strengthened Indonesia's links in the production and distribution value chains that have been driving manufacturing output in other Asian countries.

[258]The most recent report of the US Trade Representative (www.ustr.gov/sites) highlights the literally dozens of ways that Indonesian officials have been jigging the rules to provide particular sectors and local firms an edge relative to foreigners in existing domestic markets. This is yet another example of the failure to distinguish comparative from dynamic comparative advantage.

[259]The Wall Street Journal has become increasingly scathing in reporting developments in Indonesia. It has written about rising protectionism, economic nationalism, corporate corruption, Indonesia's place in the G20, the apparent arbitrary dispossession of foreign miners of their assets, and alleged army brutality in Papua (Bellman 2011, 2012; Brill and Glassman 2012; and Mahtani 2012).

Japan have taken their complaints to the WTO.[260] But more important, there is a far simpler and more effective means of substituting for imports. This approach, which as noted in Chapter 1 has been widely used across Asia for the last several decades, is to realign favorably (in Indonesia's case, devalue) the exchange rate. One of the puzzles is why this tactic is not being used in Indonesia, given that an appropriately valued exchange rate was fundamental to the policies that enabled industry and manufacturing to boom from the mid-1980s until the *Krismon*-induced collapse.

Dismantling Employment Regulations: A plethora of employment regulations related to hiring, wages, benefits, lay-offs, and firing have raised the costs and reduced the incentives for formal, large-scale employers to expand labor-intensive activities.[261]

With international interest rates historically low and the exchange rate overvalued, it has been an opportune time to substitute capital for labor.[262]

This helps explain why Indonesia has experienced relatively rapid capital accumulation, together with slow formal sector employment expansion, or "jobless growth."

---

[260]Reports suggest that Japan was to ask the WTO to rule on Indonesia's nickel ore processing requirements (Suga and Susuki 2012; Jakarta Post July 7, 2012). The United States has filed a complaint with the WTO on Indonesia's restrictions on imports of meat and other products (EIU 2013; BBC News, January 10, 2013).

[261]World Bank (2012); OECD (2012) Despite the provisions with respect to minimum wages, decent hours, work security, equal opportunity, occupational safety, and health and other benefits, only a small share of workers in Indonesia is covered (ILO 2011, Tables 3,4,7,8, 10.1). These regulations reinforce informal employment.

[262]In 2000, gross capital formation was 22 percent of GDP. By 2010, it was 33 percent, and over the period 2000-2010, gross capital formation grew by 6.1 percent per annum. During the prior decade, GCF had declined at an annual rate of 0.6 percent p.a. (*WDI* 2012, Table 4.8, p.243; Table 4.9, p. 247).

Raising Labor Productivity by Improving the Quality of Higher Education

Indonesia has made impressive gains by extending the benefits of education throughout the country.[263] The Human Development Index was 0.42 in 1980 and, as shown in Figure 4.5, had risen to 0.63 by 2012.[264] Figure 4.6 places Indonesia in a regional context. Given where it started from, with estimates that there were only 1000 university graduates at Independence, Indonesia has made exceptional progress. Participation rates at the primary, secondary and tertiary level in 2010 were 118 percent, 77 percent, and 23 percent of the relevant population cohorts.[265] This is well beyond the achievements of lower middle income countries, Indonesia's direct comparators, and close to that of upper middle income countries.

---

[263]World Bank (1992, pp.122-123); Suryadarma (2011); Hill and Thee (2012, pp.130-135).

[264]The HDI combines data showing a "long and healthy life" (measured by life expectancy at birth), "knowledge" (a composite of adult literacy and school enrolment), and a "decent standard of living" (measured by GDP in PPP terms). Regular reports appear in www.hdrstats.un.org/en/countries/profiles/idn. The BPS reports HDI for the nation and all provinces, although these are the old (non-revised) HDI series, which give higher estimates. UNDP revised the computation method in 2010. It led to a reduction in overall HDI estimates (Majerova 2012).

[265]WDI (2012, Table 2.12, p. 87).

Figure 4.5: HDI Index Trend Over Time

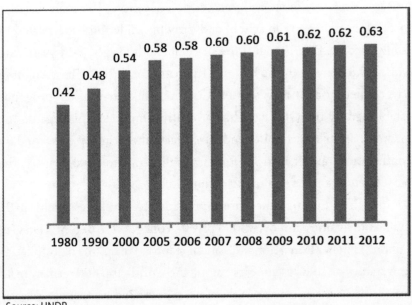

Source: UNDP

Figure 4.6: HDI Index Regional Benchmark, 2012

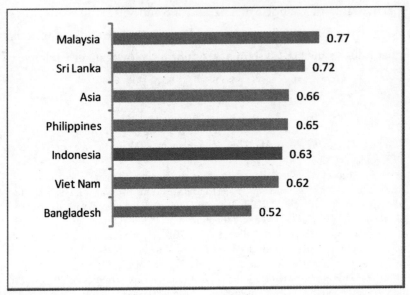

Source: UNDP

Data from UNICEF on girls' education show that there are no significant gender differences in access to education. The main barriers to children remaining in school and thriving while there are related to family income. One barrier is the share of children aged 7-14 years who work – 8.8 percent for boys and 9.1 percent for girls.[266] These children have difficulty attending school. Conditional cash transfer programs established by the GOI have had a positive impact in this regard. The income barrier to school attendance affects the primary to secondary continuation rate. It is lower for rural children, and rural girls are the most likely not to continue their education.[267]

In higher education there are approximately 4 million students in 92 public universities and over 3000 private colleges.[268] A recent *Times* (of London) Higher Education assessment recorded that none of Indonesia's universities or colleges appears among the world's top 400 tertiary institutions.[269] Another source, Webometrics compiled by Google Scholar, ranks universities by web "presence." By this measure, the University of Gadjah Mada was 30th in Asia and 381st in the world. Another two institutions, University of Indonesia and Bandung Institute of Technology, had respective ranks of 33 and 56 in Asia, and 508 and 569 in the World. These rankings have risen over recent years. Despite these trends, Indonesia's Higher Education (HE) system has significantly lower quality relative to

---

[266]*WDI* (2012, Table 2.6, p. 64). These data relate to 2000 and may be out of date.

[267]Suryadama (2006)

[268]The most recent detailed information from the European Higher Education Fair (EHEF) noted that in 2006 there were 3441 HE institutions with 3.7 million students. At that time, approximately 32,000 Indonesians were studying abroad with more than 10 thousand in Australia and close to 9 thousand in the United States (Source: www.ehef-indonesia.org/market-info/). Hill and Thee (2012, p.240) note: "In 2010, approximately 5 million students were enrolled in Indonesia's higher education institutions, up from the estimated 2000 at the time of independence in 1945."

[269]http://www.timeshighereducation.co.uk/world-university-rankings/2012-13/world-ranking/region/asia/range/001-200/page/1/order/region%7Casc

Asia, let alone those of the rest of the world.[270] Indonesia's underinvestment in people was identified in the first Harvard Kennedy School study as a significant constraint to the widespread implementation of institutional transformation.[271]

A key factor blocking the expansion of employment is the low skill levels of graduates when they enter the labor market. The education system inadequately prepares high school graduates for the rigors of university education, while the universities, in turn, have lowered their standards (or allowed their standards to drop) in ways that fail to prepare their graduates to contribute efficiently during their professional careers.[272] The following discussion examines how education can be improved.

Economic Growth and Higher Education

Economic growth and improvements in higher education are mutually inter-dependent. Box 4.4 describes some of the connections, and their mutual dependence is an opportunity for accelerating national capacities (skills, knowledge, and aptitudes). One approach is by raising the quality of formal education. Another is through expanded support for "extracurricular learning," which is stimulated by a vibrant, dynamic economy that is growing rapidly and inclusively.

Recognizing and building upon the links between higher education and economic growth has the further advantage of keeping in perspective the fetish with formal qualifications that drives bureaucratic promotions and perceptions of ability. By focusing on a joint approach through

---

[270]Suryadarma (2011); Sianipar (2012); Arshad (2012); Hill and Thee (2012, pp.234-235).

[271]Saich *et al.* (2010, pp. 82-85).

[272]World Bank (2010); Suryadarma (2011) provides evidence on the generally low quality of education and skills of newly trained workers. This is not a new problem. It was described in a report on human resources and growth two decades ago (World Bank 1992, pp.134-137).

which the country can enhance the capabilities of all of its workers, Indonesia can develop the means by which it can begin to "catch up" to its competitors and comparators. That task will be exceedingly difficult and far more time consuming if official attention remains focused on improving HE alone.

The proposition that HE and economic growth are inter-dependent is not widely accepted by Asian HE administrators and education scholars. Their predominant view is that HE "drives" economic growth.[273]

Box 4.4: The Educational Effect of Economic Growth

"Economic growth is educational because most (some would argue, all) human activity – whether a success or failure – provides an opportunity for learning.

As the economy expands, a growing number of workers are exposed to increasingly diverse tasks and a wider range of work experiences. They develop new skills and talents, discover that effort, diligence and discipline are rewarded, that personal and social progress require initiative, flexibility, and adaptability, that "getting ahead" (and "getting along") require continuous learning, and that innovation, creativity and risk-taking to acquire additional knowledge and information are possible and profitable.

---

[273]Atkinson (1996), Bollag (2003), Hanushek (2004; 2005, p.15), NIU Outreach (2005), Hanushek and Woessmann (2007), Fischer (2009), Benditt (2009), Mankiw (2013). This view often determines government policy. For example, governments in some countries with high tertiary enrolments (Singapore, South Korea, Taiwan) have been concerned that their HE achievements may not be sufficient to sustain economic growth. To rectify this, they are actively engaged (along with several other countries) in boosting financing for HE so as to raise its quality (Fischer 2009). If they took notice of their own experience, policy makers in these countries would discover that growth-oriented policies would also be effective in raising the quality of their HE.

In the process, workers develop attitudes (dedication, commitment to hard work, perseverance) and behave in ways (save, invest, take risks) that stimulates further economic growth.

As a result, economic growth rewards the individuals and families, through higher wages, productive employment, and improved welfare, who are willing to invest in boosting their capacities. At the same time, it generates the resources, private and public, to support additional investment in the education of current and future generations.

Notwithstanding the positive educational effects of economic growth, the lack of economic growth (or stagnation) is educational as well.

Unfortunately, many of the lessons are counterproductive. Conditions of slow economic growth or economic stagnation demonstrate that initiative and innovation rarely pay off; personal and family connections are more important for advancement than individual skill or merit; investment in education and capacity enhancement has low returns; hard work, individual effort, and risk taking offer few rewards; the broader society is unable to generate the conditions enabling all those who are willing to work to do so; and that conservative behavior (or coping) provides more security than seeking novel approaches to pressing problems. (McPherson, 2005)

At one level, the evidence appears to support this interpretation. International data show that the richest countries have the highest HE participation and poor countries the lowest.[274] Furthermore, empirical studies

---

[274]High-income countries (i.e., those with per capita incomes above $12,276 in 2010 prices) the gross enrolment rate in tertiary (i.e., post-secondary) education in 2010 was 70 percent. Corresponding data for low-income countries (i.e., incomes below $1005 in 2010 prices) was 7 percent and for middle income countries, 24 percent (*WDI* 2012, Table 2.12, p.88). For lower middle income countries, it was 16 percent. As noted, for Indonesia it was 23 percent.

based largely on post-1960 data show that education (defined as years of schooling, the highest level of education attained, or some related measure) is a statistically significant determinant of economic growth. Countries that have higher average years of schooling (after adjusting for initial effects of income and quality of schooling) tend to have more robust rates of growth than countries with fewer average years of schooling.[275]

These are three problems with this interpretation.

First, the international data offer an alternative explanation. Countries with the highest incomes (i.e., those which have grown on a sustained basis) have high tertiary education enrolment.[276] The relationship also holds at the bottom of the income scale – countries with low tertiary enrolment have low incomes (i.e., they have not grown on a sustained basis) and vice-versa.[277] That is, both rich and poor countries show the same direct connection between economic growth and HE. The clincher, however, is the group of countries with high tertiary enrolments which have low incomes. This group includes the Russian Federation, Poland, Hungary, Cuba, Belarus, and several others.[278] If HE "drove" growth, that situation would not exist.

---

[275]The literature is typified by the work of Barro (1996, 1999, 2001); Hanushek and Kimko (2000); Krueger and Lindahl (2001); and Hanushek *et al.* (2008). Pritchett (1996, 2001) enquired "where has all the education gone" when he failed to find a positive significant relationship between years of schooling and economic growth. Sanders (2003) obtained similar results using a different empirical approach. Ciccone and Jaroncinski (2008) showed that the relationship between education and economic growth is sensitive to the time period examined. Others researchers argued that Pritchett erred by treating years of schooling as being equivalent across countries. Once they allow for differences in education quality, the positive relationship re-emerges (Breton 2002, Dessus 2003).

[276]Although this pattern has predominated in the post WWII period, it can be traced back to the dawn of "modern economic growth" (Kuznets 1966, pp.286-294).

[277]*WDI* (2012, Table 2.12, p.88).

[278]World Bank (2012, Table 2.12, p.86-89).

Second, a major branch of economics literature, which modern writers trace back to Adam Smith, links human capital[279] rather than education to economic growth.[280] This literature acknowledges that formal education (particularly HE) contributes to the formation of human capital by developing skills, expanding knowledge, and shaping attitudes. But that literature shows that formal education is only one of numerous factors that generate, maintain, and improve human capital during a person's "formative years" and throughout their lifetimes.[281] In practice, the majority of what people come to know (and use productively) is gained outside formal education settings.[282] And, perhaps more important, the capacity and motivation for lifelong learning is directly related to the degree to which the economy and society stimulate enquiry, reward adaptation, encourage enterprise and innovation, and promote progress more generally.[283]

The third point is a technical matter regarding the statistical problems of relating a rate of change (economic growth) to a level (educational attainment). The details are discussed in Annex 6.

---

[279]"Human capital refers to the productive capacities of human beings as income producing agents in the economy" (Rosen 1998, p.681).

[280]Modern contributions began with Schultz (1959, 1963) and include Becker (1964), Freeman (1977), Mankiw, Romer and Weil (1992), Kremer (1993), United Nations (1996), AfDB (1998), Temple (1999), Johnson (2000), FRBD (2004), and Jones and Schneider (2005).

[281]Heckman (2006) and Heckman and Masterov (2004) emphasize the social benefits of ensuring that non-cognitive as well as cognitive skills are developed from an early age.

[282]Outlook (2001). One estimate suggests that the average person spends less than 5 percent of their lives "at school" (FRBD 2004). It also accounts for the emphasis over the last two decades (primarily by development agencies) on lifelong learning (Fulmer 2000; Willums 2001; World Bank 1999, 2003; Kochan 2004; FRBD 2004), a point recently reemphasized by Pearson (2012).

[283]The point is reinforced by the attention given to the numerous "learning-by" approaches such as learning-by-doing, engaging, participating, failing, trading, trial-and-error, and networking among others (McPherson 2005, n19). It combines the individual's motivation and the incentives for learning with the rewards and encouragement provided by the social and economic setting.

The interdependence between economic growth and HE has major implications for policy. For example, it highlights the value of creating a culture of learning from the top of society to the bottom. It reaffirms the value of life-long learning in which every experience, success and failure, offers an opportunity for improvement and change that can boost productivity and competitiveness.[284] It also underscores, as explained further below, the fundamental importance of matching opportunities for skill development or capacity improvement to the life-style of every worker or learner. These adjustments will help move the society beyond the notion that formal qualifications measure skill, to the idea that tasks are accomplished through competence and aptitude. Such an adjustment would be reinforced by the increasing acceptance of the effectiveness of having workers improve their capacities by taking courses of varying length that complement their work and life experiences. It would allow the idea of "continuing education" to become an acceptable and practical means for upgrading skills and expanding capabilities.

The above changes take advantage of economic growth and broader social changes to stimulate the enhancement of skills, capacities, and aptitudes, and to raise worker productivity. This point brings us back to the discussion of governance in Chapter 3 and the question raised there of the "signals" that the structure and trends within society and patterns of administration and governance provide to the general population. If the Government aids and abets corruption, leaves impunity and dereliction of duty unpunished, and stifles transparency and accountability, the general public will learn that these particular behaviors are tolerated and adjust accordingly.

If, by contrast, the Government establishes clear, open procedures, emphasizes merit over group connections, and transparently administers public resources for the public good, different economic and social behaviors will emerge. The implication is that the quality of governance

---

[284]O'Rourke (2002).

helps determine the quality of extra-curricular learning. The quality of that learning will also determine the attitudes of the general public to the types of changes needed to boost economic growth – enterprise, entrepreneurship, innovation, discipline, striving, trust, confidence, and cooperation. Students in formal HE classes can be taught the value of all of these attributes. Whether they learn their value and act accordingly depends on the degree to which the students' experiences reaffirm them in everyday social and economic interactions. Rapid, sustained, and in-clusive growth specifically reinforces this pattern of learning.

Reforming Higher Education Institutions

Part of the dynamic described above depends on feedback and cumulative causation.[285] Inclusive economic growth provides a setting that stimulates extra-curricular learning. This has important benefits for HE. But, as noted above the relationship runs the other way as well. For economic growth to be sustained, HE needs to improve as well.[286]

Several types of improvements in HE in Indonesia would help boost, or at least strengthen the foundation for inclusive growth. They include the:[287]

- quality of the programs in which students are taught;

---

[285]Gunnar Myrdal used the term "cumulative causation" to describe how a grow-ing economy creates the conditions which stimulate further growth (Ricoy 1998). For example, optimism about growth prospects boosts investment and productive capacity which, in turn, stimulates growth further. This spill-over effect was captured in endog-enous growth models which focus on how increasing knowledge supports the conditions for the further expansion of knowledge, investment, and growth (Romer 1986; Lucas 1988).

[286]The Outlook Update from the ADB (2012) could be used as a basis for action. It reviewed the role of service sector expansion as a driver of future growth in Asia. Its main argument is that countries that do not upgrade the quality of their education systems and human capital formation will not keep up, let alone hope to catch up.

[287]This section should be supplemented by the excellent suggestions for improve-ment provided by Hill and Thee (2012). They highlight issues related to HE funding, administration, quality of teaching and research, facilities, networks, remuneration and course loads.

- quality of the teaching in HE institutions (HEIs);
- excellence of the research undertaken within the HE establishments; and
- overall quality and coherence of academic management.

Every HEI in Indonesia could benefit from actions in each of these areas.[288]

The first and fourth items are handled through the overall quality assurance exercises to which HEIs are periodically subject. Academic quality and administrative competence cannot be imposed from outside. They have to emerge from within the organization, even if those involved draw on outside support.[289]

In practical terms, the Board of Higher Education in Indonesia will need to encourage HEIs to undertake institutional audits and quality assurance assessments as a means of raising their standards. These regular self-assessments, which could usefully be linked to formal accreditation procedures, should be based on international guidelines while Indonesia is upgrading its capacities in this area.[290] In this way, higher education standards in Indonesia can begin to mirror international better practice, even if international standards are a long way from being met.[291]

A further modification that is needed in Indonesia is a range of en-

---

[288]During visits by our team to UI, UGM, IPB, Hassanuddin University, and discussions with staff members of the Universities of Malang, Surabaya, and Riau, we learned that some of these changes are underway.

[289]Indonesia could productively learn from South Africa, which has used quality assurance to forcibly upgrade its whole system of higher education (Russo and McPherson 2006).

[290]Indonesia already has in place quality assurance and accreditation processes (Nizam 2009). Much could be learned about these processes from international experience. See for example, Mishra (2006), Curvale (2007), and references in Russo and McPherson (2006).

[291]Both anecdotal and press reports highlight the counterproductive practices that persist in HE. The Board of Higher Education is well aware of these. It has been exceedingly difficult inducing HEIs to raise their standards. Setting international standards or using technical support from international agencies would help boost the capacities of the Board of Higher Education.

try and exit points for students. There is widespread evidence that the skills students acquire are often inadequate to the employment they obtain. Part of the problem is that the programs offered are too rigidly orchestrated to enable students to acquire a functional set of skills. This problem has been addressed in many countries by providing several academic paths for students. Some lead to formal degrees. Others allow students to build up their skills piece-meal in ways that are consistent with their personal circumstances and match their experience and work requirements. By providing students access to tertiary education in a more flexible way, the HE system can cater more effectively to the development of careers rather than crank out, "cookie cutter" style, a relatively uniform set of graduates, whether in law, economics, psychology or other disciplines.

This adjustment recognizes that only some people will want, or have the capacities, including time and financial resources, to pursue conventional undergraduate and graduate programs. Many will find that their circumstances (income, work schedules, family situation, residential arrangements) preclude full-time study. At present, most of these students either forego further tertiary education or they attend a vocational college, often intermittently. Modifications to teaching and scheduling within HEIs would enable a large number of people, who otherwise would miss out, the opportunity to progressively enhance their capacities. As in many programs in the colleges and universities of the developed world, these students could gain additional formal education through different means and modes (in modules, on-campus or on-line, short courses, weekend retreats, and so on).[292]

---

[292]This is one of the major advantages of the community college system in the United States, which has been and is being widely copied in rich and developing countries alike (e.g., Australia and India, and more recently China). The essential feature of this education is its flexible scheduling. Another is its direct link to the career path and opportunities of the student. A third is that the learning experience is closely tied to the needs of local communities.

The emphasis should be on making higher education as accessible as possible to all segments of the population. Adult education could be readily handled in this way through further or continuing education programs. This approach would provide worker-students with second, third, and subsequent chances to improve their skills in ways that boost their income and welfare.[293] This effort could be supported within HEIs by adapting teaching and learning methods to engage student in activities that reinforce habits of critical analysis, enquiry, and lifetime learning.[294]

Another constructive change would be for HEIs to pay more attention to the quality and content of primary and secondary education. Formal education is a system in which, in principle, all levels should interact and to which all levels should contribute. In particular, the graduation standards from one level need to be consistent with the entrance requirements of subsequent levels. HE is best placed among the three levels to ensure consistency in this respect by promoting collaboration among the different administrators, undertaking relevant research, and designing approaches to help remedy deficiencies, whether of teaching methods, administration and management, or course content, within the education system as a whole.

All too frequently, including in Indonesia, administrators in HE remain aloof from issues they perceive as not directly related to their sector or level. This is short-sighted since lack of attention to the quality of teaching and learning at lower levels of the education system undercuts the success of

---

[293]World Bank (2003; 2006).

[294]This would require most higher education organizations to de-emphasize (and fruitfully jettison) the "chalk-and-talk," top-down, "professor has the answers approach." Efforts should be made to encourage student participation, group discussion, and collective enquiry. Moreover, in order for students to develop the "21st Century skills" that will enable them to adapt to changing social and economic conditions, they need to develop capacities in networking, social interaction, learning how to learn, a second language, social engagement, professionalism, leadership, teamwork, and critical and independent thinking. Much of this can be nurtured and reinforced by social interaction.

HE itself. Indeed, in their own interests, HE administrators need at least to act as if they recognize that underprepared tertiary graduates become primary and secondary teachers who then perpetuate the cycle of low quality education. This wastes resources at all levels of the education system not just in HE.[295] Perhaps if more state support went directly to students in the form of scholarships that could be used wherever they were admitted rather than in the form of university budget subsidies, universities would be compelled to pay more attention to the preferences of their "customers."

The GOI could give HE a major boost by initiating a program to educate a generation of Indonesians abroad in advanced skills. The initiative would accelerate the upgrading of the local HE system by raising academic and professional standards through the country.[296] Such an effort could be supported by agencies within the country, state-owned and private, which would benefit from medium and longer term improvement in skills, knowledge, and aptitudes within Indonesia. The success that other Asian countries have had with similar programs is evidence that such a program pays off.[297] With fewer than 40,000 students studying abroad each year, Indonesia is far from accumulating a critical mass of returning students to provide the necessary range of better practices – peer-reviewed research, improved teaching skills, externally driven quality assurance and accreditation, and effective HE administration. It

---

[295]Bastian (2013) was heavily critical of the lack of preparation provided by Indonesia's education system. This is a general problem for education systems. A major report on improving education quality in the United States (Callan *et al.* 2007, Pt. I) emphasized the need to improve "… productivity in the educational pipeline" by simultaneously ensuring that high school students are "college-ready" and that college courses are appropriately structured to seamlessly continue from where high school education left off.

[296]Hill and Thee (2012, p.241) highlight two major problems with current staffing of HEIs in Indonesia. There is minimal mobility of teachers from one organization to another and few of the senior teaching staff has internationally recognized PhDs.

[297]Indonesia already has some experience in this issue when the Ministry of Finance and Bank Indonesia sent large numbers of staff for training abroad (Hildebrand and Thomas 1997).

is these that will enable the country to take advantage of, and profitably build upon local and global knowledge.[298]

As a final point, the HE system needs to revamp its system of appointments, promotions, and research support. Weaning the current participants away from business-as-usual transactional arrangements may be difficult. Many within the existing system have a vested interest and substantial financial investment in its continuation. Nonetheless, cronyism, nepotism, and favoritism have never led to high quality academic appointments or to high quality academic research. Merit-based, transparent selection processes based on international procedures are readily available that Indonesia could learn from and adopt.

Synergies in Broad-Based Initiatives

There are multiple synergies in broad-based initiatives to develop and utilize human resources.

Sustained increases in productive work, improvements in the quality of learning, both formal and non-formal, and rapid inclusive growth are mutually reinforcing.

Furthermore, both the scope and amount of productive work would be increased by improvements in hard and soft infrastructure, as well as enhanced governance and institutional changes that reduce restrictions on enterprise and entrepreneurship.

A key challenge in Indonesia will be to raise the productivity of all work, irrespective of whether it is formal or informal. The productivity and competitiveness from which sustained rapid inclusive growth will be

---

[298]None of the data is flattering. Indicators for achievement in science and technology for Indonesia are weak (WDI 2012, Table 5.13, p.333) For example, Indonesia's expenditure on R&D is .08 percent of GDP. For lower middle income countries, it averages .61 percent of GDP. Receipts for royalty and license fees in 2010 were $60 million; payments were $1.6 billion. There was no evidence the Indonesians filed any patents.

derived will need to involve all Indonesian workers. Indeed, through improvements in governance and strengthened institutional arrangements, the GOI would remove many of the barriers that currently fragment labor markets, raise transaction costs, and limit the degree to which the domestic economy can be extended and prosper.

A more concentrated focus by the GOI on raising productivity would help workers overcome the difficulties they now face gaining a livelihood by having to cobble together several jobs or occupations. Policies that raise the rate of inclusive growth would help boost incomes more generally, providing workers with an opportunity to specialize in fewer activities. This would raise their productivity and increase their ability to compete.

The Government could make a useful start raising labor productivity and improving living standards through policies that foster efficiency and equity. One of these is the removal of subsidies, such as for fuel and electricity, which blatantly favor the well-to-do. Providing additional resources so that agricultural research can respond to the challenges facing an aging rural population and work force would have significant pay-offs in terms of farmer income and rural welfare. Provision of complementary capital, particularly infrastructure, to enable all workers, notably those with several fragmented jobs, to reduce travel, time, and inconvenience costs associated with employment, would also help.

These efforts could be readily supplemented by actions that stimulate improvements in education, especially HE. These include upgrading the content of HE programs, enhancing the quality of teaching and learning within HEIs, elevating standards of research and scholarship, and revamping the system of academic management. These changes would be reinforced by improvements in transparency and accountability, and academic advancement on the basis of merit. Greater attention to increasing the effectiveness of quality assurance and accreditation are also needed. These areas would be considerably enhanced if the Government, together with supportive private entities, initiated a large-scale, long-term program to train abroad a generation of Indonesian students.

HE is only part of the process by which learning occurs, knowledge accumulates, and skills develop. Rapid, sustained, and inclusive growth provides an appropriate setting for the enhancement of "extracurricular learning." Indeed, this completes the circle. Higher rates of economic growth, stimulated by improvements in hard and soft infrastructure, lead to the expansion of productive work. This directly raises productivity and improves competitiveness. These changes, in turn, increase the incentives for, and boost the rewards from increased learning and skill development at all levels, including a revamped higher education system. This broad-based learning has major role in generating and sustaining rapid inclusive growth.

CHAPTER FIVE

Getting Things Done:
The Politics of Doubling Shared Prosperity

*It has been said that democracy is the worst form of government
except all the others that have been tried.*

WINSTON CHURCHILL

A key challenge in promoting rapid, sustained, and inclusive growth
in Indonesia is identifying policies that have a reasonable prospect
of being implemented. Recent studies by the World Bank argue that development specialists should pay more attention to the political context
within which policies are formulated and implemented.[299] Conventional
approaches to policy tend to neglect this dimension by focusing on the
content of policies and the capacities required for implementing them,
but not addressing the politics of getting things done.

The Government's development plans and programs will remain well-
documented intentions unless they are implemented. That will involve
some hard-core politicking – negotiation, consensus-building, horse-

---

[299]World Bank (Blum, Manning and Srivistava 2012; Mansuri and Rao 2012).

trading, compromise, confrontation, brinkmanship, periodic review, and renegotiation. All of these will be reflected in the collaborative interactions by politicians, individually and in groups, as they seek the best deal for themselves and their constituents, given what they perceive to be the resources available, and the limits and opportunities confronting other politicians with whom they must deal.

There is a widespread perception that Indonesia's technical economic issues are well understood and relatively easy to deal with, but the politics are difficult. This assessment misrepresents the problem. Neither the political implications of the economic proposals for promoting rapid, sustained, and inclusive growth, nor the economic consequences of the political maneuvering required to achieve that goal, is well understood by the bureaucrats, business executives, academics, and politicians involved. Moreover, many of the political and economic issues will emerge only as the details emerge of what is required to accelerate sustainable, inclusive growth, and short-term effects are understood and weighted far more than long-term effects, who full benefits may not be appreciated.

In this chapter we examine several features of Indonesia's political system and how they relate to the goal of promoting rapid, sustained, and inclusive growth.

We begin with a brief review of the political benefits of higher rates of inclusive growth, a premise on which the rest of this chapter is based.

We then examine the horizontal politics of getting things done. This focuses on interactions between the executive and legislative branches of government, as well as some of the issues that must be addressed so that the relevant policies can gain both legislative approval and necessary budget appropriations for their implementation.

However, passing laws and providing funding are only part of the process. Accordingly, the discussion shifts to the vertical politics of getting things done. This focuses on the intergovernmental relations and bureaucratic reform required to enable efficient implementation of the relevant programs and policies. The operational context needs to be clear for bureaucratic reform to be effective. Since the Law on Decentralization was introduced in 1999, administrative arrangements between the center, provinces, and districts/cities have been regularly modified, both explicitly and implicitly. For rapid and inclusive growth to materialize and be sustained, these arrangements need to be rationalized so that each level of government has the incentive to act in ways that boosts growth and development.

An example of what that rationalization might involve is provided by a mining case study. It demonstrates how the central and local governments reached a "political settlement" that accommodated the need of the center to reaffirm its constitutional authority over natural resources, as well as the importance of local government obtaining additional revenue to support local development and capture a larger share of "their" resources to use locally.

The chapter concludes with reflections on the likelihood that Indonesia's nature of transactional (*quid pro quo*) clientelistic politics will facilitate or block the implementation of the inclusive growth agenda.

Political Benefits of Inclusive Growth[300]

Rapid, sustained, and inclusive growth in Indonesia will have broad benefits. There are obvious gains for the poor and marginalized. The advantages for the political elite – at the national and local levels – of peace and security derived from inclusive growth are also clear. Inequality between groups and poverty in ethnically divided contexts have been major sources of ethno-communal and secessionist violence.[301] Em-

---

[300]Adapted from Toha (2012).

[301]"Ethno-communal" covers groups defined by ethnicity, religion, language, and region. The term "ethno-communal" violence was used by Varshney, Tadjoeddin, and Panggabean (2008) to describe clashes in Indonesia in the late 1990s and early 2000s. The literature refers to this type of violence as "ethnic riots," which are "intense, sudden, though not necessarily wholly unplanned, lethal attacks by civilian members

pirical evidence from Indonesia and other parts of the world has shown that relative deprivation[302] and exclusion from political and economic resources[303] along ethnic lines have increased the prospects of violence. The resultant clashes have been deadly, costly, and have seriously disrupted economic growth and political development. They create distrust and division amongst the local population. Box 5.1 discusses aspects of conflict in Indonesia.

Box 5.1: Sources of Violence in Indonesia

There have been many theories to explain the ethno-communal violence in the late 1990s and early 2000s.

Some believe that riots in Indonesia were an artifact of the country's transition to democracy, representing a "critical juncture" where the elite's continuing access to resources is being renegotiated and the uncertainty of the outcome increases the likelihood of violence (Bertrand 2004; Sidel 2006). Others argue that the violence was a result of a post-Suharto scramble for political and economic power, both at the national and local levels (van Klinken 2007; Davidson 2008). Still others have focused on the legacy of violence from the New Order regime (Colombijn and Linblad 2002).

One of the most compelling explanations of ethno-communal violence in Indonesia is inequality between culturally, or ethnically defined groups,

of one ethnic group on civilian members of another ethnic group, the victims chosen because of their group membership" (Horowitz 2001, p.1). Examples of such clashes in Indonesia include the Christian-Muslim riots in Maluku and Central Sulawesi, the anti-Madurese violence in West and Central Kalimantan, and the violence against ethnic Chinese minorities.

[302]Gurr (1970).

[303]Wimmer, Cederman, and Min (2010).

commonly referred to as "horizontal inequality". Incidents of violence tend to increase with rising horizontal inequality across districts (Gurr 1970). For instance, the larger the intergroup differentials in child mortality, a hyper-sensitive indicator of deprivation, the higher the number of clashes in a given district in Indonesia (Mancini 2008).

This adverse effect of group inequality also seems to apply to routine violence as well. Unlike ethno-communal and separatist violence, which are high-profile, episodic, and massively violent, routine or everyday violence is regular destruction that often lacks explicit political aims and rarely makes the headlines. In Indonesia, routine violence is typically found in Java in the form of vigilante killings, lynching of petty criminals, and inter-neighborhood and village brawls (Tadjoeddin and Murshed 2007; Welsh 2008).

Indonesia has also had separatist rebellions. Following the country's independence, regions outside of Java complained that the country's centralized policies disproportionately favored Java. Appointments to regional government administrative posts, which were made in Jakarta, were typically given to Javanese instead of local leaders. Furthermore, the foreign exchange rate was overvalued, favoring groups that relied heavily on imports and discriminating against exporting regions, which are mostly outside of Java (Feith 1962).

While these animosities towards the central government fostered the PRRI/Permesta rebellions in Sulawesi and Sumatra in the 1950s, the same sentiments have been evident over recent decades in Aceh, Papua, Riau, and East Kalimantan.

Aceh organized the Free Aceh Movement (GAM) and Papua the Free Papua Movement (OPM). By comparison, separatist agitations in East Kalimantan and Riau were minor and did not escalate into armed confrontation. The common argument in these regions has been that since they have abundant natural resources, they are entitled to a larger share of the revenue distribution (Tadjoeddin 2011; Aspinall 2007). Some argue, however, that separatist sentiments in Aceh and Papua escalated into organized and armed groups because Aceh and Papua both claim to have a unique ethnic and religious identity that consolidates the group and justifies their claim to secede from the rest of the Republic (Aspinall 2007). East Kalimantan and Riau, on the other hand, cannot claim such distinctions. They continue to debate who is "truly indigenous" (Ford 2003; Schiller 2007). Secessionist aspirations in these contexts had difficulty gaining traction because groups were more fragmented and lacked the historical narrative that foments violence (Aspinall 2007).

These issues are being addressed as part of the decentralization process.

Some of the distrust and division is being overcome through the decentralization process.[304] Regional autonomy provides local actors with greater fiscal and political control. The central government is required to distribute fiscal transfers (DAU and DAK) to districts and cities, and to allocate a greater share of revenues from natural resources to the producing regions.[305] Local leaders are now directly elected through *Pilkada* (in contrast to the New Order regime's practice of central appointments). This has given broader discretion to the populations of each district/city to pursue local priorities. The splitting of districts and municipalities has increased the number of administrative units in the country,[306] opening up more leadership opportunities and political offices for aspiring local

---

[304]Diprose (2009); Tadjoeddin (2011).

[305]Resource rich regions gain significantly from these transfers and revenues. Since 1999, in Aceh, Papua, East Kalimantan, and Riau, local revenues have increased on average by a factor of 19. Revenues in other regions have increased only by a factor of 9 (Tadjoeddin 2011).

[306]Booth (2011); Fitrani, Hoffman and Kaiser (2005).

actors.[307] Thus, for local elites at least, decentralization has accommodated their demands for larger shares of economic and political resources.

A common danger is that when the population is ethnically divided and inequalities between groups are stark, competitive elections can encourage politicians to manipulate ethnic loyalties in order to mobilize voters.[308] In doing so, they increase the likelihood of ethno-communal violence. Delineating new jurisdictions by ethnicity exacerbates these tendencies. Implementing policies that encourage inclusive growth throughout the whole of Indonesia would benefit both the poor and marginalized, most of whom have been excluded from the gains of recent growth, and the elites who control Indonesia and need peace and stability to govern sustainably and continue gaining access to the benefits of rapid growth.

The Horizontal Politics of Getting Things Done: Executive-Legislative Relations[309]

Musyawarah-Mufakat – *Decision-Making by Consensus*

The shift to the presidential system in 2004 focused attention directly on executive-legislative relations in policy making and implementation. The reality of multiparty politics in the DPR (the Indonesian Legislature)[310] is

---

[307]Diprose (2009); Aragon (2007); Quinn (2003); Subianto (2010). Some scholars have noted that since decentralization, the majority of the leaders comprise former bureaucrats or other affiliates of the New Order regime. They are not new actors who were previously shut out from power (Malley 2003; Hadiz 2010; Vel 2007).

[308]Wilkinson (2004).

[309]This section draws freely on Hanan (2012).

[310]*Dewan Perwakilan Rakyat*, or The People's Representative Council. In the 1945 Constitution, the *Majelis Permusyawaratan Rakyat* or MPR (the People Consultative Assembly) was the highest State body. That changed with the 2002 amendments. The MPR now ranks equally with the President, DPR, DPD (*Dewan Perwakilan Daerah* or Regional Representative Council), MA (Supreme Court), MK (Constitutional Court). The main tasks of the MPR are: 1) to inaugurate the President and Vice President; and 2) to process amendments to the Constitution. The members of DPR and DPD are automatically members of MPR.

that all policy making and implementation in Indonesia requires participants to conform to democratic norms. That conformity occurs as they accommodate the interests of multiple actors, especially potential veto players, whose exchanges largely determine how the executive and legislative bodies interact (see Box 5.2).

Box 5.2: Legislative Leadership Constellation in Indonesia's Emerging Democracy

The legislature's multi-party structure makes cohesive leadership and direction difficult to achieve.

Most political parties in Indonesia have weak organizational structures and party networks. They have limited capacity to generate votes (Tomsa 2008). The governments of Abdurrahman Wahid and Megawati were coalitions. Since every party was included, there was no organized party opposition and little vertical accountability (Slater 2004). By winning 60 percent of the vote in 2004 and 2009, President Yudhoyono should not have felt pressure to co-opt members of rival parties. Nevertheless, he included members of all significant parties in his cabinets, with PDIP being the only exception.

Four sets of decision makers have leadership positions, namely the leaders of the DPR, the political parties, the fraksi, and the commissions.

DPR: The leadership of the DPR has several roles with respect to executive-legislative relations. They involve: coordination of agenda-setting and implementation of the activities of all internal organs of DPR, including committees; control over the DPR's annual operating budget; representation of the DPR in its dealings with all other institutions; and consultation with the President on behalf of DPR.

Political parties: The leaders of political parties are often members of the DPR as well as leaders of the parties in the DPR (fraksi). Political party leaders in Indonesia are not necessarily the party chair. The leader can be someone who is outside the executive structure of the party but plays a decisive role. For example, President Yudhoyono leads the Parti Demokrat. The party leaders control decisions about the party's direction, or whether controversial issues will be raised. They also draw the DPR's attention to major concerns of the general public.

Fraksi: The leaders of the fraksi head the political parties in the DPR. Each DPR member must join a fraksi. Each party typically forms its own fraksi, although a fraksi must have at least 13 members. Small parties join with others to reach the required minimum size. The leaders of fraksi represent their parties in the DPR and serve as heads of commissions and ad hoc and working committees. They also directly lobby the Executive.

Commissions: Commissions are integral to DPR operations – they are where almost all DPR decisions are made. Only issues that cannot be resolved in a commission or a combination of commissions will be substantively debated in the plenary session. The leaders of the commissions ensure that disagreements and differences in points of view are appropriately mediated and resolved.

Implementers also need to recognize the limitations imposed by their goals.[311] This will help them understand what they need to do for their ideas to be accepted while, at the same time, minimizing or deflecting opposition to the changes that are needed to get things done.

Hill and Zhuang have argued that a development strategy designed to promote higher rates of inclusive growth should be "...anchored on two pillars: one is to create and expand economic opportunities through high and sustained growth, and the other is to broaden access to op-

---

[311]This point, already noted in Chapter 3, builds on a theme of a World Bank (1997) study on state capacity.

portunities for all members of... society."[312] Creating these conditions involves both economics and politics.

A World Bank study asserted that the required development policies will not be made and implemented without an increasingly capable, credible, and committed government supported by strong political leadership. Specifically, the policy makers:

> ...have to choose a growth strategy, communicate their goals to the public, and convince people that the future rewards are worth the effort, thrift, and economic upheaval. They will succeed only if their promises are credible and inclusive, reassuring people that they or their children will enjoy their full share of the fruits of growth.[313]

This view, though apt, is the counsel of perfection. Indonesia is a new, messy democracy that is still coming to grips with the opportunities and limitations of participation and representation[314] as it seeks to develop operational procedures, acceptable to the voting public, on how to respond to emerging events. The whole democratic exercise, particularly the decentralization of administrative responsibility, is still unfolding. There are few concrete lessons to guide central and local administrators. Moreover, debates about policies regularly generate additional concerns that were not anticipated, or for which there is little accumulated experience.

One point, however, stands out. Accelerating the rate of inclusive growth will require Indonesia's leaders to adopt a longer term perspective.[315] Current political arrangements will make that difficult. Consequently,

---

[312]Hill and Zhuang (2012, p.2).

[313]Growth Commission (World Bank 2008, p.3).

[314]As discussed below, debate continues over differences between the "democratic" (i.e., indirect) and "direct" (i.e., popular) election of governors.

[315]As noted by Ianchovichina and Lundstrom (2009), the emphasis needs to be on the [long term] improvement of "...the productive capacity of individuals and creat-

moving the country forward will most likely involve a series of short-term government actions. There will be set-backs along the way as priorities change and political loyalties shift. Learning, strategic forgetting, regular re-calibration, negotiation, and accommodation will all be part of the process.

However, as noted in our first report, electoral reform that addresses the most grievous aspects of Indonesia's current worst combination of electoral systems could have dramatic results: "Change the rules governing how politicians are elected to office, and you can change their behavior." For example, Indonesia could adopt a mixed system, similar to Germany's, in which a portion of the legislature is elected via closed-list proportional representation under Indonesia's current 77 multi-member districts and the remainder is elected through 560 single member districts. This would allow for legislators with a national perspective (those elected under pro-portional representation) and legislators more accountable to their consti-tuents (those elected under single-member districts). It would also allow for a mix of legislators from large and small political parties, and address some of the worst aspects of "money politics." Even more modest reform, such as simply using a common system for both national and subnational elections, would greatly reduce current electoral complexity.[316]

Bill deliberation is fundamental to the process of lawmaking.[317] This

---

ing [a] conducive environment for employment" and not the [short term] gains from income redistribution.

[316]Saich *et al.* (2010, pp. 135-140).

[317]There are two levels of bill deliberation that comprise the general process of lawmaking. Level one (*pembicaraan tingkat satu*) is conducted by a commission (stand-ing committee/*komisi*), combination of commissions (*gabungan komisi*), in the legislative council (*Baleg*), special committee (*pansus*) meetings, or budget committee (*Banggar*), or meetings together with the minister/ministers representing the President. Level two (*pembicaraan tingkat dua*) is deliberation of the bill in the plenary session of DPR, which formally approves or disapproves the bill derived from the first level. The decision on whether a bill will be deliberated by a *komisi*, combination of *komisi*, *baleg*, or *badan anggaran* is determined by the deliberation council (*Bamus*) – a steering committee in the DPR with members from all parties. Sometimes this *Bamus* is considered as a "mini DPR". The discussion is based on the *Daftar Inventaris Masalah* or DIM (Problems In-

requires close involvement of the Executive and the Legislature from the start, when a bill is put onto the agenda, through to its completion, where both the President and DPR jointly approve the resulting legislation. A bill can be initiated by the President, the DPR, or both. Most economics-related bills originate with the Executive. The bills on the annual state budget always come from the Executive.

Except as decided otherwise, all agreement in the DPR is based on consensus, commonly referred to in Indonesia as *musyawarah-mufakat* (see Box 5.3). Although consensus-based deliberation appears to favor a minority (veto players), it is also an effective tool for the majority to include the opposition in a decision. All small parties have the opportunity to be heard, often at length.[318]

This consensus-based approach makes it difficult for parties to pursue strong disagreements, or for the DPR and the Executive to be wildly at odds. Action can be readily blocked by one party even when all other parties agree. When issues appear unresolvable, the discussion is typically moved to a smaller group such as *panja* (working committee), or the so called "*lobi*" (lobby) or "consultation" mechanism.[319] As a result, legislative deliberation can usually reach only general agreement. When controversial issues arise, such as reducing the fuel price subsidy, the details are handled by the Executive as part of its implementation authority and not part of policy making.

---

ventory List), which consists of basically all items in the bill. It can start with the title of the bill and go all the way to the end of the bill, such as closing clause.

[318]Larger parties do not wish to be accused of being intolerant of small parties, each of which is treated as an integral part of the Indonesian political family.

[319]To adopt, adapt to, and implement consensus principles, the deliberation process has several stages. From the plenary meeting, the process goes to Commission or *Pansus* (special committee – combination of representatives of several committees) then to working committee (*panja*), then to formulation team (*timmus*), and then to synchronization team (*timsin*). Along the way, the process can be interrupted by the "lobi" or lobbying process where the meeting tries to find ways of resolving disagreements that cannot be dealt with through regular/formal meetings/deliberation.

The implication is that a general policy such as the promotion of rapid, inclusive growth should easily gain legislative approval. Moreover, since the policy will be passed by consensus, it will be claimed as a national policy rather than that of a particular party or political bloc.

Box 5.3: Consensus in Indonesian Politics

Since independence, consensus in the political process has been defined by the Indonesian term musyawarah-mufakat (deliberation-agreement) or decision-making by consensus. Its development has been associated with decision by unanimous consent, in contrast to decision by voting or majority rule.

Anthropologists (Kartohadikoesoemo 1953; Koentjaraningrat 1967) have argued that the idea and practice of consensus dates back to the traditional social life in Indonesian villages. Logsdon (1978, p. 95) noted: "Decision making by unanimous consent is only reached when all sides are in agreement. Thus, it usually implies considerable discussion and compromise. But the compromise involved here is frequently viewed differently from the need to build a coalition in the majority-rule systems. The basic assumption is that there is a common interest in society, rather than competing interests, which all sides will learn to recognize through discussion. There are no "losers' in this form of decision making, which results in the good of the whole rather than the good of the greater number."

One question is whether the emphasis on consensus serves a democratic purpose, i.e., majority rule, or whether it is a strategic ploy. In the latter case, the notion of consensus is often used by the small and large parties to ensure that nothing can get done (i.e., it protects the status quo). Critics often suggest that consensus politics is politics of the lowest common denominator that does not reflect "the will of the majority." Others argue that Indonesian democracy will only mature if and when it moves beyond the notion of consensus.

The legislative foundation for emphasizing rapid, inclusive growth will be reflected in the programs and priorities of the national budget. The executive will need to convince the legislature of the value and virtue of specific policies related to the objective.

Some of the groundwork has been laid, since a general framework for rapid inclusive growth is already part of the current five-year plan and MP3EI. However, to make its case, the Government will need a coherent strategy. Despite the five-year plan and MP3EI's commitment to inclusive growth, the Government's fuel subsidy pre-empts expenditure on activities that could otherwise be used to raise the rate of economic growth. Worse, the subsidy exacerbates inequality, undercutting inclusive growth. The electricity subsidy drives up demand when supply is woefully short – and less funds for PLN means fewer households are connected at all.

Besides bill deliberation, the legislature and executive have numerous complicated exchanges to approve the annual budget. The budget is developed in several stages. The first is to establish the level of resources available. This is led by the Fiscal Policy Office in the Ministry of Finance (part of the Executive). It is assisted by a committee of technical experts comprising other parts of the Ministry of Finance, BAPPENAS (the National Development Planning Agency), BPS, BI, the Ministry of Energy and Mineral Resources, and the coordinating Ministry for Economy, Finance and Industry. This committee, chaired by the Ministry of Finance, formulates the basic assumptions for the budget and prepares the revenue estimates.[320]

These assumptions provide limits within which the budget discussions take place. It is politically expedient for the Executive to allow the DPR some discretion, while fiscally prudent to retain control of total spending. The DPR is at a disadvantage because it lacks the technical capacity to determine how the limits were derived.[321]

---

[320]Blondal, Hawkesworth and Choi (2009, pp.14-15).
[321]This difficulty of checking the assumptions is compounded for the DPR because

BAPPENAS, also in the Executive, takes the lead in establishing priorities for new programs. In the pre-budget discussions with parliament, the Ministry of Finance and the Budget Committee of DPR examine broad macroeconomic and fiscal policy objectives, especially the key economic assumptions and revenue forecasts. Meanwhile, spending ministries discuss their work plans with their DPR commission partners. Once these discussions are completed, the Executive prepares the detailed budget implementation guidance, which readies the document for the formal process of budget deliberation between the Executive and the DPR.

The proposed budget is considered by the relevant subject-matter commission, after which the bill is sent to the *Badan Anggaran* (budget committee) to be reconciled and finalized. The bill is then moved to the plenary session (level two of the deliberation process) for final approval. The above occurs within a pre-determined timetable.[322] The process is exacting and exhausting, and one for which the members of the DPR are ill-equipped. A major problem is the DPR's limited institutional support.

Weak DPR Institutional Capacities

The technical capacities available to the DPR are low. This contrasts with the demanding nature of the DPR's lawmaking authority and its extensive oversight responsibilities. For the DPR to derive and formulate substantively better policies *and* increase the efficiency of the lawmaking process itself, its members require the appropriate expertise and technical support. Much of the institutional assistance for the DPR was established before the advent of democracy. In principle, the Secretariat

---

the macroeconomic models upon which the budget is based are not provided (Blondal, Hawkesworth and Choi 2009).

[322]The budget process is time-constrained and well-orchestrated. It begins in May (around May 20), the draft is introduced by the President in a speech on August 15 or 16 (just before Independence Day), and the Budget Bill needs to be finalized by the end of October.

General of DPR plays this role, but in practice, it has not (see Box 5.4). Members have far more personal assistance than technical and professional support.[323]

The result is that DPR members have difficulty gaining access to well-informed analysis on relevant subjects and related policies. When dealing with substantive, technical issues such as promoting inclusive growth, the DPR's limited capacities affect the quality of policy making and lawmaking and the outcome of policy formulation.

A recent example is the debate over fuel subsidies, in which DPR members generally lacked a credible analysis of the benefits and costs of continuing the fuel subsidy vis-à-vis policy alternatives. Particularly unclear to DPR members were economic efficiency and social equity problems posed by higher fuel consumption, versus prospective productivity and competitiveness gains from using subsidy funds for expanded investment in basic public infrastructure and rationalization of public transport. Lacking such analysis, the issues end up being decided by the apparent "needs" of the moment, including reactions to the demonstrations by supporters, and opinions of the issues' advocates.

One area where technical support is vital is government oversight. When policies related to inclusive growth are implemented, they will be overseen by the DPR. High quality government review is meant to ensure that the program or policies are implemented procedurally as planned, and in ways that enable the anticipated goals to be achieved. The DPR is well known for its willingness to scrutinize the implementation of government policies and agendas, but because it lacks the relevant institutional capacities, the constitutional requirement of high quality oversight has not yet been achieved.

---

[323]These points were confirmed by members of the DPR interviewed for this study. Members sit on multiple commissions but lack the staff to help them prepare for the issues being raised. Support from the DPR technical pool is generic rather than specific, so few of the questions that arise during discussions of legislation can be dealt with in detail.

As noted above, interactions among members within the DPR and between the DPR and the President are often time-consuming. Consensus-driven dialogue has multiple stages, and each DPR member can participate during any one of these steps. Several proposals are being considered to shorten the interactions.[324]

Box 5.4: The Capacities of the DPR Secretariat General

The DPR Secretariat General has more than three thousand staff. However, despite the large number of employees, DPR members receive limited substantive technical support from their Secretariat General, for the following reasons:

- In 2010, staff included 560 personal assistants, 1637 administrative staff, 636 partisan expert staff, 123 non-partisan expert staff, 81 non-partisan researchers, and 27 legal drafters. These data underscore the imbalance in the number of technical and expert staff. Personal assistants and administrative staff, comprising almost three-quarters of the total, are for administrative support.

- The qualifications of non-partisan expert staff and researchers are poor. Few highly qualified technical staff members work for the DPR, since the salaries they receive are based on the scheme of the general civil servant (PNS). These are relatively low.

- The non-partisan researcher's work is evaluated by Indonesian Institute of Science (LIPI) and not according to DPR criteria. LIPI uses academic research-related standards. Consequently, the researchers produce long, technical research reports and other material that rarely relates to the day-to-day policy-related work of DPR members.

---

[324]One issue is determining when, and on what issues, members of each Fraksi might speak. No guidelines are presently available for such determinations.

- The legal drafters are recruited as PNS members. Most of them are young. Some are new graduates of Indonesian law school who lack experience - law school is an undergraduate program in Indonesia, so their qualifications are at the B.A. level.

- Partisan expert staff members are appointees with little attention given to competence. Often these partisan experts are the relatives or close friends of DPR members. Again, because of the low salaries and the type of work involved, few highly qualified people apply for these jobs. A person with a PhD, if recruited as an expert staff, will be paid less than $700 per month, while if he/she works outside, the salary is around $2000 per month, often more.

- Although some well qualified and highly respected PhDs have been recruited as partisan experts, they typically treat this work as a side job. The outcome is that the technical issues being examined by DPR members are not his/her highest priority.

Thus far, policies related to economic issues such as the annual national budget (APBN) always have been jointly approved by the Executive and Legislative through the consensus mechanism. As Indonesia modernizes and matures politically, it is likely to move to a democratic (majority-determined) mechanism. With this shift, policy makers will have the opportunity to concentrate more on issues, with less attention to parliamentary maneuvers. Designing and implementing policies and programs to promote higher rates of inclusive growth may be an important means of encouraging (or even forcing) change in parliamentary procedures.

The Vertical Politics of Getting Things Done: Intergovernmental Relations[325]

Decentralization in Indonesia dramatically changed the political system. The shift from a centralized to a decentralized government was largely in response to the authoritarian regime of Suharto, and the decentralization focus on districts and municipalities rather than provinces was to counteract secessionist challenges by the resource-rich regions of Papua, East Kalimantan, and Riau. The urgency of the situation required that Law 22 of 1999 be enacted quickly.

This Law devolves central government "authorities" rather than functions to the lower (sub-provincial) levels of government. Under Article 7(1), the central government retains responsibility for national defense, international relations, justice, security, religion, and monetary and fiscal policies. To fulfill these authorities, the central government maintains an organizational structure in the provinces. It also continues activities such as national planning, intergovernmental fiscal policies, state administration, human resource development, natural resource utilization and conservation, and national standards.

In principle, the provinces are meant to coordinate among the local governments and carry out functions that affect more than one local government. Law 22 stipulates that there is no hierarchical link between the province as an autonomous region and the districts and municipalities. The governor (not the province) is responsible for de-concentrated central tasks, and represents the central government in the regions. Implementing regulations (Government Regulation 25 of 2000) further define the roles of the central and provincial governments, which include the setting of standards for public service delivery.[326]

---

[325]This section is based on interviews by team members in East Java, Bali, Jakarta, East Kalimantan, Batam, South Sulawesi, Riau and Yogjakarta. It includes contributions by Prasetyawan (2012) and Howitt (2012).

[326]One problem is that while the DPR produces the laws (the approved bills), the

The local governments implement all authorities except those allotted to the center and the provinces. Local governments have to deliver services in sectors such as health, education, public works, environment, communications, agriculture, industry and trade, capital investment, land, cooperatives, manpower and infrastructure services. Local governments may return to the province functions they cannot perform. Law 22 has been replaced by Law 34 of 2004, but the basic arrangements between the central and local governments remain the same.

Over recent years, the State Ministry of State Apparatus and Bureaucracy Reform (MENPAN-RB) has promoted a BR strategy and work plan in each central ministry/agency. The goal is to expand the effort to the sub-national level, and a set of local governments have been selected to participate in a BR pilot effort. In practice, however, there has been little support from all levels of the national civil service for BR because they see BR as a threat to their jobs. BR strategies and work plans have therefore been completed but not widely implemented.

In general, administrative performance at the sub-national level has been disappointing. Local government officials regularly announce that "we generate employment by hiring more civil servants." Corruption in the recruitment process is relatively common in many provinces, districts, and municipalities. For example, there is evidence indicating that a new civil servant in a district in East Java had to pay Rp 100-150 million ($11,100 to $16,700) to be recruited in 2010. Moreover, anecdotal evidence suggests that promotion and rotation of high-level local government officials have been based on political considerations, including how much is paid, rather than needs and qualifications.[327]

Notwithstanding these difficulties, several local governments—

---

bureaucracy often takes years from the time the bills are passed to produce the implementing regulations. This delay undercuts the law's intention.

[327]Kristiansen and Ramli (2006) provide data and insights on the market for civil service positions in Indonesia.

headed by reform-minded leaders—have implemented some aspects of BR. A "zero civil servant growth" policy has been applied in some districts. The prominent recruitment of young, capable, and reformist civil servants in a growing number of local government units indicates that some local governments have been initiating BR.[328]

A further positive example is the establishment of the one-stop shops (OSS) for business licensing that consolidates the requirements and services in one office. Although the main driver behind OSS has been to cut business costs, these services created the opportunity to apply "better practices" in public services.[329] They include open and transparent staff recruitment, participatory formulation of standard operating procedure (SOP) and service standards, transparency of licensing requirements (including information on processing time and costs), and the establishment of a complaint response mechanism. Although the general performance needs improvement,[330] this OSS development could be a model of BR for other sectors. E-procurement has been another incubator of BR at the local level.

Few leaders at the national and local levels have an incentive to promote BR. The first five years (the term of elected officials) of the reform would be full of problems that are politically unpopular, while the outcomes would only be enjoyed after their terms end. For BR to be supported and successful, it will be necessary to create incentives for the relevant politicians. Technically, BAPPENAS should be the government

---

[328]Wijayanto (2011); Buehler (2012).

[329]OSS Monitoring conducted in 2011 by MOHA and supported by the Asia Foundation show that of the 252 local governments responding to the questionnaire, 207 have established OSS with full authority to issue licenses ("one-door" OSS) and another 32 provide integrated front office assistance with technical departments continuing to process the license applications ("one-roof" OSS).

[330]Roughly half of "one-door" OSS are only authorized to issue fewer than 20 percent of the business licenses under the authority of the local governments (totaling about 100). The official time to issue licenses is still longer than the national government regulations prescribe.

agency promoting BR through both long- and medium- term development plans (RPJP and RPJM), and the party consistently monitoring implementation against the plans. The political parties could create incentives for the politicians to promote BR. At present, none of them has developed clear programs on the issue or consistently followed them.[331] Thus, in terms of influence and advocacy, BR falls to civil society – researchers, NGOs, engaged academicians, and the media.

The national government, however, has an important means of creating the incentives for BR at the sub-national levels. The high degree of dependence of district and municipal governments on fiscal transfers from the center makes it easier to create fiscal incentives for those promoting BR. The MOF has started allocating "Incentive Funds" for the local governments that performed well in the last few years. The amounts involved are small, with criteria mainly focused on the results of the State Audit Agency (BPK) and timeliness of the sub-national budget approval. This would be enhanced if BR were included as one of the criteria, although measurement of reform is always difficult and contentious.

While there are several clear dimensions of BR that can be pushed, such as budget reallocation, better governance, improvements in the investment climate through OSS, the over-riding issue is to reconfigure central-subnational roles and responsibilities. Some specialists in government highlight the devolution of authorities to the district level, bypassing the provincial governments, as a major weakness in the Indonesian decentralization architecture because it Balkanizes public policy and public administration. Others claim that it is efficient and effective for most basic services to be provided at the local level, as it fosters government transparency and accountability through participatory governance.

---

[331]This may be changing. Although voter identification with a party and its leadership is strong (Liddle and Mujani 2007), recent evidence related to PKS success indicates that voters are paying more attention to platforms rather than personalities (Hamayotsu 2011).

Nonetheless, there are some services and, more importantly, particular activities related to the promotion of economic growth, such as watershed management, pollution abatement, environmental mitigation, and electrification, that require the attention of provincial governments or some other type of cross-jurisdictional authority. The central government sought to enhance the role of provincial government through revision of the autonomy law (No. 33/2004) by authorizing provincial governments to review local governments' budgets, land use plans, and local regulations on taxes and revenues. However, its implementing regulations, particularly Government Regulation No. 38/2007 on the division of authorities, does not give significant authority to the provincial governments.

The autonomy law is currently being revised. But rather than attempting to clarify and rationalize center-subnational relationships, the draft legislation instead makes the provincial governments more accountable to the central government as an extension of the central government apparatus. It does little to expand their autonomy or provide them with more significant roles and functions. It is proposed, against significant resistance, that the governor be indirectly elected by the provincial legislative council (DPRD). The rationale is to save the costs of direct elections. Most observers have concluded that indirectly elected governors would have little legitimacy in the eyes of local government and the electorate. As now structured, the revised law on sub-national autonomy is likely to be a significant setback to decentralization and democratization, leaving district and municipal officials convinced that the national government is seeking to re-centralize control. An alternative would be to enhance the decentralization architecture by keeping the existing law but revising its implementing regulations.

Promoting Local Investment: The Mining Sector[332]

General Legal and Institutional Context

The implementation of the Law on Decentralization in 2000 significantly changed the conditions under which mining investment in Indonesia could be promoted, and would be monitored and overseen. The devolution of authority encouraged local representatives to be more insistent that the central government address their concerns.

This change is an example of the profound adjustments that have occurred in political accommodation, or "political settlement,"[333] in Indonesia. It has implications for attempts to accelerate inclusive growth. The type of political settlement that is achieved, including how it is modified over time, is directly related to both the institutional arrangements that are created as part of the political process, and the resulting distribution of political and economic benefits. Such concerns were less pressing during the authoritarian era, when power was concentrated with central bureaucrats, state-owned agencies, or shared with cronies.[334] However, in a democratic society the accepted (and acceptable) roles and responsibilities of all parties need to be based on negotiations and maintained through regular, open, and agreed procedures.

Promoting conditions favorable for investment requires stability derived from the equitable sharing of benefits among the various economic

---

[332]This section draws on Prasetyawan (2012), supplemented by material in Prasetyawan (2005, 2006).

[333]Khan defines a *"political settlement"* as "...an interdependent combination of a structure of power and institutions at the level of a society that is 'sustainable' in terms of economic and political viability" (Khan 2010). He argued that if a combination of institutions and power structure cannot survive, it is not a political settlement.

[334]Authoritarian regimes also foster political accommodation, with some authoritarian regimes being relatively competitive (Levitsky and Way 2002). Dictators often have to appease their winning coalition either providing public services and goods or cash transfers (Bueno de Mesquita *et al.* 2003).

and political actors, including investors and the general public. With decentralization, the challenge has been to ensure that the institutional mechanisms which protect the public interest are sustained during the transition from full central control to a workable blend of central-subnational roles and responsibilities. Key public interest issues have included preventing over-exploitation, repairing mining damage, adopting appropriate environmental management, and ensuring occupational safety.

Most observers recognize that there have been difficulties, excesses, and deficiencies. For example, many central government officials and academics regularly refer to the disruptions associated with decentralization created by the loss of central authority over property rights, mining, and forestry. They see this as an adverse development that the central government needs to reverse, or at least strictly control.

The reality is that decentralization was meant to be disruptive. Indeed, many politicians and bureaucrats in the central government were shocked by the degree to which decentralization diluted their power, and many local authorities regularly interpret central regulations as an attempt to undermine the process of decentralization.

Part of the required "political settlement" moving forward is for the central authorities to shift their focus from how much power they have lost to how much influence they will gain if Indonesia does begin to grow rapidly and inclusively and become the thriving upper middle income country envisioned in the national development plans. Political accommodation or an appropriate political settlement would help remedy the problems while laying the foundation for future inclusive growth. This requires attention to efforts that strengthen the institutional framework supporting development, even while it is recognized that the pattern of development and the institutional arrangements which emerge are jointly-determined.[335]

---

[335]Institutional issues have been widely studied. North (1990, 1992) referred to institutions as "rules of the game" i.e., the socially devised and derived constraints which shape human interactions. Coase (1960) had earlier argued that the human interactions

The challenge in policy formulation and implementation, and promoting development more broadly, is determining what issues need to be pushed, when, by whom, and how forcefully. One approach is to recognize the limits and opportunities provided by political settlement.

A favorable investment climate[336] helps foster rapid economic growth since it encourages investors to use their specialized knowledge in ways that will generate a profit.[337] This requires negotiation and accommodation. Democratic societies negotiate the means by which national goals such as inclusive growth can be supported within a structure of recognized property rights, contract enforcement, respect for legal processes, public accountability, and the minimization of impunity.[338] Since there is a high probability that local political actors are from different political parties, central government actors should expect to negotiate with local political actors over natural resources and other relevant issues. In fact, the willingness to negotiate and compromise is the essence of political accommodation and political settlement.

A widely discussed impediment to creating a favorable investment climate is the rising "transaction costs" of doing business (see Box 3.2). Under

---

determine the "game" and the rules by which it is played. Both of these scholars recognized that scarcity and competition (core features of economics) were basic to human behavior and hence how humans conducted their social and economic exchanges and interactions.

[336]The World Bank has paid close attention to the notion of "investment climate." One of its reports argued that "...a good investment climate provides opportunities and incentives for firms – from micro enterprises to multinationals – to invest productively, create jobs, and expand" (World Bank 2005, p.1). Growth and poverty reduction are featured as well. Although the Report does not specify what might be done, it stresses that "...government policies and behavior play a key role in shaping the investment climate" (ibid.).

[337]A similar point was made in an interview by Chatib M. Basri following his appointment as chair of the Investment Coordinating Board (BKPM) (Jakarta Post August 27, 2012).

[338]The literature, specifically North (1990), Ostrom (1990), Williamson (1996) and subsequent contributors, describe how the relevant conditions are generated and maintained.

the New Order regime, regulatory authority and the corruption derived from it were centralized. The common complaint now is that regulatory authority and its associated corruption have been decentralized. But what no one has yet shown is that corruption in Indonesia is worse now than formerly, in terms either of greater financial cost or increased business uncertainty. Until that evidence emerges (perhaps as the Churchill Mining case unfolds in international court, the financial flows behind the fuel subsidies are exposed, and reasons for the weak performance of Batam are revealed), the burden of proof remains with those who wish to dispense with or dilute decentralization. In other countries undergoing rapid decentralization, there has been a short-term spike in overall corruption, but this has been followed by a long-term decline as local government capacity has increased and local civil society had strengthened as a counterweight to corruption.

Decentralization and the Mining Sector

The passage of Law 11/1967 and Law 11/1970, which revised Law 1/1967 on Foreign Investment, was partly in response to efforts by the international financial community and foreign investors to induce Indonesia to liberalize its investment climate.[339] The Sukarno regime's nationalization program had made Indonesia hostile to foreign investors and had de-linked Indonesia from the international economy.[340] For example, by 1965, the government could not service its debt of around $2.5 billion and the central bank could not honor letters of credit.[341] Under the new laws, the GOI signed Contracts of Work (COW) with foreign investors specifying the conditions for their investment, including the time period (up to 30 years) for which the investment was protected.

---

[339]They abolished Law 78 of 1958 on foreign investment and Regulation 37 of 1960 on basic mining, both of which deterred foreign investment.

[340]Crouch (1988).

[341]Hill (1996, p. 65).

Indonesia had large reserves of natural resources, but the Indonesian private sector and government lacked the finance and technical capabilities to develop them. The liberalization of investment rules recognized these problems. The investment response was dramatic, producing a major expansion of natural resource exports. These exports boosted foreign exchange earnings and government tax receipts. The recent decade has been typical. The exports of fuels and ores and minerals were 30 percent of merchandise exports in 2000 and 40 percent in 2010. Taxes on goods and services, which are largely taxes on extraction and production of minerals, contributed 29 percent of central government revenues in 2000 and 23 percent in 2010 [342]

An important but perplexing problem has been how to rationalize the control over and ownership of natural resources.

An example from Nusa Tenggara, the COW for which was agreed in 1986, illustrates overlapping interests at the local and central level. Under its investment agreement, the company PTNTT (PT Newmont Nusa Tenggara) was required to divest part of its shareholdings in 2010. The negotiations proved difficult because they involved the GOI, the company, the Nusa Tenggara administration, and a large Indonesian conglomerate.[343] The issue was resolved with the central government, demonstrating that it was ready to compromise with local political players while sustaining a climate conducive to investment and protection of property rights.

Other cases, however, have been more difficult. For example, while the central government has provided generous incentives to local political players, it has announced its intention of retaining a 7 percent share in local resources. This has created unease and even discord at the local level.

A recent example illustrates the point. The central government is be-

---

[342]*WDI* (2012, Tables 4.4, 4.14, pp. 227, 267).
[343]Prasetyawan (2012) describes the circumstances.

ing sued by a UK investor, Churchill Mining, at the International Center for Settlement of Investment Disputes, over an investment in East Kalimantan from which Churchill was dispossessed by local authorities.[344] Irrespective of its ultimate outcome, the dispute highlights problems that continue to arise in coordinating mining policy between the central government and local political actors.

Notwithstanding these difficulties, there are several reasons for optimism over the central government's capacity to credibly commit to the protection of property rights and enforce its regulations.

First, at the same time as it has dealt with the cost and intricacies of creating new institutional arrangements such as decentralized administrative structures, the central government has generally succeeded in protecting property rights.

Second, by accommodating local interests, the central government has committed itself to a more open distribution of benefits. This action is establishing acceptable "rules of the game," both formal and informal. The agreement over a minimum distribution of benefits is helping to create a sustainable foundation for long term economic development.

Third, compromise between central and local actors generates the type of accommodation that will assist in future negotiations. This will not eliminate future disagreements, but it does set the stage for resolving contentious issues without reversion to violence or threats of secession. That is, decentralization has been part of a political settlement that has allowed local political actors to voice their concerns. In the process, Indonesia has been maintaining a generally favorable investment climate for both local and foreign investors.[345]

Fourth, when the central government is able to consolidate its power, enforcement is improved. But in order to retain its influence, the central

---

[344]*The Economist* (October 1, 2011); Bellman (2011); Taylor (2011); Soeriaatmadja (2011); Schonhardt (2012): Mattangkilang (2012).

[345]Case studies in Prasetyawan (2005, 2006) provide details.

government has had to listen, be open to negotiation, and be ready to compromise. With these responses, it has created more room to accommodate the concerns of local political actors in the management of mining resources. At one level, it appears as though the central government bowed to interests of local political actors. But in a democratic society, voices from regional level need to be heard, and heeded.

Politics, Investment, and Effective Decentralization

Formulating and implementing long-term policies to promote rapid, sustained, and inclusive growth have several requirements. They include: inducing agreement between the Executive and the Legislature on the substance of development policies and strategies; ensuring that the policies are acceptable to all parties in the Legislature; establishing mechanisms so that the policies will be implemented over extended periods; and achieving the above within the context of the short-term orientation of DPR members (see Box 5.5 for an empirical analysis of the political economy of policy reform in Southeast Asia).

Box 5.5: The Political Economy of Policy Reform in Southeast Asia

A recently completed analytical survey of both major and incremental economic policy reform in Southeast Asia (Hill 2013) identified the following nine recurring themes in these reforms, albeit with the caveat "that it is difficult to generalize across a highly diverse set of institutional circumstances, development stages, and policy issues":

- ideas are needed to articulate and promote an intellectual agenda underpinning reform, often formulated by technical experts working closely with political leaders;

- political leadership, whether of an individual or a group, is essential for reform, but failure to institutionalize reforms creates dependencies and vulnerabilities that can undermine the sustainability of these reforms;

- large negative exogenous shocks, economic crises, imminent cessation of external assistance, and a growing realization that "the system is broken" have all been catalysts for reform, but aid works only if accompanied by good domestic policies and it is unclear whether donors can positively influence the domestic reform agenda – the impact might even be counterproductive;

- reforms are durable only if they "deliver the goods" and thereby develop a reform constituency – poor performance dooms reform;

- reform is not a linear progression, and thus requires long-term horizons and ways to combat reform fatigue and political marginalization of reform advocates;

- the transition from authoritarian to democratic systems dramatically changes both the speed and modality of reform – reform is slower but perhaps more durable as voice, accountability, and public persuasion become critical determinants of reform success;

- although institutions are important for the sustained implementation of reform, it is not necessary to have high-quality institutions to reform;

- it is relatively easier to implement prudent macroeconomic policies and broadly open commercial policies than it is to undertake microeconomic reform; and

- there does not appear to be any clear association between the propensity to reform and the level of corruption.

Short-term policies pose particular challenges. For a start, it would be useful for the Executive and the Legislature to cooperate to orient the annual budget process towards the goals of inclusive growth. This needs to be supported by breaking down policies and programs into components that are more closely related to that goal but not tied to the budget. This will enable them to be more readily approved by the Legislature.

In the short term, the presidential decree powers (*perpu*) might prove useful. If specific policies related to inclusive growth are viewed as urgent by the government, the processes in the DPR can be circumvented, at least temporarily, by this means. The political and legal implications need to be carefully considered though.

Over the medium and long terms, it will be essential to increase the capacities of the DPR to draft and deliberate substantive bills. This will enable the DPR to more closely meet its constitutional responsibilities. Improved capacities within the Legislature would be complemented by Bureaucratic Reform that professionalizes the existing bureaucracy.

Several changes would improve the performance of decentralized administrations.

Many of Indonesia's difficulties are compounded by inefficient bureaucracy. Much of this inefficiency can be traced to unclear, overlapping and conflicting regulations, low compensation, weak incentives for cooperation, and limited oversight. Some of it can be traced to the arbitrary nature of public sector recruitment, non-merit based appointments and the transactional nature of advancement. Dealing with these problems will involve deeper BR with open recruitment, promotion based on merit, and broader oversight and accountability.

Effective implementation at all levels of government also requires appropriate incentives. Providing them on a sustained basis entails a sound monitoring and evaluation framework so that the progress of policy implementation can be regularly reviewed. A special effort is needed to improve data quality and timeliness. Under current circumstances, such an investment will have a high pay-off in terms of improved performance and local government effectiveness.

Decentralization has profoundly affected the distribution of the power and benefits to different actors across regions. The central government appears to have recognized that regional voices need to be heard and that their concerns deserve attention. The mining example illustrates the value of rationalizing center-subnational arrangements in ways that support growth and development. To ensure effective operation of the decentralized political system, the central and local governments need to reach an "equilibrium" reflected in institutional arrangements that are consistent with their particular interests. In this case, the central government has to credibly protect the property rights that are its responsibility, while the local authorities have to demonstrate to their citizens that revenues are being appropriately and inclusively shared.

An important outcome, illustrated by the accommodation reached in the case of mining, is the general acceptance that under a democratic regime, state capacity cannot be exercised through force and control.[346] As a result, there has been more attention to negotiation and the distribution of incentives in the devolution of power to sub-national levels of government.

Superficially, it appears that the settlements reached through democratic processes are fragile. The reverse is true. Those processes are resilient and adaptable. The incentives are negotiated and distributed in a manner that participants perceive to be fair. The enforcement of rules is the joint responsibility of the local political actors and the central government. The process avoids unnecessary political conflicts. So long as the political and other actors negotiate acceptable outcomes, the

---

[346]Authoritarian regimes are limited in the degree to which they can impose settlements (Bueno de Mesquita *et al.* 2003) unless they are fully closed (Diamond 2002). In a democracy, the types of outcomes reached will depend upon state capacity (or rather, the government's implementation capacity). That, in turn, depends in part on the ability of the opposition to form a credible coalition and challenge the government (Howard and Roessler 2006).

investment climate will stabilize.[347] Accommodation by the central government does not represent a weakening of its role or authority relative to local political actors.

As a final point, the discussion in this chapter intentionally does not invoke the notions of "political will" and "leadership." The former explains little and the latter is circular.[348] Huge amounts of ink are regularly spilled on these topics with minimal impact. Neither Sukarno nor Suharto, both of whom had ample means to enforce their political will, created conditions that produced sustained, inclusive growth. Instead, Sukarno's policies stalled or reserved economic development while Suharto's policies could not sustain development.

With Indonesia now democratic and decentralized, its prospects for that outcome hinge on the collective endeavors and aspirations of its population and their representatives. Indeed, some governance specialists reverse the emphasis by stressing the quality of citizen "follow-ship" in achieving national objectives. A related perspective is that politics is the art of helping to open up the path along which the general population is already headed. Indonesia's recent history, with popular support for anti-corruption efforts and the change of leaders in the 2012 elections for the governor of Jakarta, are highly positive developments. They signal a desire by the population at large and some of their leaders for a different approach to development, one that may even involve the promotion of rapid, sustained, and inclusive growth.

---

[347]This point was noted by Hinds (2005, p. 97) "While creating an investment climate that will attract investment depends on some explicitly economic factors, the *investment climate* actually refers to the quality of the ultimate non-tradable that makes a location competitive: the shape of its social order."

[348]"Political will" is a "why-because" explanation; "leadership" is circular – leadership makes countries grow and countries grow because they have leadership – again without any explanatory content. Gray and McPherson (2002) explore whether and how leadership promotes economic growth. There is little evidence that it does independently of all of the other factors that contribute to growth.

CHAPTER SIX
Moving Forward:
Reactive, Proactive, and Transformative Policy Alternatives

The best way to predict your future is to create it.
PETER F. DRUCKER

Three Development Paths

Indonesia has the potential to formulate and implement policies for accelerating sustainable, inclusive growth. The country has a plethora of natural and human resources, as well as a sound physical and institutional infrastructure, which it can develop to pursue this objective.

Indonesia's potential, appropriately managed, could enable the nation to double prosperity over the next decade by extending and integrating its domestic market, and linking a large, unified national economy to global supply and distribution value chains.

Local and global economic integration can best be achieved by: reducing the costs of logistics and transactions through improvement of hard and soft infrastructure; promoting productive employment and livelihoods through development and utilization of human resources;

and implementing rapid, sustained, and equitable growth by adroit management of the political economy of policy reform in a decentralized democracy.

Notwithstanding its considerable potential, nothing in Indonesia's history guarantees that rapid, sustained, and inclusive growth will be achieved. Over recent decades, there have been periods where sensible economic policies boosted growth by raising productivity in selected sectors, for example agriculture in the 1960s and 1970s, and manufacturing in the 1980s and 1990s. There have also been periods, such as the oil boom of the 1970s and the resource boom since 2003, when economic growth has been largely driven by external events.

However, Indonesia has yet to attain rapid, sustained, and inclusive growth. Moreover, none of these boom periods has generated the economic performance required for Indonesia to reach upper middle income status by 2025, an explicit objective of the Government. Despite presiding over intermittent periods of impressive economic development, the GOI has failed to design and implement the requisite programs on a consistent basis over an extended period of time, primarily due to the nature of Indonesia's transactional politics (see Chapter Five).

Based on Indonesia's historical context and its current economic, political, and social environment, the nation has a choice of three future development paths: reactive, proactive, and transformative. *Reactive* best describes the GOI's current "muddling through" policies; *proactive* refers to reform policies pursued by the GOI in response to major crises such as widespread malnutrition and rural poverty in the 1960s and the collapse of oil prices in the 1980s; and *transformative* characterizes the policies over the past half-century that have morphed the "Four Asian Tigers" (South Korea, Taiwan, Hong Kong, and Singapore) into high-income nations. Each of these development paths is summarized below.

Reactive: Policy by Exception

In principle, there is little difference between reactive policies and "muddling through." Lindblom (1959) described muddling through as circumstances where economic policies "evolve" as various parts of economic and social systems interact in the absence of purposeful government action. Reactive policies always have the government playing "catch-up" to situations that market responses and group interaction have largely "resolved." It is akin to "policy by exception," whereby leaders ride on past accomplishments, and overcome their inertia to formulate new policies only when existing policies do not suffice.

This approach to economic and social policy has been evident in Indonesia at three points in the last four decades. It has typically followed a period of intense, fruitful change, namely: the push for improved food security in the late 1960s; the manufacturing export boom of the 1980s; and post-*Krismon* democratization and decentralization.

There has been no clear pattern to the policy regression. Reform fatigue, complacency, and political gridlock have all been involved. A feature common to the reactive approach has been the re-emergence of exaggerated rates of "surplus extraction" by the political and business elites and their enablers. The three episodes have coincided with the rising oil affluence of the 1970s, the financial excesses of the mid-1990s, and the resource boom that began in 2003. In each of these phases, the increased availability of finance and government revenues eroded and largely scuttled the reforms that had been adopted when the economy was under stress.

Indonesia has not been alone in putting itself through periodic stop-start reform. Since the oil, food, and debt shocks of the 1970s, much of the development literature has described and analyzed the general inability and unwillingness of developing countries to promote economic and social reform. As a consequence, a large part of the work of the IMF, the World Bank, and numerous other international agencies over recent decades has involved coming to grips with and responding to this pattern of truncated reform.[349] Indeed, a sub-text of the World Bank's Commission on Growth is that without their regular bouts of recidivism, many more poor countries, including Indonesia, would be well on their way to upper middle status.

Indonesia's history is consistent with international experience. It specifically confirms that a reactive approach to policy does not promote rapid, sustained, and inclusive growth. At best, it represents a period of drift during which the effects of earlier reforms linger even as the excesses and distortions associated with growing surplus extraction, KKN practices, and other impediments set the stage for economic and social disruption. The noted economist Prof. M. Sadli once quipped, in describing Indonesia's post-*Krismon* policy, "Indonesia wasn't even 'muddling through' – it was just muddling."

Current policy in Indonesia is reactive. Complacency has re-surfaced among political, business, and civil society leaders. Although they understand that the country's current development path is unsustainable, they also believe that neither President Yudhoyono nor his administration will actively promote economic reform during the remainder of his term. This view is also common in the literature.[350] The current policy stasis parallels the final years of the Suharto regime.

The resource boom is one reason, but there are others. As noted in Chapter One, Indonesia is widely seen as an emerging "giant" in Asia

---

[349]The series of studies prepared by the World Bank on Sub-Saharan Africa recounted the economic regression due to the general unwillingness of countries to sustain reform (World Bank 1981, 1984, 1986, and 1989). Each report examined the problems and suggested ways to resolve them. Most of the remedies were ignored. The sub-continent as a whole stagnated for three decades. Across SSA, real per capita incomes were the same in 2000 as they had been 1969 (ERS 2012).

[350]EIU (January 2013); Cornwall and Anas (2013, pp.8-9).

and a potential BRIC. The country's debt has been upgraded.[351] These changes have produced a sense of self-assurance, self-satisfaction, and over-confidence in the upper echelons of government.

External accolades also partially account for revival of the 1950s notions of "economic democracy" and "economic nationalism." The latter is producing increased government intervention and has provoked international backlash.

They also help explain: growing official acceptance of the view that an over-valued exchange rate is an index of national strength rather than future economic weakness; political gridlock that tolerates the public expenditure of five percent of GDP on energy subsidies and less than three percent of GDP on infrastructure; and a national commitment to agricultural R&D and S&T research that is among the lowest of any middle income country.

This reactive approach has placed Indonesia on its present development trajectory: still growing,[352] but not fast enough and in an unsustainable manner, with intensifying inequality, and 120 million Indonesians outside the economic mainstream.

The next changes in policy are predictable. There will be some reorganization of expenditure when the deficit hits its three percent legal limit, and some emergency reductions in credit growth in response to balance of payments and inflationary pressures. Social protection expenditure is likely to rise, particularly with the roll-out of the anti-poverty program MP3KI, and there may even be some limited borrowing to

---

[351]Moody's and Fitch rating services upgraded Indonesia's debt in December 2011 and January 2012; S&P did not. The upgrade was widely interpreted in Indonesia as validation of the country's current economic policies (CFR 2009; Indrawati 2011).

[352]The Asian Development Outlook 2012 Update (ADB 2012) projected growth in Indonesia of 6.3 percent in 2012 and 6.6 percent in 2013 (*ibid.*, p.xix). This was the highest in Southeast Asia but just below that of Developing Asia as a whole. Corresponding data for inflation were 4.4 percent and 4.5 percent, respectively. This is roughly the same rate as for Developing Asia.

jump-start infrastructure projects. This option will become more attractive as Government officials increasingly realize that the public-private partnerships upon which MP3EI's major activities are based will not materialize.[353] Yet, this patch-work response will not foster and sustain rapid, inclusive growth.

Proactive: Sporadic Reform

A second potential policy path for the Government is to promote vigorously selected changes that will raise the rate of economic growth and reduce inequality, or at least prevent inequality from worsening. Such changes should be relatively attractive to political and business leaders. Raising the rate of growth will enable Indonesia to remain a dynamic member of the G-20, while simultaneously defusing the possibility of urban disruption that might accompany a growth slow-down. Avoiding a further deterioration in inequality would deflect agitation at the sub-national level for additional transfers from the center, or for increased local autonomy.

Indonesia is familiar with proactive responses, especially in response to crisis. It was how the New Order regime dealt with the hyperinflation and food shortages at the end of the Sukarno era. It was also how the Suharto regime handled the collapse of oil prices in the early 1980s.[354] Similar fundamental economic and political changes were adopted in the aftermath of *Krismon*.

---

[353]One of those projects could be the Sunda Straits bridge (Antara News August 28, 2012; Lin Che Wei 2012). This initiative will raise public investment spending. But the potential impact on growth, particularly given the much smaller cost and more immediate impact of an expanded ferry service, is problematic. A recent report on India (*Economist*, December 15, 2012) under the headline "RIPPP" outlines that country's disaffection and lack of success with PPPs. Indonesia could usefully take note of India's experience.

[354]Hill (1996); Booth (1998); Thee (2002, 2012).

Proactive reforms need to be selective if they are to be implemented. This approach creates the "political space" for change. International experience shows that both politicians and the public lose their willingness to continue reforms once the basic responses to the crisis have been made.[355] Selective reforms are the easiest to defend and, if appropriately packaged, can be sold politically. Broad-based reforms offer the prospects of dramatic change, but they quickly encounter widespread resistance. Too many changes are difficult to organize and implement and, being disruptive, they are more easily diluted and deflected.

The earlier discussion indicates four changes that would significantly boost Indonesia's productivity and competitiveness and raise its rate of growth:

- sharply *increase public investment in infrastructure* and sustain it for the next decade;

- *re-focus attention on agriculture* as a means of raising the productivity of work and improving rural welfare, including the elimination of food insecurity;

- *rationalize center-subnational relations* so that each level of government works for, and not against, *national* development; and

- *raise the quality of higher education*, as well as learning more generally.

The problem with this package of reforms is there is no pressure for action. The economy is still growing robustly, international admiration for Indonesia's performance remains full-throated, and both local voters and business leaders continue to work around the economy's bottlenecks. Assessments of the economy by the IMF, World Bank, OECD,

---

[355]Stein *et al.*(2005, esp. Chs 2,12).

and EIU do not indicate any need for substantial change, at least over the next five years. For instance, the EIU report projects real annual GDP (non-inclusive) growth above 6.4 percent, a stable exchange rate, low inflation, declining unemployment, a reduced budget deficit, and basic balance in the trade account.[356]

Nevertheless, there are several potential tipping points.

One possible trigger is fiscal. The rejection of efforts to reduce the fuel subsidy and other distortions in government expenditure is placing stress on the budget.[357] The stresses will intensify as commodity prices soften.[358] As the budget deficit approaches its three percent limit, the Government will be forced to cut other budget items or raise additional revenue, both of which will encounter political resistance.

A second trigger could be an adverse shift in the flow of foreign investment in response to local restrictions. Combined with the rapidly rising demand for imports to satisfy the "new consumer class," this will result in what senior officials are likely to see as an "unacceptable" erosion of foreign reserves.[359]

---

[356]OECD (2012); Oberman *et al.* (2012); Bellman (2012); EIU (January 2013, p.7).

[357]Many senior officials were unsettled by Nigeria's unsuccessful attempts to modify its fuel subsidies (*The Economist*, January 21, 2012). They wish to spare Indonesia similar disruptions.

[358]A World Bank (2012) study on trade development suggested that high commodity prices are now the "new normal" for Indonesia and argues that Indonesia could use natural resource extraction as a growth strategy. Curiously, the study ignores the problem of growing inequality, the lack of inclusiveness, and the large number of Indonesians who are marginalized by the related impacts of natural resource exploitation. It also provides no advice on how to handle the fact that exports (from all sources) have been growing significantly more slowly than the overall economy. *WDI* (2012, Table 4.8) data show that from 2000 to 2010, exports as a share of GDP fell from 41 percent to 25 percent. Natural resources will allow growth to continue; they will not enable Indonesia to reach upper middle income status as envisioned by its leaders.

[359]A sharp reduction in foreign exchange reserves may induce international agencies to reassess the country's debt rating. Reserve depletion would be accompanied by a marked upward adjustment in the exchange rate, raising the costs of imports and reducing the real purchasing power of the "new consumer class". Formal sector workers would agitate for higher wages.

A third trigger could be the realization among residents of Greater Jakarta (and other increasingly cluttered urban areas) that rising traffic congestion, increased commuting times, and worsening pollution represent economic regression rather than economic progress.[360] A similar awakening might be happening in China where pollution, though not congestion, is worse.

Though the timing is difficult to predict, at some point the central government will be forced to begin rebalancing the economy by shifting resources from subsidizing consumption to boosting investment, initiating a structured program to realign the exchange rate (among other measures) to raise productivity and improve competitiveness, and seeking workable arrangements with the provincial and local administrations to distribute efficiently responsibilities and resources. While the last-mentioned would take the most effort, it offers the potential for enabling inclusive growth to occur across the entire country and not, as at present, only in areas where local authorities use central government transfers in socially productive ways.[361]

Transformative: Fundamental Metamorphosis

Neither of the first two options will fundamentally modify Indonesia's economic structure and administrative arrangements. They will not sub-

---

[360]The intense efforts by Sao Paulo, Rio de Janiero, Mexico City, and other major cities to restore urban livability underscore the challenges which lie ahead of the Greater Jakarta Area (Brillembourg 2006; Urban Age 2009; wpsa 2012). Their collective experience shows that urban conditions continue to deteriorate even though remedial steps are being taken. This point has recently been reaffirmed by the extreme pollution in Beijing (*Economist* January 14, 2013; Ma 2013; BBC News 21 January 2013; Wong 2013).

[361]Visitors to most provinces and districts will contrast the extravagance of the local administrative buildings and facilities with the general under-provision of other public amenities such as electricity, potable water, accessible health clinics, roads, ferries, and bridges.

stantively change the present allocation of public expenditure or revenue generation, significantly raise the amount of productive work being undertaken, or meaningfully improve the coherence of what each level of government is attempting to achieve. Both approaches involve the least amount of change consistent with avoiding major social disruptions, alienating the powerful, or forcing the most vocal and potentially troublesome urban-based groups to moderate their demands.

By contrast, transformative change seeks to sustain the reforms that extend and integrate the domestic market through measures that raise and sustain productivity and competitiveness. The critical difference between proactive and transformative change is that the latter involves the regular recalibration and redirection of the reforms as experience accumulates and learning occurs. Transformative change explicitly builds upon the initiatives identified in the proactive scenario. Earlier chapters made the case that these initiatives were critical to raising productivity throughout the economy. Yet, unlike in the proactive case where the changes are one-off, the transformative approach regularly modifies and adapts them in ways that enable rapid inclusive growth to continue. Proactive reform aims to avoid troubles; transformative reform embraces the costs of reform to create a better future. It requires an energized coalition with a vision.

In short, a transformative development policy would comprise integrated, evolving, and sustained reforms to promote synergistic, dynamic, and lasting change.

It would include the following six key elements:

- Adopt economically and socially feasible measures to *extend and integrate the domestic market, and to link this expanded and unified national market to global production and distribution value chains*. Local and global economic integration will raise productivity and competitiveness, providing a foundation for rapid, sustained growth that all Indonesians contribute to, participate in, and benefit from. This can be done by decreasing economic distance and diminishing barriers to trade and exchange.

- *Reduce logistics costs* by expanding public investment in roads, bridges, ports, harbors, water, power, and sanitation facilities through budget reallocation from consumption to investment. This reallocation should be complemented by the prudent expansion of public borrowing, and the provision of incentives that induce the private sector to engage fully in boosting infrastructure and logistics-related investments.

- *Reduce transaction costs* by normalizing operations of the financial system, modifying regulations that entrench privilege and reinforce economic discrimination, and persevering in the campaign against corruption and public waste. Reducing judicial arbitrariness and bureaucratic discretion would complement this process.

- *Stimulate productive work for all Indonesians* through expansion of the private sector. This will require the appropriate incentives. Improved infrastructure through higher rates of private investment will help. Efforts to rebuild confidence in the financial system will be important as well. The productivity of work would also be reinforced, initially at least, by shifting public service recruitment to merit-based, open competition.

- *Increase worker productivity by enhancing the quality of knowledge and learning*. Potentially large pay-offs are available by restructuring higher education. Within higher education, merit-based appointments, peer-reviewed research, external accreditation, and institutional audits to promote quality assurance should become the norm. This process should be accelerated by a joint public-private program to educate a generation of Indonesians abroad in advanced skills.

- *Realign center-subnational administrative and fiscal arrangements* in a most appropriate allocation of respective roles and responsibilities. Since intergovernmental relations will remain works-in-progress for the foreseeable future, formal procedures for regular negotiation, experimentation, and reconfiguration of activities should be adopted.

The Road Not Taken

The *reactive* approach will produce much the same performance as the last decade—steady but unspectacular and *largely jobless growth* with *declining competitiveness* and *rising inequality*.

Growth can be preserved by actions to rebalance the budget through reductions in energy subsidies and the allocation of more resources to public investment, or by tightening controls over credit creation to reduce the demand for imports as export revenues soften.

These measures will not enhance competitiveness nor reduce inequality. For that to happen, the private sector will need to increase substantially its demand for labor so that employment and income, both formal and informal, can expand through increased labor productivity.

The growth projections derived by the IMF and data from Annex 1 suggest that average GDP growth is likely to remain in the range of 5-6 percent per annum, or roughly 4 percent per capita. This implies that it will take 12-15 years to double GDP, and that by 2025-28, real per capita income in Indonesia will be around $5,300, significantly below the $14,000 plus envisioned in MP3EI.[362] Indonesia will be well short of its goal of being among the 10 largest economies in the world. This tepid performance will also undercut Indonesia's status within the G-20.[363]

The *proactive* approach will stimulate rapid growth in Indonesia for at least a decade. Inequality will not worsen, and may even decline.

Outcomes in other countries show that such one-off reforms typically boost economic performance at several levels. A large-scale effort in infrastructure would have multiple payoffs. Construction activity would expand the opportunities for productive work and boost incomes. The additional investment would have multiplier effects in related industries

---

[362]At 4.5% annual growth, $3000 will reach $5300 in 2025.

[363]CFR (2009). Some commentators argue that Indonesia does not meet the criteria relevant to membership of the G-20 (PRNewswire June 14, 2012).

and activities. The increased employment would raise consumer welfare and well-being. By reducing the real resource costs of moving goods, people, and providing services (including the transfer of information), the increase in capital stock would have productivity-enhancing and income-generating effects that reverberate throughout the economy. The induced expenditure would further stimulate industry and enterprise producing additional rounds of expenditure.

The major challenge with pushing a few reforms in response to an actual or anticipated difficulty such as a sharp deterioration in the balance of payments or rising inflation is that, once undertaken, the effects of the reforms tend to fade and are often reversed as special interests stiffen their resistance.

The New Order reforms in the 1980s that produced the boom in manufacturing exports are an example. By the mid-1990s, tax reform was on hold, the prudential regulations intended to limit financial excess were being ignored, and large parts of the market were being re-partitioned as cronies and members of the Suharto family expanded their business empires. Even so, per capita manufactured exports in 2000 were about equal to China's – something that is forgotten or denied now that Indonesia's level is only one-quarter of China's.

The advantage of the *transformative* approach is that it would, for the first time in Indonesia's history, move the economy onto a robust, sustainable, and equitable growth and development trajectory. None of the Asian countries that have attained middle or high income status over the last four decades—Japan, Korea, Taiwan, Hong Kong, Singapore—or other countries that have moved rapidly up the various development scales when measured in terms of per capita income, improvements in their HDI, or admission to the OECD, have done it through truncated, stop-start, or tentative reforms. Indonesia will not be the exception. The country's well-publicized and thoroughly commendable goals of reaching upper middle-income status by 2025 will only be achieved through sustained, deep-rooted reform. The reactive and proactive approaches outlined above, or some version of them, are inadequate to this purpose.

The goal determines the strategy. If the political and business estab-lishments want Indonesia to make rapid advances towards upper middle-income status, the required strategy is transformative. By not choosing such a strategy, the country's leaders will be simultaneously deciding that Indonesia will continue along its present trajectory. It will grow in ways that generate exaggerated wealth for a select few, rising income for some, continued income and food insecurity for many, with the growth path punctuated by resource-driven balance of payments booms and busts and periodic problems with inflation and local and foreign debt. The domestic market will not be extended and integrated in ways that raise productivity and competitiveness, nor will it be linked to global production and distribution value chains. That is, growth in Indonesia will not be rapid, sustained, or inclusive.

Since this has been the general description of Indonesia's history for the last three centuries, its current political and business leaders might find useful to ask: "Should this historical trend continue on our watch? Why or why not?" It would be encouraging if they responded to these questions by deciding that, to paraphrase the American poet Robert Frost, "Three roads diverged in a wood, and I took the one less traveled by, and that has made all the difference."

If Indonesia's leaders believe that change is needed, much needs to done. One initial task will be to convince various stakeholder groups and the general public that, this time, reforms will be sustained. This will not be easy with government credibility so limited and trust so low.

None of the difficulties the GOI will face in promoting and sustain-ing the reforms needed to achieve rapid and inclusive growth is insur-mountable. The key challenge will be to seriously pursue robust, sus-tained economic reform in the interests of the whole population rather than particular individuals or select groups, while getting influential stakeholders to support both transformative policies and government resistance to special interest pushback.

Meeting this challenge offers the opportunity to launch the nation on a development trajectory that will enable it to join the ranks of upper middle-income countries by 2025. This would be the finest legacy Indonesia's leaders could bequeath to future generations.

Annex 1: Indonesia – Selected Indicators

	1995	2000	2005	2007	2008	2009	2010	2011
Population								
Total, million	194.8	206.3	220.9	224.2	227.6	234.4	237.6	241.0
Age distribution (per cent)								
0-14	33.1	30.2	28.5	27.7	27,4	27.0	26.7	26.4
15-64	62.7	65.0	66.3	66.9	67.2	67.4	67.7	67.9
65+	4.2	4.7	5.2	5.4	5.5	5.6	5.6	5.7
Absolute poverty rate (per cent) [1]	-	19.1	16.0	16.6	15.4	14.2	13.3	12.5
Gini coefficient	0.36	-	0.36	0.36	0.35	0.37	0.38	0.41
Net enrollment ratio (secondary education, per cent)	-	46.7	56.0	65.7	64.5	65.1	67.3	-
Employment and inflation								
Employment (million)	80.1	89.8	93.4	99.9	102.6	104.9	108.2	109.7
Informal employment (per cent of employment)	-	-	69.5	69.5	69.6	69.3	66.9	62.2
Unemployment rate (per cent)	-	6.1	11.2	9.1	8.4	7.9	7.1	6.6
CPI inflation (per cent, end-of-year)	9.0	9.3	17.1	6.6	10.2	2.8	7.0	3.8
Supply and demand								
GDP (current trillion rupiah)	454.5	1,389.8	2,774.3	3,950.9	4,948.7	5,606.2	6,436.3	7,427.1
GDP (current USD billion)	202.4	166.1	285.6	432.2	512.7	543.3	708.8	846.1
GDP growth (real, per cent)	8.2	4.9	5.7	6.3	6.0	4.6	6.2	6.5
GDP per capita growth rate (real, per cent)	6.1	4.5	4.4	5.3	4.9	3.6	2.3	5.4
Demand (growth, per cent)								
Private consumption	12.6	1.6	4.0	5.0	5.3	4.9	4.7	4.7
Public consumption	1.3	6.5	6.6	3.9	10.4	15.7	0.3	3.2
Gross fixed investment	14.0	16.7	10.9	9.3	11.9	3.3	8.5	8.8
Exports	7.7	26.5	16.6	8.5	9.5	(9.7)	15.3	13.6
Imports	20.9	25.9	17.8	9.1	10.0	(15.0)	17.3	13.3
Supply (per cent of nominal GDP)								
Agriculture	-	15.6	13.1	13.7	14.5	15.3	15.3	14.7
Mining	-	12.1	11.1	11.2	10.9	10.6	11.2	11.9
Manufacturing	-	27.7	27.4	27.0	27.8	26.4	24.8	24.3
Services [2]	-	44.6	48.3	48.1	46.8	47.8	48.7	49.1
Public finances (state government, per cent of GDP								
Revenue	15.7	14.8	17.9	17.9	19.8	15.1	15.5	16.3
Expenditure	14.4	15.9	18.4	19.2	19.9	16.7	16.2	17.4
Nominal balance	1.3	(1.2)	(0.5)	(1.3)	(0.1)	(1.6)	(0.7)	(1.1)
Gross debt	-	88.8	47.3	35.2	33.1	28.4	26.1	24.3
External sector (per cent of GDP)								
Trade balance	3.2	15.1	6.1	7.6	4.5	5.7	4.3	4.1
Current account balance	(3.2)	4.9	0.1	2.4	-	1.9	0.7	0.2
In USD billion	(6.4)	8.0	0.3	10.5	0.1	10.6	5.1	1.7
International reserves (gross, USD billion)	-	-	34.7	56.9	51.6	66.1	96.2	110.1
Outstanding external debt (end-of-year)	-	85.3	45.8	31.6	30.2	31.8	28.6	26.5

Source: Statistics Indonesia, Government financial statement (audited), World Bank and OECD

Notes:

(1) Per cent of people below the national poverty line, where the latter is the value of per capita expenditure per month needed for a person to stay in decent living conditions.

(2) Includes electricity, gas, water and construction

Annex 2: Labor, Capital, and Total Factor Productivity in Indonesia

Background and Summary: This Annex examines the potential contribution to growth of education-augmented labor, capital, and productivity improvements. Growth in capital and labor, including the effects of education, is likely to support annual GDP growth in Indonesia of around 5 percent over the next decade. Estimated changes in Total Factor Productivity[364] from 1970-2007 were negative, i.e., GDP growth was less than the growth of inputs. However, in the period since 2000, TFP has increased by 1.7 percent a year.[365] If continued, this would support annual GDP growth of 6-7 percent. The movement of additional new workers into high-productivity sectors might raise total GDP growth to 7-8 percent.

Labor: Indonesia's labor force growth rate, currently 1.7 percent a year, continues to slow. Within a decade, the "demographic dividend" will be exhausted. From 2000 to 2010, the prime working age population (15-54 years) increased by 1.5 percent a year. It is projected to grow at 0.9 percent a year from 2010 to 2020, and by 0.4 percent a year from 2020 to 2030. The population over 55 years will grow at a much faster rate (the "longevity transition"). Many of those who are over 55 years are retired and semi-retired. Since they generally have lower levels of education than younger workers, they will not add to productivity growth. The changes indicate that shifts in the composition of the prime working age population, by themselves, will reduce the growth rate of GDP by around 0.5 percent a year.

---

[364]Total Factor Productivity (TFP) is growth of GDP that is neither from labor or capital growth. It is the growth resulting from the combined productivity of labor and capital and can be attributed to better education, improved technology, economies of scale and scope, higher rates of utilization, and removal of cost-increasing regulations.

[365]van der Eng (2009).

Labor productivity will rise if workers are transferred out of lower productivity jobs – agriculture, informal trade, and personal services – into higher productivity activities like manufacturing and high-end services. The share of the labor force in agriculture, trade and personal services is now just over 71percent, while their contribution to non-oil GDP is 44 percent. Since 85 percent of farmers are over 45 years old, mass movement out of agriculture is unlikely. Older workers are less likely to move, although they may switch occupations. From 2007 to 2012, the number of workers in low productivity agriculture, trade and personal services rose by 5.3 million, nearly half of the total 10.9 million increase in the total workforce. In effect, there has been minimal movement of workers out of low-productivity sectors.

Improvements in education and skills boost the effective labor supply. Workers with higher secondary education or above earned 72 percent more than those with lower qualifications.[366] If education levels continue to increase, the effective labor force would grow significantly faster than the physical numbers of workers. An increase in average schooling of the entire workforce by one year during the 2010-2020 decade will boost output by 1 percent a year.[367]

Capital: Increases in capital stock contribute to growth. Gross investment/GDP ratios of 33-38 percent a year are likely over the next decade. If capital stock were two times GDP and depreciation were 10 percent of capital,[368] then with GDP of roughly $600 billion in 2010, the

---

[366]Ridao-Cano and Umpathi (2008).

[367]The years of schooling of those over 15 years rose from 4 to 5 years from 1990 to 2000. A similar improvement is possible. In fact, by 2005, the average years of schooling had increased to 6.1.

[368]The *World Development Indicators* 2011, Table 4.10, estimated that depreciation of fixed capital was 10.9% of gross national income for Indonesia in 2009. Natural resource depletion was 6.5 percent of GDP. van der Eng (2005) estimated capital stock at roughly two times GDP. Van der Eng (2009, p.13) reported, respective, labor and capital shares of around 50 percent.

capital stock would be $1200 billion, investment would be $200 billion and depreciation would be $120 billion. Net investment would be $80 billion, leading to capital stock growth of 6.7 percent a year. (Mineral wealth depletion is not included in this estimate.) Since the estimated share of capital is one half (see below), capital growth of 6.7 percent a year contributes 3.35 percent a year to GDP growth.

GDP Growth Rate: Combining the growth of labor, education, and capital yields the following:

- Contribution from capital growth of 6.7% /year = 3.35% (weight of capital in output is one-half)
- Contribution from labor force growth of 0.9%/yr. = 0.45% (weight of labor in output is one-half)
- Contribution from education (+1 grade, 2010-20) = 1.0%

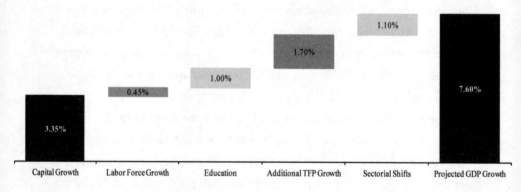

If there were no increase in productivity from other sources, real GDP would grow at around 4.8 percent a year from 2010-2020. Annual growth above this level would require faster productivity growth and/ or much higher investment levels (to boost the contribution of capital). The estimated TFP growth of 1.7 percent a year from 2000 to 2007 **excluded** the impact of education (it was already in the quality-adjusted labor force) but included the reallocation of labor across sectors. Additional factors could include better infrastructure, economies of scale,

removal of barriers to enterprise, and technical progress. If the 1.7 percent rate of TFP improvement persists, it would raise total real GDP
growth to 6.5 percent.[369] If infrastructure barriers were progressively
reduced and investment efficiency increased, a higher share of workers
could move to high productivity sectors. This would support growth of
7 to 8 percent per annum. This is, after all, what India has realized over
the past decade with an average 32 percent investment ratio.

How Much Growth from Inter-Sectoral Shifting of Workers? As noted,
the number of workers in low productivity sectors has expanded rapidly
over recent years. In 2007, these workers accounted for 74 percent of the
workforce but only 43.6 percent of non-oil GDP. That is, their productivity per worker was only 27 percent of that in the higher productivity
sectors. By 2012, the share of these low productivity workers had fallen
to 71 percent of total workers while their productivity has risen to 31
percent of the output per worker in the high productivity sectors. How
much more output could have been gained if *all* new workforce entrants
managed to join the higher productivity sectors?

It is a straight-forward calculation. The increase of 5.3 million jobs in
the low productivity sector is cancelled and their contribution to output
is subtracted. However, these same 5.3 million are assumed to produce
as much as the average higher productivity worker. The net gain is equal
to about 1 percent per year of 2012 non-oil GDP. This additional shifting of workers would boost GDP growth from 6.2 to 7.3 percent a year.

Higher Sustained Growth? Sustaining rates of growth above 7 to 8
percent in Indonesia for a decade or two would require unprecedented
improvements in TFP. During its period of fastest growth, between
1960 and 1989, South Korea's annual TFP growth was 3.1 percent. This
included the favorable impacts of inter-sector labor reallocation and

---

[369]That is, we expect 4.8 percent growth a year including education but excluding
the inter-sector shift which is included in the 1.7 percent a year figure. Adding 4.8
percent and 1.7 percent gives a total of 6.5 percent a year.

rising education.[370] We have already included the contribution of education and past and projected rapid reallocation of factors across sectors (yielding 3.8 percent per year). Hence, Indonesia is already credited with 3.8 percent TFP and education growth in GDP, or 0.7 percent extra TFP growth compared to Korea's golden period. It is hard to see how Indonesia could do better than Korea. Equaling the Korean performance would be an exceptional achievement. The implication is that even with the boost provided by improved policy and infrastructure, it will be hard for Indonesia to raise its growth above the 7 to 8 perent range. The only possibility would be if the investment/GDP ratio rises well beyond .35. Though technically possible, it has never been sustained in Indonesia.

Factors reducing growth will be the slowing of the labor force (i.e., the end of the demographic dividend) and the diminished gains as more workers transfer out of agriculture. The latter effect is unlikely to be significant. Many agricultural workers are on the "Outer Islands" and cannot so readily transfer to higher productivity activities on other islands. Moreover, given the high average age of most agricultural workers, they have few incentives to migrate.

In summary, Indonesia has the potential for higher rates of growth for the next two decades. This would have a major impact on income and welfare. At 6 percent growth, real GDP will roughly triple over twenty years. At 8 percent, GDP would increase 4.7 times. That is, real GDP would be 50 percent higher in twenty years if the Indonesian economy could use capital as efficiently as is now the case in India. Rapid growth will be difficult to sustain after 2030. The "extra" source of growth from transferring labor out of agriculture and the growth of the workforce will both diminish. Education is one area that could make a large contribution. But, the rate of growth of capital stock will decline as capital per worker and capital per unit of output rises. With lower rates

---

[370]World Bank (1993, p. 56). Only Taiwan managed nearly 4 percent TFP growth.

of capital stock and labor force growth, growth in Indonesia is likely to slow down parallel to the experience in countries such as Thailand and Malaysia. Growth would decline to around 4 to 5 percent a year as the country approaches upper middle income status.

Annex 3: What are Public Private Partnerships?

Indonesian infrastructure plans have accorded a central role to Public Private Partnerships (PPPs). Indonesian policy makers have repeatedly referred to the limited budgetary capacity of the national government to build necessary infrastructure and have therefore concluded that the private sector would have to bridge the financing gap. This justifies the need for PPPs.

Based on Indonesian regulations, a working definition of PPPs derives from the financial viability of projects. The principal criterion is whether the financial rate of return of a project exceeds its private financing cost. Using this criterion, projects that are financially viable are concessions, those not financially viable are public projects, and those which are only marginally viable are PPPs. While there is not one single structural definition of PPP in the broader literature, the following working definition of PPPs from the International Monetary Fund[371] highlights that PPPs are more effectively defined using their functional characteristics.

According to the IMF, a PPP is an arrangement in which the private sector, comprising one or more partners, participates in the supply of assets and services traditionally provided by the government. The arrangements typically involve:

- An agreement between a government and the private partners whereby they undertake to deliver an agreed upon quantity and quality of service.
- In return for the delivery of the agreed quantity and quality of service, the partners receive either a unitary charge paid by government

---

[371]Akitoy, Hemming, and Schwartz (2007).

or a user charge (e.g., a toll) levied by the private partners on the direct recipients of the service.

- An emphasis on a whole-of-life approach. The private partners are usually responsible for both the construction and operational phases of the project.

- Some degree of risk sharing between the public and private sector that in theory should be determined on the basis of which party is best able to manage each risk.

It is perhaps even more useful to contrast a PPP with the alternative mechanism that is commonly adopted for infrastructure development, public procurement. A PPP is a single, long-term, service delivery contract, with payment linked to performance and risks shared between public and private entities over the life cycle of the infrastructure asset. By contrast, public procurement has been traditionally undertaken through multiple, shorter contracts that are segmented across the different stages, such as construction and operation, in ways that leave much of the risk with the public sector. The identification of these specific features in PPPs is necessary because international experience suggests that they are the value drivers of PPPs. Thus mere juxtaposition of public and private resources, or simply private (off public budget) financing, does not make a PPP.

Realizing successful PPPs: Embarking on a PPP program is a challenging undertaking. Building the necessary level of expertise in the public and private sectors can take numerous iterations and refinements over many years. Even well-planned PPP projects have to respond to changing needs, as well as unforeseen events. Indonesia has sought to develop an elaborate framework of decrees and regulations for evaluating and executing PPPs that reflect the theory very well, but few infrastructure PPP projects have taken off to date.

Not every project is suitable to be procured through a PPP. Nor does every government or market have the requisite capacity in the public and private sectors to join together as partners in a PPP. And even if all of these are in place, the right process is essential to draw out the benefits of a PPP arrangement and keep its limitations in check.

The starting point for considering PPP as a form of procurement is to identify a project that: is economically viable; can be clearly segregated from surrounding projects; offers scope for innovation and real efficiency gains in construction and operation; and allows the writing of incentive contracts based upon verifiable performance-based, service-delivery indicators. It is important to note that financial viability is not a prerequisite because that can be altered using subsidies and/or taxes.

Next, PPPs require private entities that possess the innovative capacity and expertise to bring about real innovation and efficiency gains, not only in traditional engineering and management skills related to construction, operations and technology, but also those related to contracting, financing and governance. Furthermore, private entities must have the experience, reputation and size to be able to bear the sizeable and long-term risks that they take on by participating in a PPP.

Finally, for the benefits of PPPs to be fully realized, they need to be structured and implemented through an objective, competitive, and transparent process. A necessary feature, and one that does not figure prominently in traditional public procurement, is protracted and complex negotiations between public and private partners. Vigilant monitoring though competent public agencies and a credible regulatory framework are required to ensure that performance targets are met and the risk transfer is enforced. At the same time, it has to be accepted that long-term contracts are incomplete, and a renegotiation may be required to adjust to shifting conditions.

Most public agencies possess experience in preparing and tendering projects that have been structured as traditional public procurement. Preparing PPP projects requires different skills and greater capacity at the outset since the contract to be put together and negotiated is much more complex. Furthermore, PPP project-related operations typically span a variety of different ministries of the government, some of which might view it as a threat to the traditional public procurement. On this count, coordination among the different units of government is essential.

Risk Transfer and Risk Capital: The mere presence of the scope for efficiency gains and the capacity to deliver them does not guarantee that those gains will necessarily be realized. For that to happen, it is imperative to devise a project structure that aligns the incentives of the partners in a manner that promotes the success of the project. Moreover, the mechanism through which incentives are shaped is optimal risk sharing. The incidence of risk needs to be balanced against return, in the form of rewards and penalties, and coupled with control mechanisms that allow the party which bears the risk to take the actions necessary for its own benefit, and thereby for the benefit of the PPP project.

One attraction of developing infrastructure through PPPs is that it facilitates the use of private capital to build and operate public projects. But the role of private capital is not just about financing the project. Indeed, governments usually access finance on cheaper terms than any private entity, making private finance a more expensive source of capital, and therefore a disadvantage of PPPs. The role of private capital in PPPs emerges from the centrality of risk transfer. Financial investors are valuable because they are paid back only when the infrastructure project begins operating and performing successfully. The incentive-alignment property of this long-term engagement makes the financial investors share in the life-cycle perspective that is one of the most attractive features of a PPP.

Therefore what is needed for a successful PPP is not just private capital, but capital that is subject to risk related to the performance of the project over its life, or "risk capital." Mere private capital will not unleash private expertise to realize efficiency gains. Risk capital creates the incentives by which financial investors exert necessary oversight on different participants in the project special purpose vehicle to shape incentives and deliver expected outcomes.

A PPP involves a number of different parties that bring different skills but also interests. Even if the rationale for a PPP project is self-evident, it should be subjected to a feasibility analysis and a value for money analysis and the results shared with the private sector and the public at large. Similarly, the process of negotiating how risks should be allocated and making sure that the final contract reflects these agreements is a lengthy undertaking—it should not be rushed by political pressure or the market.

Annex 4: Where Has All the Garlic Gone?[372]

Indonesia used to produce large amounts of garlic, but no longer does. Production per capita averaged 0.7 kg in the early 1990's and .06 kg from 2008 to 2010. That is, production per capita dropped by over 90 percent from the beginning of the 1990s. By contrast, garlic imports from China increased sharply over the same period. They were around 21 thousand tons a year in the early 1990's, but rose to 202 thousand tons in 2001-03 and to 387 thousand tons in 2007-09, the most recent years available. The graph below illustrates:

Indonesian Garlic Production and Imports from China, Thousand Tons

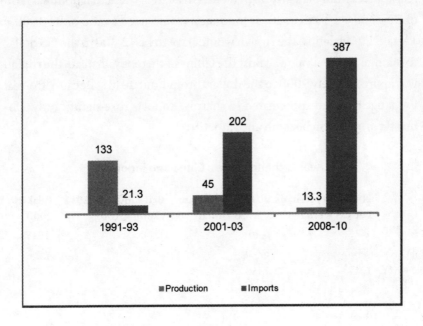

___

[372]Adapted from David Dapice (2012) "Where has all the garlic gone?" Paper prepared for this study, Ash Center Harvard Kennedy School, April.

Notes: From FAO database. "Imports" are recorded imports of garlic from China. The final year is 2007-09 for imports.

What is happening? There is growing domestic demand for garlic. The total supply (i.e., local production and imports) grew from 150 thousand tons in the early 1990's to 400 thousand tons recently. Yet Indonesian production has collapsed. Why?

One reason is the real (inflation-adjusted) exchange rate of Indonesia appreciated relative to the Chinese yuan, especially since 2000. Although Indonesia benefited from expanding tree crop exports such as coffee, rubber and palm oil, other less competitive farm products – such as garlic[373] -- did poorly. From 2000 to 2011, prices in Indonesia nearly tripled but prices rose only 56 percent in China. There were 1017 rupiah per yuan in 2000, which translated into an inflation-adjusted 723 Rp/Yuan in 2011 – a real appreciation of nearly 30 percent. (Instead of the actual nominal ratio of Rp 1358 = 1 Yuan in 2011. Indonesia would need a ratio of Rp 1900 = 1 Yuan. Equivalently, the rupiah would have to be 12,300 to the US dollar to maintain its real value against the Chinese currency. Instead, the rupiah was approximately 9000 to the dollar throughout 2011.) Because the real exchange rate had appreciated so sharply, imports rose significantly. Domestic production became uncompetitive.

Real Exchange Rates: China and Indonesia

	2000: Rp or Yuan Per US Dollar	2011: Rp or Yuan Per US Dollar	Price index in 2011 (2000 = 100)	Real Rp/Yuan 2000	2011
China	8.28	6.46	156	1017	723
Indonesia	8422	8770	293		
Nominal Rp/Y	1017	1358			

---

[373]The appreciating real rupiah also caused per capita manufactured exports of Indonesia to be essentially flat from 2000 to 2010 while China and Vietnam quadrupled their per capita manufactured exports.

Sources: Asian Development Bank *Key Indicators 2011* and *Economist Intelligence Unit*, April 2012. The real Rp to Yuan exchange rate in 2011 is equal to the nominal Rp/Yuan rate in 2011 times the Chinese price index divided by the Indonesian price index in 2011.

A second reason is differential technical change. This is illustrated by changes in garlic yields in China and Indonesia. The following graph shows that Indonesia's yields barely increased. Moreover, they did not even match the average yields in China from two decades earlier. China managed to nearly double yields over the same period. The cost of all garlic imports (and not just from China, though China is the major supplier) rose from $18 million a year in the early 1990s to $51 million a year in 2001-03 to an average of $148 million a year from 2007-09. Indonesia has responded to its lack of technical progress by proposing protectionist measures for local producers. This, to echo a sub-theme of this study, is a static response. Viewed in dynamic terms, Indonesia needs to invest in upgrading its production techniques as well as move its exchange rate to a competitive level.

Yields of Garlic in Tons/Hectare, China and Indonesia

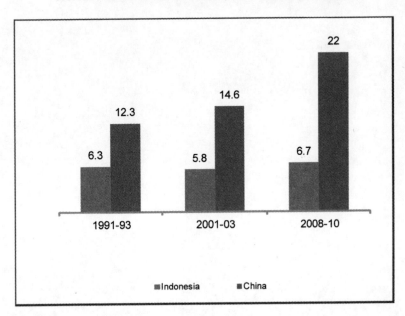

Source: FAOStat Database

Does Garlic Matter?

Garlic is not a major crop or consumer item. Does it matter? What is wrong with Indonesia exporting palm oil and importing garlic? Isn't that just specialization and free trade? Unfortunately, it is not so simple. Garlic symbolizes much more than one small crop. It could be replaced by many goods, agricultural and non-agricultural, that are losing competitiveness due to inappropriate macroeconomic policies and inadequate research and development spending or acquisition of appropriate technology. Java has some of the richest soils in the world and a favorable climate. Indonesia's wage rates are lower than China's. The cost of transport into the country (or even among islands) is relatively high. Indonesia's inability to compete in garlic raises questions about its ability to compete for many other goods. Garlic is an example and a warning of why Indonesia is failing to expand its manufactured exports and why its leaders are discussing a ban on food imports rather than looking for a way to produce them more cheaply. The present outcome represents, at best, represents policy confusion; at worst, policy failure.

Annex 5: State Capacity, Governance, and Credibility

The World Bank's 1997 World Development Report "The State in a Changing Society" helps place in perspective Indonesia's goals of promoting sustained, rapid, and inclusive growth and attaining upper middle-income status by the middle of next decade. That Report pays detailed attention to the features of a "capable state." Such a state matches its development agenda to its financial, institutional, physical, organizational, and political capacities. The international experience examined in Chapter One indicated that capable states do not over-extend their capacities by attempting to achieve everything immediately. Rather, they focus on the few key issues that will enable the country to progress and then build on that success, including learning from and adapting to things that did not work.

Indonesia could follow a similar path. For that, its policymakers will need to realistically assess the country's existing capacities for promoting rapid, sustained, and inclusive growth and the rate at which they can be enhanced.

The following list, drawn from an extensive examination of cross-country evidence, is a guide to the types of capacities that will need to be strengthened and/or developed.[374] They include:

1: set and sustain key development priorities
2: target the use of resources where they are most effective
3: innovate when existing policies have failed
4: coordinate conflicting objectives in a coherent way
5: when necessary for the greater good, impose losses on powerful groups

---

[374]Stein *et al.* (2005, Box 6.1, p. 132).

6: represent diffuse, unorganized groups and not just those which are vocal, organized, and concentrated.

7: effectively implement government policies once they are formulated

8: maintain policy stability so that policies have time to work

9: make and honor international commitments for the State's long-term well-being

10: manage political cleavages so as to prevent social degeneration

11: adapt policies when circumstances change

12: ensure policy coherence so that new policies are consistent with existing ones

13: maintain effective policy coordination among different actors who are instrumental for policy formulation and implementation

Efforts are underway in Indonesia to enhance and strengthen many of these capacities. So far, however, the available capacities have not been organized or used in ways that promote rapid sustained inclusive growth. While this is a drawback to meeting the Government's ambitions, there is a more formidable problem of restoring credibility.

At present, few in Indonesia expect the Government to sustain any of the reform programs it initiates. This expectation has been reconfirmed on numerous occasions over the last several decades. Irrespective of whether Indonesia has an autocratic or democratic government, economic reforms have never been sustained. In view of this track record, no one (including the policy makers and bureaucrats) has any reason to believe that the Government will continue to implement any of the economic changes it makes. Under present circumstances, an announcement by the GOI that it intends to encourage and sustain particular reforms will fail.[375]

---

[375]There has been voluminous research on credibility under several topics including "time inconsistency," "political trust," "policy credibility," and "reputation" among others (Kydland and Prescott 1977; Goodhart and Huang 1998; Hetherington 1998; Grabel 1999; Mishler and Rose(2000; Cox and McCubbins 200); Forder 2001; Belemann 2005; Stein et al. 2005, Ch. 6; and Ferguson 2005).

The main credibility challenges are unlikely to arise when the Government initiates the reform, particularly if there is some major distortion or emerging crisis that needs attention. The principal challenge (and the feature that distinguishes the proactive from the transformative approach discussed in Chapter 6) will come when the Government seeks to adapt and modify the reforms to sustain rapid and inclusive growth.

Taking their cue from past experience, most interest groups (businesses, bureaucrats, and members of the general public) will anticipate that the Government's commitment to reform will diminish over time and it will revert to a reactive muddling through approach. Perhaps more important, some interest groups (especially large businesses and state-owned enterprises) will presume that the recidivism will occur and begin anticipating it. For example, they may begin to position their operations to take advantage of increased government intervention. This is similar to what has occurred with the resurgence of "economic nationalism" over the last decade, or the effects of distortions in the national budget as support for consumption takes precedence over public investment, or growing resistance to the exchange rate movements required to assure international competitiveness.

The issue of credibility is beset by the same problem that arises with respect to trust and confidence, namely, it is circular: programs succeed because they are credible; programs which do not succeed, were not credible.[376] Dealing with this issue requires pragmatism. There is nothing the GOI can do about its past performance and the expectations that have been generated by that performance. Yet, *if* the GOI is determined to move beyond a pattern of stop-start reform, it needs explicit measures

---

[376]Hetherington (1998); Grabel (1999) Hamid (2012) provides a recent overview of political developments in Indonesia, highlighting problems the Government is finding in generating credibility.

to ensure that it performs in ways that enable the reforms to continue.[377] This is where the experience of the "high-growth economies" recounted by The Growth Commission is so useful. None of them found that sustaining reform was straightforward or easy. All of them began from conditions characterized by limited trust, minimal confidence, and widespread skepticism. Nonetheless, all of these Governments discovered that credibility (trust, confidence, and reputation) are endogenous. They are generated and sustained by the way the economy is managed and how it performs.

The lesson is that improvements in economic management provide a basis for increased credibility, and vice-versa. The two are inter-dependent and reinforce each other.[378] The reverse holds as well as many countries, including Indonesia, have found when economic management deteriorates.

There are plenty of actions for the GOI to begin rebuilding its credibility. The current study has numerous suggestions and other research highlights more. For example, the Government could explicitly modify its administrative procedures to achieve the "debottlenecking" that MP3EI emphasizes is essential. There is also plenty of time to work on becoming credible. If the Government is to succeed in this endeavor it has the whole future to work with.

---

[377]This is exactly what the Bank Rakyat Indonesia devised through its KUPEDES program to enable borrowers to establish creditworthiness. They borrowed a small amount (limiting the potential losses of the lender). When they repaid the amount was increased ("repeat borrowing"). In this way, the borrower established a credit history based on his/her repayment record (Patten and Rosengard 1991, pp.23-26).

[378]As Schelling (1978) noted the micro behavior of individuals (increasing confidence/trust) cumulate to have macro impacts (improved macroeconomic outcomes). In turn, these reinforce confidence/credibility.

Annex 6: "HE Drives Growth" – Empirical Issues

In addition to the data and conceptual issues highlighted in the text, the econometrics used to demonstrate that "HE drives growth" is inappropriate. The conventional single equation estimation methods that relate economic growth to a range of selected determinants (such as measures of education), from which the basic empirical results are derived, are unsuitable for modeling and understanding such a complicated long term relationship.[379] Moreover, from a statistical perspective, economic growth (a rate of increase) is not determined, driven, or whatever quasi-causal term is used, by years of schooling (a level) or some equivalent measure.[380]

In effect, the empirical methods used to show education "drives" growth are misleading at best and counterproductive at worst.[381] Determining how higher education and economic growth are related require a multi-equation, multi-variable framework that incorporates the relevant inter-dependencies, feed-back, and knock-on effects, including the fact that over periods which are relevant to policy formulation and implementation, economic growth is its own determinant.[382]

---

[379]The only value single equation "models" of this type can have is if the period being examined is so short that feedback from economic growth (i.e., rising income) to education can be neglected.

[380]There is no dispute that at the micro level individuals with more education earn on average more than those with less education (Psacharopoulos 1995; Psacharopoulos and Patrinos 2002). This relates individual income to education attainment (or vice-versa). The issue here is the macro relationship between education attainment/participation and economic growth.

[381]The intense focus by growth specialists on single equation methods leads them to systematically overlook the point (which is a theme of the present study) that economic growth is the result of the dynamic interaction of elements which propel the economy forward and those which hold it back (McFadden 2008; Lutz, Cuaresma and Sanderson 2008; Ciccone and Jaroncinski 2008). There is nothing linear about economic growth.

[382]The mainstream economic literature lacks examples of multi-equation statistical models which relate higher education to economic growth. The framework in Appiah

What happens when economic growth and higher education are examined within such a framework? Few formal empirical models have examined these links.[383] A broad historical overview, however, highlights the key relationship in question.

The experience of the United States during the twentieth century is illustrative. The rate of growth in the decades bracketing 1900 and 2000 was roughly the same, 3.4 percent in the former period and 3.3 percent in the latter. For the century as a whole, the share of population with formal post-secondary (i.e., tertiary) qualifications increased from around 5 to almost 40 percent. The average years of schooling for all Americans increased from 7 years at the turn of the twentieth century to roughly 15 years at the turn of the twenty-first century.[384]

Readers wanting other examples can obtain similar results for Japan after WWII, and China after its reforms began around 1980.[385] Indeed, Indonesia's experience from the time its growth accelerated in the last 1960s and early 1970s is further affirmation of the point.[386]

---

and McMahon (2002) traces many of inter-relationships among all levels of formal education, economic growth, health and other variables.

[383]The same points about the interdependence between education and growth are illustrated by McPherson and Rakovski (2002) who studied the commonly held view that "trade drives growth." When placed within a broad multi-equation, multi-variate relationship, the apparent one-way causation disappeared, replaced by mutual feed-back.

[384]GDP data are from Historical Statistics of the United States Millennial Edition Online, with special reference to "National Product Before 1929." Education data are from Goldin (2002) and UNESCO Education For All Global Monitoring Report (annual since 2001).

[385]China's average rate of growth over the period 1980 to 2010 has been on the order of 10 percent per annum (WDR 1994, Table 2, p.164; WDI 2012, Table 4.1, p.214). Post-secondary enrollment in China in 1980 was 1 percent (WDR 1994, Table 28, p.216) of the relevant cohort while in 2010 it was 26 percent (WDI 2012, Table 2.12, p.86). Over the period of Japan's most rapid economic growth, i.e., from the end of WWII until 1990, tertiary enrolment increased from less than 1 percent of the relevant population to 31 percent (Watanabe 2000; Godo and Hayami 2003; World Bank 1994, Table 28, p.217).

[386]Data in Chapter 1 for Indonesia indicate that over the last four decades the average annual growth of GDP has been on the order of 6 percent with growth rates roughly

The implication is that neither years of schooling (which doubled) nor share of population in post-secondary education (which increased eight times) could have been "driving" economic growth (which remained roughly constant). In these countries (and many others)[387] economic growth was associated with changes in a range of other variables which included formal education and learning and knowledge generation more broadly.[388]

---

the same at the start as at the end. WDI data show that in 1980 tertiary enrolment in Indonesia was 4 percent of the relevant cohort. Recent census data show that roughly 5 percent of the population has education qualifications beyond secondary school. Over that period the average years of schooling has roughly tripled. This repeats the pattern for the US, Japan, and China referred to above. Growth has not accelerated, yet all of the education variables have increased sharply.

[387]Canada, UK, Australia, Germany, Sweden are obvious examples among the rich countries; Singapore, South Korea, Turkey, and Taiwan are examples among countries which started from low income levels in the post-WWII/post-colonial periods.

[388]This is consistent with the findings of the Commission on Economic Growth (World Bank 2008; Brady and Spence 2010) referred to earlier. The factors which affect economic growth (and vice versa) differ as a country's circumstances change. This point has been widely confirmed (Brunner 1985; Matthews 1986; Bailey and Eicher 1994; Frankel 1997; Temple 1999; and Nicolae and Alina 2007).

References

ADB (2012) *Asian Development Outlook 2012 Update Services and Asia's Future Growth,* Mandaluyong City: Asian Development Bank

ADB (2012) "Republic of Indonesia: Inclusive Growth through Improved Community Connectivity Program," *Asian Development Bank Concept Paper,* Project no. 46093-001-INO, May

ADB (2005) "Connecting East Asia: A New Framework for Infrastructure," *Asian Development Bank and Japan Bank for International Cooperation,* March 16

AfDB (1998) *African Development Report 1998 Human Capital Development* New York: Oxford University Press for the African Development Bank

Abdussalam, Andi (2011) "News Focus: Export Ban to Disadvantage Rattan Farmers?" *Antara News,* October 29

Acemoglu, Daron, and Robinson, James (2012) *Why Nations Fail: The Origins of Power, Prosperity and Poverty,* New York: Crown Publishing

Adam, Latif (2010) "Four Reasons Why Indonesia's Infrastructure is on Shaky Ground," *Jakarta Globe,* July 19

Adler, Gustavo (2012) "Volatility in External Demand: Indonesia's Commodity Boom and Overall Competitiveness," Chapter 4 in ed. Thomas Rumbaugh *Indonesia Sustaining Growth During Global Volatility,* Washington D.C.: International Monetary Fund

Agarwal, Bina (2011) "Food Crises and Gender Inequality," *DESA Working Paper* no. 107, (Economic and Social Affairs), ST/ESA/2011/DWP/107, June

Agunias, Dovelyn R. and Christine Aghazarm (2012) "Labour Migration from Colombo Process Countries: Good Practicies, Challenges and Way Forward," *Issue in Brief* no. 1, International Organization for Migration (IOM) and Migration Policy Institute, May

Akitoy, Bernadin, Richard Hemming, and Gerd Schwartz (2007) "Public Investment and Public Private Partnerships," International Monetary Fund, *Economic Issues,* no. 40

Alexander, Carol and John Wyeth, (1994) "Cointegration and Market Integration: An Application to the Indonesian Rice Market," *The Journal of Development Studies,* vol. 30, no. 2, January, pp. 303-328

Anas, Titik (2012) "Indonesia's New Protectionist Trade Policies: a Blast from the Past," *East Asia Forum,* June 18

Anderson, Perry (2011) "Lula's Brazil," *London Review of Books,* vol. 33, no. 7, March 31, pp. 3-12

Andrews, Matt (2013) *The Limits of Institutional Reform in Development Changing Rules for Realistic Solutions,* Cambridge: Cambridge University Press

Antara News (2012) "Sunda Strait bridge not to burden state budget," (Editor: Heru) August 28

Appiah, Elizabeth N. and WalterW. McMahon (2002) "The Social Outcomes of Education and Feedbacks on Growth in Africa" *The Journal of Development Studies* vol. 38, no. 4, April, pp. 27-68

Aragon, Lorraine (2007) "Elite Competition in Central Sulawesi," in *eds.* Henk Schulte Nordholt and Gerry van Klinken, *Renegotiating Boundaries: Local Politics in Post-Suharto Indonesia,* Leiden: KITLV Press, pp.39-66

Arrow, K.J. (1959) "Toward a theory of price adjustment" pp.41-51 in *ed.* M. Abramovitz *The Allocation of Economic Resources* Stanford: Stanford University Press

Arshad, Alina (2012) "Indonesia's Universities are the Weakest Link," *The Jakarta Globe,* August 29

Aryo, Bagus (2011) "Inclusive Growth in Indonesia: Another Neoliberal Project? A case study of National Program for Community Development," PowerPoint presentation, Department of Social Welfare, University of Indonesia

Asia Sentinel (2012) "Economic Nationalism Catches Up with Indonesia," October 3

Aspinall, Edward (2007) "The Construction of Grievance: Natural Resources and Identity in a Separatist Conflict," *Journal of Conflict Resolution,* vol. 51, p. 950-972

Atkinson, R.C. (1996) "Universities and the Knowledge-based Economy," Remarks by the President of University of California, Berkeley, California State Senate Fiscal Retreat, February

Athukorala, Prema-chandra and Hal Hill (2010) "Asian Trade and Investment Patterns and Trends," Chapter 2 in *ed.* Prema-chandra Athukorala, *The Rise of Asia Trade and investment in global perspective,* London: Routledge Taylor & Francis Group

BAPPENAS (2010) *Regulation of the President of the Republic of Indonesia no.5 of 2010 Regarding the National Medium-Term Development Plan* (RPJMN) 2010-2014, Jakarta: Republic of Indonesia

BAPPENAS (2011) "Infrastructure Development Strategy in Indonesia," PPoint Presentation, Ministry of National Development Planning, National Development Planning Agency, Jakarta, January 13

BBC News (2013) "US Takes Indonesia to WTO over import restrictions," Asia Busines, January 10

BPS (2011) *Trends of Selected Socio-Economic Indicators of Indonesia,* Jakarta: Republic of Indonesia, August

BPS (2011) *BPS Strategic Data,* Jakarta: Statistics Indonesia

Bacchetta, Marc, Ekkehard Ernst, and Juana P. Bustamante (2009) *Globalization and Informal Jobs in Developing Countries,* Geneva: World Trade Organization and International Labour Organization

Bailey, Thomas and Theo Eicher (1994) "Education, Technological Change and Economic Growth," *Inter-American Review of Educational Development,* no. 119, 3, pp.461-81

Baskoro, Faisal Maliki (2011) "Port of call," *The Jakarta Globe,* May 11

Bank of Canada (2013) "The Economy and Economic Policy," at www.bankof-canada.ca/ (access February 3, 2013)

Bank of Indonesia (2008) "Inflation Targeting Framework (ITF)," at www.bi.go.id (accessed September 2012)

Barajas, Adolfo, *et al.* (2012) "Workers' Remittances: An Overlooked Channel of International Business Cycle Transmission?" *IMF Working Paper,* WP/12/151, International Monetary Fund, October

Barro, R. J. (1996). *Determinants of economic growth: a cross-country empirical study.* Cambridge, MA: National Bureau of Economic Research, NBER Working Paper 5698. Prepared for the Lionel Robbins Lectures, delivered at the London School of Economics, February 20-22

Barro, Robert J. (1999) *Determinants of Economic Growth A Cross-Country Empirical Study* Cambridge: The MIT Press

Barro, Robert J. (2001) "Education and Economic Growth," in John F. Helliwell, ed., *The Contribution of Human and Social Capital to Sustained Economic Growth and Well-Being*, OECD, Keynote speech, OECD Symposium: *The Contribution of Human and Social Capital to Sustained Economic Growth and Well-Being*. Canada, Château Frontenac, Québec City, March 19-21, 2000

Basri, M. Chatib (2012) "Indonesia's Role in the World Economy: Sitting on the Fence," Chapter 3 in *ed.* Anthony Reid *Indonesia Rising The Repositioning of Asia's Third Giant*, Singapore: ISEAS Publishing [Institute of Southeast Asian Studies]

Basri, M. Chatib and Gustavo Papanek (2013) "Dutch Disease and Employment in Indonesia," *Working Paper*, LPEM, University of Indonesia, Jakarta

Basri, M. Chatib and Hal Hill (2008) "Trade Policy Review 2007," *The World Economy*, vol. 31, no. 11, pp. 1393-1408

Bastian, Aqbal Qowi (2013) "Education System Letting Students Down," *JakartaGlobe*, March 27, p.6

Becker, Gary S. (1964) *Human Capital* Princeton: Princeton University Press

Bellman, Eric (2011) "U.K. Miner Challenges Indonesia," *The Wall Street Journal*, December 2

Bellman, Ian (2012) "Indonesian Boom Starts to Stall," *The Wall Street Journal*, July 16

Benditt, L. (2009) "Higher Education Key to Minnesota's Economic Growth," Growth and Justice www.mn2020hindsight.org, November 17

Berlemann, Michael (2005) "Time inconsistency of monetary policy: Empirical evidence from polls," *Public Choice*, no. 125, pp. 1–15

Bertrand, Jacques (2004) *Nationalism and Ethnic Conflict in Indonesia*, New York: Cambridge University Press

Black, Stanley (1989) "Seignorage," in eds. John Eatwell, Murray Milgate, and Peter Newman *The New Palgrave Money*, New York: W.W. Norton

Blanco Armas, E., C. Gomez Osorio, and B. Moreno-Dodson (2010) "Agricultural Public Spending and Growth: The Example of Indonesia," *Economic Premise*, no. 9, April

Blanco Armas, Enrique *et al.* (2012) "Agriculture Public Spending and Growth in Indonesia," Policy Research Working Paper no. 5977, East Asia Region, The World Bank, February

Bland, Ben (2012) "Indonesia: Archipelago Apprehension," *The Financial Times*, August 29

Blöndal, Jón R, Ian Hawkesworth and Hyun-Deok Choi (2009) "Budgeting in Indonesia," *OECD Journal on Budgeting*, vol. 2009/2 (Organization for Economic Cooperation and Development)

Bloomberg (2012) "Indonesia June Forex Reserves Fall to $106.50 billion," *Bloomberg News*, July 5

Bloomberg (2013) "Corn Leads Grain Plunge as U.S. Reserve Tops Analysts Estimates," Bloomberg News at www.bloomberg.com, March 28

Blum, Jurgen, Nick Manning, and Vivek Srivastava (2012) "Public Sector Management Reform: Toward a Problem-Solving Approach," *Economic Premise*, World Bank Poverty Reduction and Economic Management Network, No. 100, December

Bollag, Burton (2003) "Study Documents Economic Benefits of Secondary and Higher Education in the Developing World," *The Chronicle of Higher Education*, Today's News, February 19

Booth, Anne (1998) *The Indonesian Economy in the Nineteenth and Twentieth Centuries - A History of Missed Opportunities*, London: Macmillan Press

Booth, Anne (2011) "Splitting, Splitting, and Splitting Again: A Brief History of the Development of Regional Government in Indonesia since Independence," *Bijdragen tot de Taal-, Land- en Volkenkunde* vol. 67, p. 31-59

Brady, David and Michael Spence (2010) *Leadership and Growth Commission on Growth and Development*, Washington D.C.: The World Bank

Breton, Theodore R. (2003) "Education, Human Capital and National Income," EER 2003-115, George Mason University, July 27

Brill, Alex and James K. Glassman (2012) "The G-20 needs better admissions standards," *The Wall Street Journal*, June 19

Brillembourg, Carlos (2006) "The Artist's Voice Since 1981, Jose Castillo," *Bombsite*, BOMB 94, Winter

Brunner, Karl (1985) "The Poverty of Nations" *Business Economics* vol.20, no.1, January, pp.5-12

Bruno, Michael (1972) "Domestic Resource Costs and Effective Protection: Clarification and Synthesis," *The Journal of Political Economy*, vol. 80, no. 1, January/February, pp.16-33

Budhrani, Ricky (2010) "As Costs Rise, Indonesian Airlines Must Fly Smarter," *JakartaGlobe*, March 21

Buehler, Michael (2012) "Countries at the crossroads Indonesia," Freedom House, Washington, D.C.

Buehler, Michael (2013) "A False Hope? Indonesia's Economic Miracle," *The Diplomat Blogs,* February 5

Bueno de Mesquita, Bruce, *et al.* (2002) "Political Institutions, Policy Choice, and the Survival of Leaders," *British Journal of Political Science* vol. 32, pp. 559-590

Bueno de Mesquita, Bruce, *et al.* (2003) *The Logic of Political Survival,* Cambridge: The MIT Press

CFR (2009) "The Group of 20," Council on Foreign Relations, Washington, D.C., March 30

Callan, Patrick M. *et al.* (2007) "Good Policy, Good Practice Improving Outcomes and Productivity in Higher Education: A Guide for Policymakers," A joint report from The National Center for Public Policy and Higher Education and The National Center for Higher Education Management Systems, Washington D.C., Report #07-4

Carney, Diana *ed.* (1998) *Sustainable Rural Livelihoods: What Contribution Can We Make?* London: Department for International Development

Castle, James and Andri Manuwoto (2013) *Indonesia: Political Pulse 2012,* Jakarta: CastleAsia

Castle, James and Andri Manuwoto (2013) *Indonesian Business: The Year in Review 2012,* Jakarta: CastleAsia

Chenery, Hollis B. and Moises Syrquin (1975) *Patterns of Development 1950-1970* London: Oxford University Press for the World Bank

Chinn, Menzie D. (2006) "A Primer on Real Effective Exchange Rates: Determinants, Overvaluation, Trade Flows and Competitive Devaluation," *Open Economies Review,* pp.115-143

Ciccone, Antonio and Marek Jaroncinski (2008) "Determinants of Economic Growth: Will Data Tell?" European Central Bank, Working Paper Series, no. 852, January

Claessens, Stijn, Simeon Djankov and Larry H.P. Lang (2000) "The Separation of Ownership and Control in East Asian Corporations," *Journal of Financial Economics,* vol. 58, pp.81-112

Coase, Ronald H. (1960) "The Problem of Social Cost," *Journal of Law and Economics,* vol. 3, October, pp.1-44

Cole, David C. and Betty F. Slade (1993) "How Bank Lending Practices Influence Resource Allocation and Monetary Policy in Indonesia," *Development Discussion Papers,* n. 444, Harvard Institute for International Development, April

Cole, David C. and James S. Duesenberry (1994) "Financial Development," in eds. David Lindauer and Michael Roemer, *Asia and Africa: Legacies and Opportunities*, San Francisco: ICS Press

Collier, Kate *et al.* (2009) "Effecting cultural change in government agencies," Australia Indonesia Governance Research Partnership, Jakarta

Collier, Kate *et al.* (2009) "Enhancing the Integration of Workplace Learning Through the Use of SMS in Peer Learning Groups – An Indonesian Case-Study," Australia Indonesia Governance Research Partnership, Jakarta

Colombijn, Freek, and J. Thomas Lindblad (2002) "Introduction," in *eds.* Freek Colombijn and J. Thomas Lindblad, *Roots of Violence in Indonesia: Contemporary Violence in Historical Perspective*, Leiden: KITLV Press, pp. 1-32

CME (2011) (2011) "Master plan Acceleration and Expansion of Indonesia Economic Development 2011-2025," Jakarta: Coordinating Ministry for Economic Affairs, Republic of Indonesia

Corden, W. Max (1966) "The Structure of a Tariff System and the Effective Protective Rate," *The Journal of Political Economy*, vol. 74, no. 3

Cornwell, Katy and Titik Anas (2013) "Survey of Recent Developments," *Bulletin of Indonesian Economic Studies*, vol. 49, no.1, pp.7-33

Crone, Theodore M. (2007) "A Pattern of Regional Differences in the Effects of Monetary Policy," *Business Review*, Federal Reserve Bank of Philadelphia, Q3, pp.9-19

Crouch, Harold (1988) *The Army and Politics in Indonesia*, Ithaca: Cornell University Press

Curvale, Bruno (2007) "Quality culture and adaptability," European Association for Quality Assurance in Higher Education, PPoint presentation, Yerevan, June 4-5

Damuri, Yose Rizal (2012) "Indonesian Trade Policy and the Search for Added Value," *The Jakarta Post*, August 9

Dapice, David (2012) "Indonesian Energy Policy in Disarray," Paper contributed to this study, Harvard Kennedy School, May

Dapice, David (2012a) "Where has all the garlic gone?" Paper prepared for this study, Ash Center, Harvard Kennedy School, April

Davidson, Jamie (2008) *From Rebellion to Riots: Collective Violence in Indonesian Borneo*, Madison, WI: University of Wisconsin Press

Deane, Phyllis (1965) *The First Industrial Revolution*, Cambridge UK: Cambridge University Press

Deep, Akash (2012) "Indonesia's Infrastructure Gap," Paper prepared for this study, Harvard Kennedy School, October

Demopoulos, Katherine (2009) "Indonesian Banks target 48 million low income earners," *Financial Times*, October 15

Denison, Edward F. (1962) "United States Economic Growth" *The Journal of Business* vol.25, no.2, April

Denison, Edward F. (1967) *Why Economic Growth Rates Differ: Postwar Experience in Nine Western Countries* Washington D.C.: The Brookings Institution

Dessus, Sebastian (2002) "Human Capital and Growth: the Recovered Role of Educational Systems," The World Bank, draft working paper

Dervis, Kemal (2012) "Convergence, Interdependence and Divergence," *Finance & Development*, September, pp.10-14

Diamond Larry J. (2002) "Thinking About Hybrid Regimes," *Journal of Democracy*, vol.13, no.2, pp.21–35

Dick, Howard W. (1985) "Interisland Shipping: Progress, Problems and Prospects," *Bulletin of Indonesian Economic Studies*, vol. 21, no.2, pp.95-114

Dick, Howard W. *et al.* (2002) *The Emergence of a National Economy, An Economic History of Indonesia, 1800-2000,* Honolulu: Allen & Unwin and University of Hawaii Press

Dick, Howard W. (2002) "State, nation-state and national economy," Ch. 1 in Howard Dick *et al. The Emergence of a National Economy, An Economic History of Indonesia, 1800-2000,* Honolulu: Allen & Unwin and University of Hawaii Press

Dick, Howard W. (2002) "Formation of the nation-state, 1930s-1966," Ch. 6 in Howard Dick *et al. The Emergence of a National Economy, An Economic History of Indonesia, 1800-2000,* Honolulu: Allen & Unwin and University of Hawaii Press

Diprose, Rachael (2009) "Decentralization, Horizontal Inequalities, and Conflict Management in Indonesia," *Ethnopolitics* vol. 8, p. 107-134

Dorfman, Robert (1969) "An Economic Interpretation of Optimal Control Theory," *American Economic Review*, vol. 59, no. 5, pp. 817-831

Dorfman, R. (1997) *Economic Theory and Public Decisions Selected Essays of Robert Dorfman* Brookfield US: Edward Elgar

Dorfman, Robert, Paul A. Samuelson, Robert M. Solow (1987) *Linear Programming and Economic Analysis (Dover Books on Computer Science)* Mineola: Dover Publications

Duesenberry, James S. (1964) *Money and Credit: Impact and Control,* Englewood Cliffs, N.J: Prentice-Hall

Duggan, Victor, Sjamsu Rahardja and Gonzalo Varela (2013) "Can Open Service Sector FDI Policy Enhance Manufacturing Productivity? Evidence from Indonesia," *Economic Premise,* no. 106, World Bank Poverty Reduction and Economic Management Network (PREM), February

EIU (2012) *Country Report Indonesia,* London: Economist Intelligence Unit [December]

EIU (2013) *Country Report Indonesia,* London: Economist Intelligence Unit [January, April]

ERS (2012) "Real Historical Gross Domestic Product (GDP) Per Capita…Baseline Countries/Regions (in 2005 dollars) 1969-2011" Economic Research Service, US Department of Agriculture International Macroeconomic Data Set (www.ers.usda.gov), January 16

ESCAP (2011) "Emerging issues in transport: Inter-island shipping Note by the Secretariat," Economic and Social Commission for Asia and the Pacific, Expert Group Meeting on Preparations for the Ministerial Conference on Transport, Bangkok, July 14-15

East Asia Analysis Unit (2000) *Indonesia Facing the Challenge,* Department of Foreign Affairs and Trade, Canberra: East Asia Analytical Unit

Economist, The (2009) "A golden chance A special report on Indonesia," September 12

Economist, The (2011) "Mining in Indonesia Now You Own It, Now You Don't," Asia, October 1

Economist, The (2012) "Let Them Have Fuel," Middle East and Africa, Jan 21

Economist, The (2012) "Economic policy in Brazil Sparking recovery," September 15, p.35

Economist, The (2012) "A sense of place Special Report Technology and Geography," October 27

Economist, The (2012) "India's love affair with public-private partnerships faces a stern test," December 15

Economist, The (2012) "India's love affair with public-private partnerships faces a stern test," December 15

Economist, The (2013) "Beijing's air pollution Blackest day," January 14

Eggleston, Karen N. and Victor R. Fuchs (2012) "The New Demographic Transition: Most Gains in Life Expectancy Now Realized Late in Life," *Journal of Economic Perspectives*, vol. 26, no.3, Summer, pp. 137-156

Eichengreen Barry *et al.* (2012), *From Miracle to Maturity: The Growth of the Korean Economy*, Cambridge: Harvard East Asian Monographs, Distributed by Harvard University Press

Emmerson, Donald K. (2012) "Is Indonesia Rising? It Depends," Chapter 4 in *ed.* Anthony Reid, *Indonesia Rising The Repositioning of Asia's Third Giant*, Singapore: Institute of Southeast Asian Studies (ISEAS)

Engel, Bob (2011) "10 best practices you should be doing now," *CSCMP's Supply Chain Quarterly*, no. 1

FAO (2006) "Food Security," Food and Agricultural Organization of the United Nations, *Policy Brief*, Issue 2, June

FAO (2013) "FAO Cereal Demand and Supply Brief," Food and Agricultural Organization of the United Nations, www.fao.org/worldfoodsituation/

FRBD (2004) *A Better Way Productivity and Reorganization in the American Economy* Federal Reserve Bank of Dallas Annual Report 2003

FRBSF (2010) "Regulatory Frameworks for Financial Services in Asia," *Asia Focus*, Country Analysis Unit, Federal Reserve Bank of San Francisco, San Francisco

Fane, George and Ross H. McLeod (2002) "Banking Collapse and Restructuring in Indonesia, 1997-2001, *Cato Journal*, vol.22, no.2, Fall, pp.277-295

Farole, Thomas (2012) "Competitiveness and Connectivity: Integrating Lagging Regions in Global Markets," *Economic Premise*, World Bank PREM Network number 93, October

Fedchun, Gerald B, (1995) "Staying competitive in a changing world," *Canadian Business Review*, vol. 22, issue 3, Autumn, p.37

Feith, Herbert (1962) *The Decline of Constitutional Democracy in Indonesia*, Ithaca: Cornell University Press

Findlay, Ronald (1998) "comparative advantage," in eds. John Eatwell, Murray Milgate and Peter Newman, *The New Palgrave A Dictionary of Economics*, vol. I, London: Macmillan Reference Ltd., pp.514-517

Firdaus, Muhammad and Amalia A. Widyansanti, (2010) "Indonesian Interprovincial Trade: What can be Revealed from a Gravity Modeling?" PPoint Presentation at the Tenth IRSA (Indonesian Regional Science Association) International Conference, Surabaya July 28-29

Fischer, Karin (2009) "As U.S. Retrenches, Asia Drives Growth Through Higher Education," *The Chronicle of Higher Education*, vol.56, no.7, October 9, pp.A1, A25-A27

Fitrani, Fitria, Bert Hoffman, and Kai Kaiser (2005) "Unity in Diversity? The Creation of New Local Governments in a Decentralising Indonesia," *Bulletin of Indonesian Economic Studies*, vol.41, pp.57-79

Ford, Michelle (2003) "Who are the Orang Riau? Negotiating Identity across Geographic and Ethnic Divides" in *eds*. Edward Aspinall and Greg Fealy, *Local Power and Politics in Indonesia: Democratization and Decentralization*, Singapore: Institute of Southeast Asian Studies, pp. 132-147

Frankel, J.A. (1997) "Determinants of Long Term Growth," Meeting of the Asia-Pacific Economic Cooperation Advisors, Vancouver Canada, November 20

Franken, Josh (2011) "Analysis: Indonesian Labor: Regulations in Need of Review," *The Jakarta Post*, March 21

Freeman, Richard. B. (1977) "Investment in Human Capital and Knowledge" Ch. 4 in *eds*. Eli Shapiro and William L. White *Capital for Productivity and Jobs* Englewood Cliffs NJ: Prentice Hall Inc.

FreshFruitPortal (2012) "U.S. puts pressure on Indonesia over Jakarta port closure plans," January 26, www.freshfruitportal.com

Friedman, Milton (1971) "Government Revenue From Inflation," *The Journal of Political Economy*, vol. 79, no. 4, July –August, pp.846-856

Fukuyama, Francis (1995) *Trust: The Social Virtues and the Creation of Prosperity*, London: Hamish Hamilton

Fulmer, William E. (2000) *Shaping the Adaptive Organization Landscapes, Learning, Leadership in Volatile Times* New York: Amacom

Galbraith, John Kenneth (1979) *The Nature of Mass Poverty*, Cambridge, MA: Harvard University Press

Garnaut, Ross (2012) "Indonesia in the New World Balance," Chapter 2 in *ed*. Anthony Reid, *Indonesia Rising The Repositioning of Asia's Third Giant*, Singapore: Institute of Southeast Asian Studies (ISEAS)

Geiger, Thierry (2011) *The Indonesia Competitiveness Report 2011, Sustaining the Growth Momentum*, Geneva: World Economic Forum, June

Georgopoulos, George (2009) "Measuring regional effects in monetary policy in Canada," *Applied Economics*, vol. 41, no. 16, pp. 2093-2113

Godo, Yoshihisa and Yujiro Hayami (2003) "Catching Up in Education in the Economic Catch-Up of Japan with the United States, 1890-1990," FASID Reprint Series on International Development Strategies, no.2002-0005, January

Goldin, Claudia (2002) "The Human Capital Century and American Leadership: Virtues of the Past," Harvard University and National Bureau of Economic Research, June 19 ["The Human Capital Century" *Education Next*, Winter 2003]

Goldin, Ian (1990) "Comparative Advantage: Theory and Application to Developing Country Agriculture," OECD Development Centre, Working Paper no. 16, June

Goodhart, Charles A E & Huang, Haizhou, (1998), "Time Inconsistency in a Model with Lags, Persistence, and Overlapping Wage Contracts," *Oxford Economic Papers*, vol. 50, no. 3, July, pp. 378-96

Grabel, Ilene (1999) "The Political Economy of Policy Credibility: The New-Classical Macroeconomics and The Remaking of Emerging Economies," Kellogg Institute, *Working Paper* no. 269, June

Gray, Clive S. and Malcolm F. McPherson (1999) "The Leadership Factor in Africa's Economic Growth" *HIID Development Discussion Papers* no. 703, May Cambridge, February [published in *Economic Development and Cultural Change*, vol.49, no.4, July 2001, pp.705-740]

Grigg, David B. (1995) *An Introduction to Agricultural Geography*, Second Edition, London: Routledge

Griliches, Z. (1979) "Issues in assessing the contribution of research and development to productivity growth," *The Bell Journal of Economics*, vol. 10, no.1, Spring, pp.92-116

Griliches, Z. (1996) "Education, Human Capital, and Growth: A Personal Perspective" *NBER Working Paper* 5426, January

Griliches, Z. (2000) *R&D, Education, and Productivity A Retrospective*, Cambridge MA: Harvard University Press

Guggenheim, Scott (2012) "Indonesia's Quiet Springtime: Knowledge, Policy and Reform," Chapter 8 in *ed*. Anthony Reid, *Indonesia Rising The Repositioning of Asia's Third Giant*, Singapore: Institute of Southeast Asian Studies (ISEAS)

Gunawan, Anton H. and Reza Y. Siregar (2009) "Survey of recent developments," *Bulletin of Indonesian Economic Studies*, vol. 45, no.1, April, pp. 9-38

Gurr, Ted (1970) *Why Men Rebel*, Princeton, NJ: Princeton University Pres

Guntensperger, Patrick (2009) "Bank Bailout Scandal Rocks Indonesia," *Asian Times Online*, September 17

Hadad, Muliaman D. (2010) "Developing a financial inclusion strategy: The case of Indonesia," PPoint presentation by Deputy Governor, Bank Indonesia, The 2010 AFI Global Policy Forum, Bali, September 27-29

Hadiz, Vedi (2010) *Localizing Power in Post-Authoritarian Indonesia: A Southeast Asia Perspective,* Stanford, CA: Stanford University Press

Hamayotsu, Kikue (2011) "The End of Political Islam? A Comparative Analysis of Religious Parties in the Muslim Democracy of Indonesia," *Journal of Current Southeast Asian Affairs,* vol. 30, no. 3, pp.133-159

Hamid, Sandra (2012) "Indonesian politics in 2012: coalitions, accountability and the future of democracy," *Bulleting of Indonesian Economic Studies,* vol. 48, no.3, pp. 325-345

Hanan, Djayadi (2012) "Executive-Legislative Relations and Inclusive Growth in Indonesia," Paper prepared for this study, Harvard Kennedy School Indonesia Program

Hanifah, Abu (2013) "News Analysis: Indonesia Takes Steps to Cut Logistics Support Costs," *The Jakarta Globe,* April 11

Hakansson, N.H. (1998) "portfolio analysis," in eds. J. Eatwell, M. Milgate, and P. Newman *The New Palgrave A Dictionary of Economics,* vol. 3, K to P, New York: Stockton Press, pp. 917-9202

Hanushek, Eric A. and D. D. Kimko (2000) "Schooling, Labor-Force Quality, and the Growth of Nations," *The American Economic Review,* vol. 90, No. 5, December, pp.1184-1208.

Hanushek, Eric A. (2004) "Economic outcomes and school quality," International Academy of Education, *Education policy series,* 4

Hanushek, Eric A. (2005) "Why Quality Matters in Education," *Finance & Development,* vol.42, no. 2, June, pp.15-19

Hanushek, Eric A. and L. Woessmann (2007) "Education Quality and Economic Growth," The World Bank, Washington D.C.

Hanushek, Eric A. *et al.,* (2008). "Education and Economic Growth":It is not just going to school, but learning something while there that matters." *Education Next,* Hoover Institution, Spring, pp. 62-70

Haswidi, Andi (2012) "News Analysis: Indonesia's 'sudden shift to the left' and other fallacies," *Jakarta Post,* June 5

Hayek, F.A. (1945) "The Use of Knowledge in Society," *American Economic Review,* vol. 35, no. 4, pp. 519-530

Heckman, James J. (2006) "Catch 'em Young," *The Wall Street Journal*, opinion, January 10

Heckman, James J. and Dimitriy V. Masterov (2004) "The Productivity Argument for Investing in Young Children" Working Paper 5, Invest in Kids Working Group Committee for Economic Development, University of Chicago, October 4

Herschleifer, Jack (1989) *Time, Uncertainty, and Information* Oxford: Basil Blackwell

Hendar, (2012) "Fiscal policy, public debt management and government bond markets in

Indonesia," Bank for International Settlements, *BIS Papers* no. 67, October

Herwidayatimo (2002) "Moving toward a single supervisory agency Indonesia Initiative," PowerPoint Presentation at A Regional Seminar on Non-Bank Financial Institutions, Bangkok, Thailand, September 4-6

Hetherington, Marc J. (1998) "The Political Relevance of Political Trust," *The American Political Science Review*, vol. 92, no. 4, December, pp.791-808

Hildebrand, Mary E. and John W. Thomas (1997) "Teaching, Training and Public Policy Programs," Chapter 18 in Dwight H. Perkins *et al., Assisting Development in a Changing World The Harvard Institute for International Development 1980-1995*, Cambridge MA: Harvard University Press

Hill, Hal (1996) *The Indonesian Economy since 1966: Southeast Asia's Emerging Giant,* Cambridge UK: Cambridge University Press

Hill, Hal (2013) "The Political Economy of Policy Reform: Insights from Southeast Asia," *Asian Development Review*, vol. 40, no. 1, pp. 108-130.

Hill, Hal and Thee Kian Wie (2012) "Indonesian Universities in Transition: Catching Up and Opening Up," *Bulletin of Indonesian Economic Studies*, vol. 48, no. 2, pp.229-251

Hill, Hal, Muhammad Ehsan Khan, and Juzhong Zhuang *eds.* (2012) *Diagnosing the Indonesian Economy: Towards Inclusive and Green Growth*, London: Anthem Press

Hinds, Manuel (2005) "Reforming the Investment Climate," in *eds.* Gudrun Kochendorfer-Lucius and Boris Pleskovic *Investment Climate, Growth and Poverty,* Washington D.C.: The World Bank

Howard, Marc Morje and Philip G. Roessler (2006) "Liberalizing Electoral Outcomes in Competitive Authoritarian Regimes," *American Journal of Political Science* 50:2, p.365-381

Howitt, Arnold (2012) "Bureaucratic Reform and Regional Autonomy," Paper prepared for this study, Ash Center, Harvard Kennedy School, April

Horowitz, Donald (2001) *The Deadly Ethnic Riot*, Berkeley and Los Angeles: University of California Press

Hotelling, Harold, (1931) "The Economics of Exhaustible Resources," *The Journal of Political Economy*, vol. 39, issue 2, April, pp. 137-175

ILO (2005) "Labor Regulation Act No. 21/2000 Act No 13/2003, Act No. 2/2004", International Labour Office, Jakarta

ILO (2011) *Decent Work Country Profile Indonesia*, Geneva: International Labour Organization

ILO (2012) *World of Work Report 2012, Better jobs for a better economy*, Geneva: International Labour Organization

IMF (2010) "Indonesia Selected Issues," *IMF Country Report* No. 10/285, International Monetary Fund, Washington D.C., September

IMF (2011) "Indonesia: Selected Issues," International Monetary Fund Country Report no. 11/310, October

IMF (2011) "Indonesia 2011 Article IV Consultation," *IMF Country Report* No.11/309, International Monetary Fund, Washington D.C., October

IMF Survey (2011) "Strong Domestic Demand Cushions Indonesia from Global Uncertainty," IMF Survey online interview with Thomas Rumbaugh, October 21

IMF (2012) "IMF Executive Board Concludes 2012 Article IV Consultation with Indonesia," Public Information Notice (PIN) no. 12/112, International Monetary Fund, Washington D.C.

IOM (2010) *Labour Migration From Indonesia An Overview of Indonesian Migration to Selected Destinations in Asia and the Middle East*, Jakarta: International Organization for Migration, Mission in Indonesia

Ianchovichina, Elena and Susanna Lundstrom (2009) *Inclusive Growth Analytics: Framework and Application*, Washington D.C.: The World Bank

Indrawati, Sri Mulyani (2002) "Indonesian economic recovery process and the role of government," *Journal of Asian Economies*, vol. 13, pp.577-596

Indrawati, Sri Mulyani (2011) "Indonesia and Global Development," *East Asia Forum*, September 18

Istiqomah (2006) "Rice Market Integration Effects of Trade Liberalization," Institute of Rural Development, Goerg-August-University, Gottingen

JICA (2007), *The Study on Public-Private Partnership Scheme for Trans-Java toll Road in the Republic of Indonesia*, Final Report, Jakarta: Japan International Cooperation Agency, January

JakartaGlobe (2013) "Overhaul Education or Fall Further Behind," Viewpoint, March 27, p. 10

JakartaGlobe (2013) "Light Relief" Indonesia News on "street children", March 27, p.5

Jakarta Post (2011) "I'm Not Optimistic with the MP3EI: Economist," *The Jakarta Post*, July 25

Jakarta Post (2012) "Indonesia-Japan Relations Turn Sour," *The Jakarta Post*, July 7

Jakarta Post (2012) "JP Interviews with M. Chatib Basri: Industry Downstreaming Must Move in Stages," *The Jakarta Post*, August 27

Johnson, D. Gale (2000) "Population, Food, and Knowledge" *The American Economic Review* vol.90, no. 1, March, pp. 1-14

Johnson, Harry G. (1964) "Towards a Generalized Capital Accumulation Approach to Economic Development" in OECD Study Group in the Economics of Education, *The Residual Factor and Economic Growth*, Paris: Organization of Economic Cooperation and Development

Johnson, Simon, Jonathan D. Ostry, and Arvind Subramanian (2006) "Levers for Growth," *Finance and Development*, vol.43, no.1, March

Jones, Carlton (2010) "MEASURE Indonesia, The Enterprise Development Diagnostic Tool," J. E. Austin Associates Inc. for USAID/Indonesia, December (at www.egateg.usaidallnet.gov/bgi)

Jones, Garett and W. Joel Schneider (2005) "Intelligence, Human Capital, and Economic Growth: A Bayesian Averaging of Classical Estimates (BACE) Approach," Southern Illinois University and Illinois State University, June

Kartohadikoesoemo, Sutardjo (1953) *Desa (The Village)*, Jogjakarta: Sumur Bandung

Keidel, Albert (1981) *South Korean Regional Farm Production and Income, 1910-1975*, Honolulu: University of Hawaii Press

Kennedy, John F. (1961) "Inaugural Speech," Washington D.C: The White House., January 21

Khan, Mushtaq H. (2010) *Political Settlements and the Governance of Growth-Enhancing Institutions*, Research Paper Series on Governance for Growth, School of Oriental and African Studies, University of London, London UK

Khan, Musthaq H. (2011) "Political Economy of Inclusive Growth," Paper presented at OECD-WB Conferences on Challenges and Policies for Promoting Inclusive Growth

Klein, Lawrence (1971) *An Essay on The Theory of Economic Prediction*, Chicago: Markham Publishing Co.

Kochan, Thomas. (2004) "Education, Families, and Workplace Policies," *Challenge*, vol.47, no.6, November-December, pp.69-81

Koopmans, Tjialling C. (1975) "Concepts of Optimality and Their Uses Nobel Memorial Lecture," Yale University, New Haven, Connecticut, December 11

Koentjaraningrat (1967) *Villages in Indonesia*, Ithaca: Cornell University Press

Kremer, Michael (1993) "Population Growth and Technological Change: One Million B.C. to 1990" *Quarterly Journal of Economics*, vol. 108, no. 3, August, pp. 681-716

Kristiansen, Stein and Muhid Ramli (2006) "Buying an Income: The Market for Civil Service Positions in Indonesia," *Contemporary Southeast Asian Studies* (ISEAS) vol. 28, no. 2, pp. 207-233

Krueger, A.B. and M. Lindahl, (2001) "Education for Growth: Why and for Whom?" *Journal of Economic Literature*, vol. 39(4), pp.1101-1136, December

Krugman, Paul R. (1990) *The Age of Diminished Expectations, U.S. Economic Policy in the 1990s*, Cambridge MA: The MIT Press

Krugman, Paul R. (1991) *Geography and Trade* Cambridge MA: The MIT Press

Krugman, Paul R. (1994) "Competitiveness: A Dangerous Obsession," *Foreign Affairs*, vol. 73, no.2, March/April, pp. 28-44

Kuncoro, Haryo *et al.* (2011) "The Cost of Public Debt Services, The Case of Indonesia," *International Journal of Advanced Economics and Business Management* (IJAEBM), vol.1, no. 1, pp. 14–24

Kuncoro, Mudrajad, Tri Widodo, Ross McLeod (2009) "Survey of Recent Economic Developments," *Bulletin of Indonesian Economic Studies*, vol. 45, no. 2, pp. 51-76

Kuznets, Simon (1966) *Modern Economic Growth: Rate, Structure and Spread* New Haven: Yale University Press

Kydland, Finn E. and Edward Prescott (1977) "Rules Rather than Discretion: The Inconsistency of Optimal Plans," *Journal of Political Economy* vol. 87, pp. 473-492

LPEM-FEUI (2010) "Transportation of Goods in East Nusa Tenggara: Problems and Costs," Published by LPEM-FUEI and The Asia Foundation, Jakarta, October

Lancaster, Kelvin J. (1966) "A New Approach to Consumer Theory," *Journal of Political Economy*, vol. 74, pp.132-157

Leibenstein, Harvey (1979) "A Branch of Economics Is Missing: Micro-Micro Theory," *Journal of Economic Literature*, vol. 17, pp. 477-502

Levitsky, Steven and Lucan Way (2002) "The Rise of Competitive Authoritarianism," *Journal of Democracy*, vol. 13, no. 2, April, pp. 51-65

Liddle, R. William, and Saiful Mujani (2007) "Leadership, Party, and Religion: Explaining Voting Behavior in Indonesia," *Comparative Political Studies*, vol. 40, no. 7, pp. 832-857

Lin Che Wei (2012) "Insight: Sunda Strait Bridge and Public-Private Partnership Confusion," *Insight*, July 26

Lindblad, J. Thomas (2002) "The late colonial state and economic expansion, 1990-1930s," Ch. 5 in ed. Howard Dick *The Emergence of a National Economy, An Economic History of Indonesia, 1800-2000*, Honolulu: Allen & Unwin and University of Hawaii Press

Lindblom, Charles E. (1959) "The Science of Muddling Through," *Public Administration Review*, vol. 19, no. 2, Spring, pp.79-88

Lockwood, William W (1954) *The Economic Development of Japan: Growth and Structural Change*, Princeton: Princeton University Press

Logsdon, Martha G. (1978) "Traditional Design Making in Urban Neighborhoods," *Indonesia*, no.26, pp.95-110

Lubis, Harun Al Rasyid, S. *et al.* (2005) "Multimodal Transport in Indonesia: Recent Profile and Strategy Development," *Proceedings of the Eastern Asia Society for Transportation Studies*, vol. 5, pp.46-64

Lucas, Robert (1988) "On the Mechanics of Economic Development," *Journal of Monetary Economics*, vol. 22, no. 1, pp. 3-42

Lutz, Wolfgang, Jesus Crespo Cuaresma, and Warren C. Sanderson (2008) "The Demography of Educational Attainment and Economic Growth," *Science*, vol.319, February 22, pp.1047-1048

Ma, Wayne (2013) "Beijing Pollution Hits Highs" *The Wall Street Journal*, January 14

Mahtani, Shibani (2012) "South East Asia's Stories of 2012," *The Wall Street Journal*, South East Asia, December 30

Majerova, Ingrid (2012) "Comparison of Old and New Methodology in Human Development and Poverty Indexes: A Case of the Least Developed Countries," *Journal of Economic Studies and Research,* Article ID 290025, October

Malkin, Israel and Fernanda Nechio (2012) "U.S. and Euro-Area Monetary Policy by Regions," *FRBSF Economic Letter,* 2012-16, February 27

Malley, Michael (2003) "New Rules, Old Structures, and the Limits of Decentralisation," in *eds.* Edward Aspinall and Greg Fealy. *Local Power and Politics in Indonesia,* Singapore: Institute of Southeast Asian Studies, pp. 102-118

Mancini, Luca (2008) "Horizontal Inequality and Communal Violence: Evidence from Indonesian Districts," in *ed.* Frances Stewart, *Horizontal Inequalities and Conflict: Understanding Group Violence in Multiethnic Societies,* New York: Palgrave Macmillan, pp. 106-135

Mankiw, N. Gregory (2013) "Give me your tired, your poor and your economists, too," *The New York Times,* Business Day, February 9

Mankiw, N.Gregory., David Romer, and D.N. Weil (1992) "A Contribution to the Empirics of Economic Growth," *Quarterly Journal of Economics,* vol.107, Issue 2, May, pp.407-437

Marinescu, Ioana and Margaret Triyana (2012) "The Specificity of Human Capital in a Developing Country: Does Informality Matter?" draft University of Chicago, May

Mansuri, Ghazala and Vijayendra Rao (2012) *Localizing Development Does Participation Work?* Washington D.C.: The World Bank

Marks, Stephen V. and Sjamsu Rahardja (2012) "Effective Rates of Protection Revisited for Indonesia," *Bulletin of Indonesian Economic Studies,* vol. 48, no. 1, pp. 57–84

Matthews, Robin C. O. (1986) "The Economics of Institutions and the Sources of Economic Growth," *The Economic Journal,* vol.96, December, pp.903-918

Mattangkilang, Tunggadewa (2012) "Churchill Mining Update: East Kutai Chief Not Worried about Pending $2 billion Suit," *The Jakarta Globe,* July 13

McFadden, D. (2008) "Human Capital Accumulation and Depreciation," *Review of Agricultural Economics,* vol.30, no.3, pp.379-385

McLeod, Ross (2003) "Dealing with Bank System Failure: Indonesia, 1997-2002," *Departmental Working Papers* 2003-05, Australian National University, Arndt-Corden Department of Economics

McCleod, Ross H. (2003) "Toward Improved Monetary Policy in Indonesia," *Bulletin of Indonesian Economic Studies,* vol. 39, no. 3, pp. 303-324

McPherson, Malcolm F. (2000) "Seignorage in Highly Indebted Developing Countries," African Economic Policy Discussion Paper, no. 58, EAGER Project, July

McPherson, Malcolm F. (2005) "The Educational Effect of Economic Growth," Center for Business and Government, John F. Kennedy School of Government, Harvard University, March 28

McPherson, Malcolm F. and T.S. Rakovski, (2002) "Understanding the Growth Process in Sub-Saharan Africa: Empirical Evidence" Ch.11 in ed. M.F. McPherson *Restarting and Sustaining Growth and Development in Africa* Bethesda, MD: Franklin Press for United States Agency for International Development

McPherson, Malcolm and Christopher Vas (2012) "Productivity in Resource Dependent Countries: The Experience of Indonesia and Ghana," Ash Center, Harvard Kennedy School and H.C. Coombs Policy Forum, Crawford School of Public Policy, The Australian National University, August

Meyer, Bruce D. and James X. Sullivan (2012) "Identifying the Disadvantaged: Official Poverty, Consumption Poverty, and the New Supplemental Poverty Measure," *The Journal of Economic Perspectives*, vol. 26, no. 3, Summer, pp. 111-136

Mishra, Sanjaya (2006) *Quality Assurance in Higher Education, An Introduction,* Bangalore: National Printing Press for National Assessment and Accreditation Council (NAAC) and Commonwealth of Learning (COL)

Morales, R. Armando, Edo Mahendra and Wiwit Widyastuti, (2012) "Corporate Governance and Leverage Trends," Ch. 6 in *ed.* Thomas Rumbaugh *Indonesia Sustaining Growth During Global Volatility,* Washington D.C.: International Monetary Fund

Mordoch, Jonathan (2007) "The Unbanked: Evidence from Indonesia," financial access institute (FAI), NYU Wagner Graduate School of Public Service, March

Mundell, Robert A. (1962) "The Appropriate Use of Monetary and Fiscal Policy for Internal and External Stability," *IMF Staff Papers*, vol. 9, no. 1, March, pp. 70-79

NIU Outreach (2005) "The Role of Higher Education in Economic Development," Higher Education Alliance for the Rock River Region, May

Nasution, Anwar (2008) "Combating Corruption in Indonesia since 1997," PowerPoint presentation at Second Meeting of the INTOSAI's Working Group, "Fighting Against International Money Laundering and Corruption – FAIMLAC," Cairo, Egypt, July 29-31

Nasution, Anwar (2012) "Financial Development and the Macro Economy Since the Asian Financial Crisis of 1997," Draft paper presented at Roundtable Discussion on Indonesia's Political Economy: "How Can Indonesia Double Per

Capita Income over the Next Decade," Harvard Kennedy School Indonesia Program, Mandarin Hotel, Jakarta, January 16-17

Nasution, Anwar (2012) "Indonesia Imposes New Bank Ownership Caps," *East Asia Forum,* August 24

Nasution, Anwar (2012) "The future of the Indonesian economy," *East Asia Forum,* November 9

Nasution, Anwar (2012) "Preparing for uncertainty in the global economic recession," *The Jakarta Post,* Opinion, December 5

Nasution, Anwar (2013) "Escaping middle-income trap: the case of Malaysia," PPoint presentation, Kuala Lumpar (March 12) and Penang (March 13)

Nicolae, C.D. and C. Alina (2007) "Facts about Determinants of Economic Growth," Academy of Economic Studies, Bucharest and Media University, draft

Niehans, Jurg (1978) *The Theory of Money,* Baltimore: The Johns Hopkins University Press

Neihans, Jurg (1998) "transactions costs," in eds. John Eatwell, Murray Milgate, and Peter Newman, *The New Palgrave A Dictionary of Economics,* vol. 4, Q to Z, London: Macmillon Reference Ltd, pp. 676-679

Niehans, Jurg (1998) "Thunen, Johann Heinrich von (1783-1850)," *The New Palgrave A Dictionary of Economics, eds.* John Eatwell, Murray Milgrate, and Peter Newman, vol.4, New York: The Stockton Press

Nizam, (2009) "Higher Education Quality Assurance System in Indonesia," Board of Higher Education, Jakarta

North, Douglass (1990) *Institutions, Institutional Changes and Economic Performance,* Cambridge: Cambridge University Press

North, Douglass C. (1992) "Transactions Costs, Institutions, and Economic Performance" International Center for Economic Growth *Occasional Papers* No.30, May

North, Douglass C. (1997) "Transactions costs through time" Ch. 6 in *ed.* C. Menard *Transactions Costs Economics Recent Developments,* Cheltenham: Edward Elgar

Nugroho, Hanan (2013) "Geothermal development in Indonesia: proposal for government policies and interventions," Ash Center for Democratic Governance and Innovation, Harvard Kennedy School, April

OECD (2012) "Economic Surveys: Indonesia 2012", Geneva: Organization for Economic Cooperation and Development Publishing, September

Oberman, Raoul, *et al.*, (2012) "The Archipelago Economy: Unleashing Indonesia's Potential," Jakarta: *McKinsey Global Institute*, September

Olivia, Susan and Chikako Yamauchi (2012) "Survey of Recent Developments," *Bulletin of Indonesian Economic Studies*, vol. 48, no. 2, pp.143-171

Olson, Mancur (1965) *The Logic of Collective Action: Public Goods and The Theory of Groups*, Cambridge: Harvard University Press

Olson, Mancur (1998) "collective action," in eds. John Eatwell, Murray Milgate, and Peter Newman *The New Palgrave A Dictionary of Economics*, vol. 1, A to D, New York: The Stockton Press, pp.474-477

O'Rourke, Patrick J. (2002) "The Success of Failure" *The Atlantic Online* [*The Atlantic Monthly*, June]

Osorio, Camilo Gomez *et al.* (2011) "Who is Benefiting from Fertilizer Subsidies in Indonesia?" Policy Research Working Paper no. 5758, East Asia and Pacific Region, The World Bank August

Østby, Gudrun, *et al.* (2011) "Population Pressure, Horizontal Inequality, and Political Violence: A Disaggregated Study of Indonesian Provinces, 1990-2003," *Journal of Development Studies*,vol.47, pp. 377-398

Ostrom, Elinor (1990) *Governing the Commons: The Evolution of Institutions for Collective Actions*, Cambridge: Cambridge University Press

Outlook (2001) "The Learning Zone" (available on www.newmango.com/01iftf/learnzone/)

PRNewswire (2012) "Study Calls for Replacing Four Members of the G20, Including Argentina and Indonesia," (at www.prnewswire.com/news-releases/), June 14

Palomba, Geremia (2012) "Explaining Higher Inflation in Indonesia: A Regional Comparison," Chapter 1 in *ed*. Thomas Rumbaugh, *Indonesia Sustaining Growth during Global Volatility*, Washington D.C.: International Monetary Fund

Papanek, Gustav F, M. Chatib Basri with Daniel Schydlowsky (2010) "The impact of the world recession on Indonesia and an appropriate policy response: Some lessons for Asia," in eds. Armin Bauer and Myo Thant, *Poverty and Sustainable Development in Asia Impacts and Responses to the Global Economic Crisis*, Mandaluyong City: Asian Development Bank

Partridge, M.D. and D. S. Rickman (2007) "Persistent Rural Poverty: Is It Simply Remoteness and Scale?" *Review of Agricultural Economics*, vol.29, no.3, pp. 430-436

Patunru, Arianto A. and Christian von Luebke (2010) "Survey of Recent Developments," *Bulletin of Indonesian Economic Studies*, vol. 46, no.1, April, pp.7-32

Pearson (2012) *The Learning Curve Lessons in Country Performance in Education 2012 Report,* London: Pearson and Economist Intelligence Unit

Peiris, Shanaka J. *et al.* (2012) "Global Spillovers, Lending Conditions, and Monetary Policy in Indonesia," International Monetary Fund Indonesia, IMF Country Report No. 12/278, Selected Issues, September

Perkins, Dwight H. (2013) *East Asian Development Strategies: Historical and Modern Foundations,* Cambridge: Harvard University Press, forthcoming

Perkins, Dwight, H. (2012) "Learning from Northeast and Southeast Asian Development to Date," Paper prepared for this study, April

Pissarides, Christopher A. (1997) "Learning by Trading and the Returns to Human Capital in Developing Countries" *The World Bank Economic Review,* vol. 9, January

Porter, Michael (1990, 1998), *The Competitiveness of Nations,* New York: Free Press

Porter, Michael (2005), "What is competitiveness?" IESE Business School, University of Navarra, Jan.-April

Pradiytyo, Rimawan *et al.* (2011) "A Bridge Too Far; the Strive to Establish a Financial Service Regulatory Authority (OJK) in Indonesia," *MPRA Paper* no. 32004, (Munich Personal RePEc Archive), July 4

Prasetyawan, Wahyu (2005) "Government and Multinationals: Conflict Over Economic Resources in East Kalimantan 1998-2003," *Southeast Asian Studies,* vol. 43, no. 2

Prasetyawan, Wahyu (2006) "Unfinished Privatization of Semen Padang: The Structure of Political Economy in Post-Suharto Indonesia," *Indonesia,* no.81

Prasetyawan, Wayhu, (2012) "Re-Orienting Indonesia's Investment Climate toward Inclusive Growth: An Institutional Assessment in the Mining Sector," Paper prepared for this study, Syarif Hidayatullah Islamic State University and Indonesian Survey Institute, Jakarta

Pritchett, Lant (1996) "Where Has All The Education Gone?" Policy Research Working Paper 1581, Development Research Group, World Bank, Washington D.C.

Pritchett, Lant (2001) "Where Has All the Education Gone?" *The World Bank Economic Review,* Vol. 15, No. 3, pp. 367-391

Psacharopoulos, George (1995) "The Profitability of Investment in Education: Concepts and Methods" *World Bank, Human Capital Development and Operations Policy HCO Working Papers* no.63, November

Psacharopoulos, George and Harry A. Patrinos (2002) "Returns to Investment in Education: A Further Update" *World Bank Policy Research Working Paper* 2881, September

Quinn, George (2003) "Coming Apart and Staying Together at the Center: Debates over Provincial Status in Java and Madura," in *eds.* Edward Aspinall and Greg Fealy, *Local Power and Politics in Indonesia: Decentralization and Democratization,* Singapore: Institute of Southeast Asian Studies, pp. 164-178

Radner, R. (1998) "teams," in eds. J. Eatwell, M. Milgate, and P. Newman *The New Palgrave A Dictionary of Economics* vol. 4, Q to Z, New York: The Stockton Press, pp.613-617

Ramsey, Frank P. (1928), "A Mathematical Theory of Saving," *Economic Journal,* vol. 38, no. 152, December, pp. 543-59

Rauniyar, Ganesh and Ravi Kanbur (2010) "Inclusive Growth and Inclusive Development: a Review and Synthesis of Asian Development Bank Literature," *Journal of the Asia Pacific Economy,* vol.15, no. 41

Ravallion, Martin (2009) "The Developing World's Bulging (but Vulnerable) "Middle Class," *Policy Research Working Paper* #4816 The World Bank Development Research Group, January

Redding, Stephen (1997) "Dynamic Comparative Advantage and the Welfare Effects of trade," Draft, New College, Oxford and Centre for Economic Policy Research, November 24

Reid, Anthony *ed.,* (2012) *Indonesia Rising–The Repositioning of Asia's Third Giant,* Singapore: Institute of Southeast Asian Studies

Republic of Indonesia (2010) *Appendices Regulation of the President of the Republic of Indonesia Number 5 of 2010 Regarding the National Medium-Term Development Plan (RPJMN) 2010-2014, Book 1, National Priorities,* Jakarta: Ministry of National Development Planning

Reuters (2010) "Tensions Rise Over Indonesia Bank Rescue Probe," *Reuters International,* March 3

Ricardo, D. (1821) *On the Principles of Political Economy and Taxation,* 3rd Edition, London: John Murray [Reprinted: London: Dent 1911]

Ricklefs, Merle C. (2003) "The Future of Indonesia," *History Today,* vol. 53, issue 12

Ricoy, Carlos J. (1998) "cumulative causation" (eds.) J. Eatwell, M. Milgate, and P. Newman *The New Palgrave A Dictionary of Economics,* vol. 1, pp. 730-735

Ridao-Cano, Cristobel and Nithin Umapathi (2008) "Average and Marginal Returns to Upper Secondary Schooling in Indonesia," draft May [Published as Carneiro, Pedro M. *et al.* CEPR *Discussion Paper,* no. DP 8689 December 2011]

Ridhwan, Masagus M. *et al.* (2011) "The Regional Impact of Monetary Policy in Indonesia," *Tinbergen Institute Discussion Paper* TI 2011-081/3 (at http://www.dsf.nl/)

Ridhwan, Masagus M. (2011) *Regional Dimensions of Monetary Policy in Indonesia,* Amsterdam: Vrije Universiteit, Tinbergen Institute

Robinson, Marguerite S. (1997) "Sustainable Microfinance," Ch. 12 in *eds.* Dwight H. Perkins *et al. Assisting Development in a Changing World, The Harvard Institute for International Development 1980-1995,* Cambridge MA: Harvard University Press

Romer, Paul (1986) "Increasing Returns and Long-Run Growth", Journal of Political Economy, vol.94, pp. 1002-1037

Rosen, S. (1998) "Human capital" in ed. J. Eatwell, M. Milgate and P. Newman *The New Palgrave A Dictionary of Economics* volume 2 E to J, New York: Stockton Press Ltd., pp.681-690

Rosengard, Jay K. and Richard H. Patten (1991) *Progress with Profits: The Development of Rural Banking in Indonesia,* San Francisco: International Center of Economic Growth, ICS Press

Rosengard, Jay K, *et al.* (2007) "The Promise and the Peril of Microfinance Institutions in Indonesia," *Bulletin of Indonesian Economic Studies,* vol. 43, no. 1, April, pp. 87-112

Rosengard, Jay K. and Agustinus Prasetyantoko (2011) "If the Banks Are Doing So Well, Why Can't I Get A Loan? Regulatory Constraints to Financial Inclusion in Indonesia," *Asian Economic Policy Review,* vol. 6, no. 2, December, pp. 273-296

Ruiz-Arranz, Marta and Milan Zavadjil (2012) "Adequacy of Indonesia's Foreign Exchange Reserves," Chapter 5 in *ed.* Thomas Rumbaugh *Indonesia Sustaining Growth During Global Volatility,* Washington D.C.: International Monetary Fund

Rumbaugh, Thomas, *ed.* (2012) *Indonesia Sustaining Growth During Global Volatility,* Washington D.C.: International Monetary Fund

Russo, Sandra L. and Malcolm F. McPherson (2006) "The Transformation of Higher Education in South Africa: Dancing on Top of a Rapidly Moving River," Presentation to the Carter Center, University of Florida, Gainesville, February 27

SMH (2012) "Indonesian airlines are booming, but are they safe?" *The Sydney Morning Herald,* www.smh.com.au, August 6

Sahara, Ian (2010) *Commuting Times in Metropolitan Cities in Indonesia 2008,* University of Indonesia, Masters Program on Population and Labor Studies, Master's Thesis

Sahminan, Sahminan (2008) "Effectiveness of monetary policy communication in Indonesia and Thailand," Bank for International Settlements, *BIS Working Papers* no. 262, September.

Saich, Anthony, *et al.* (2010) *From Reformasi to Institutional Transformation: A Strategic Assessment of Indonesia's Prospects for Growth, Equity and Democratic Governance,* Cambridge: Ash Center for Democratic Governance and Innovation, Harvard Kennedy School, July

Samboh, Esther (2012) "Bank Indonesia campaigns to debunk financial inclusion myth," *Jakarta Post,* June 28

Samuelson, Paul A. (1970) "The fundamental approximation theorem of portfolio analysis in terms of means, variances, and higher moments," *Review of Economic Studies,* vol. 37, no. 4, October, pp. 537-542

Sandee, Henry (2011) "Indonesian Trade Needs to Find a Better Way," *Jakarta-Globe,* Opinion, March 7

Sandel, Michael J. (2012) *What Money Can't Buy The Moral Limits of Markets,* New York: Farrer, Straus and Giroux

Sanders, Jon (2003) "Does Spending on Higher Education Drive Economic Growth? 20 Years of Evidence Reviewed," *Goldwater Institute* Policy Report, no.181, May 12

Schelling, Thomas C. (1978) *Micromotives and Macrobehavior,* New York: W.W. Norton

Schultz, Theodore W. (1959) "Investment in Man: An Economist's View," *Social Science Review* June

Schultz, Theodore W. (1962) "Reflections on Investment in Man" *Journal of Political Economy, Supplement*: October

Schultz, Theodore W. (1963) *The Economic Value of Education,* New York: Columbia University Press

Schumpeter, Joseph S. (1954) *History of Economic Analysis,* New York Oxford University Press

Schiller, Anne (2007) "Activism and Identities in an East Kalimantan Dayak Organization," *Journal of Asian Studies,* vol. 66, pp. 63-95

Setyoko, Nur Rakhman, Ray Trewin, and David Vanzetti (2012) "Regional rice stocks, prices and food security: Implications of Indonesia," PPoint presentation, Arndt-Corden Department of Economics, Australian National University, May 22

Sidel, John (2006) *Riots, Pogroms, and Jihad: Religious Violence in Indonesia,* Ithaca: Cornell University Press

Sjafruddin, Ade, *et al.* (2010) "Policy Evaluation of Multimodal Transportation Network: The Case of Inter-Island Freight Transportation in Indonesia," *Asian Transport Studies,* vol. 1, issue 1, pp.18-32

Solesbury, William (2003) "Sustainable Livelihoods: A Case Study of the Evolution of DfID Policy," *Overseas Development Institute Working Paper* no. 217, London

Schonhardt, Sara (2012) "British Mining Firm Sues Indonesia for Asset Seizure," *The New York Times,* June 6

Schwab, Klaus ed. (2011) *The Global Competitiveness Report 2011-2012,* Geneva: World Economic Forum

Schwab, Klaus ed. (2012) *The Global Competitiveness Report 2012-2013, Full Data Edition,* Geneva: World Economic Forum

Simanjuntak, Damiana N. (2012) "Government Seeks to Boost Rattan Sales, Reclaim the Market from China," *Jakarta Globe,* June 3

Sianipar, Michael, (2012) "Indonesian Universities Rise in Asian Rankings of Best of Schools," *The Jakarta Globe,* March 27

Siregar, Reza Y. and James E. Williams (2004) "Designing an Integrated Financial Supervisory Agency: Selected Lessons and Challenges for Indonesia," *CIES Discussion Paper* no. 0405, Center for International Economic Studies, October

Slater, Dan (2004) "Indonesia's Accountability Trap: Party Cartels and Presidential Power After Democratic Transition," *Indonesia,* October

Smith, Adam (1776) *An Enquiry into The Nature and Causes of the Wealth of Nations,* New York: The Modern Library (edited with notes by E. Cannan 1937).

Smith, Vernon L. (1963) "Minimization of Economic Rent in Spatial Price Equilibrium," *Review of Economic Studies,* vol. 30, no. 1

Soeriaatmadja, Wahyudi (2011) "Dispute Over Land After Coal is Found," *Straits Times Indonesia,* November 25

Spence, M. (1973) "Job Market Signaling" *The Quarterly Journal of Economics* vol.87, no.3, August, pp. 355-374

Stein, Ernesto *et al.* (2005) *The Politics of Policies Economic and Social Progress in Latin America 2006 Report,* Washington D.C.: Inter-American Development Bank

Stewart, Frances (2008) "Horizontal Inequalities and Conflict: An Introduction and Some Hypotheses," in *ed.* Frances Stewart, *Horizontal Inequalities and Conflict: Understanding Group Violence in Multiethnic Societies,* New York: Palgrave Macmillan, pp. 3-24

Strategic Asia (2012) "Implementing Indonesia's Economic Master Plan (MP3EI): Challenges, Limitations and Corridor Specific Differences," Strategic Asia and Foreign and Commonwealth Office, Jakarta, June

Strotz, R.H. (1955-56) "Myopia and Inconsistency in Dynamic Utility Maximization" *Review of Economic Studies* vol. 23, pp. 165-180

Subianto, Benny (2010) "Ethnic Politics and the Rise of the Dayak-Bureaucrats in Local Elections: *Pilkada* in Six *Kabupaten* in West Kalimantan," in *eds.* Maribeth Erb and Priyambudi Sulistiyanto *Deepening Democracy in Indonesia? Direct Elections for Local Leaders (Pilkada),* Singapore: Institute of Southeast Asian Studies, pp. 327-355

Sumantri, Yeni and Sim Kim Lau (2011) "The Current Status of Logistics Performance Drivers in Indonesia: An Emphasis on Potential Contributions of Logistics Service Providers (LSPs)," *Journal of Asia Pacific Business Innovation & Technology Management,* vol. 1, pp.34-50

Sumarto, Sudarno and Asep Suryahadi (2010) "Conclusion: Coping with the Crisis," Ch. 10 in eds. Joan Hardjono, Nuning Akhmadi, and Sudarno Sumarto *Poverty and Social Protection in Indonesia,* Singapore, Institute of Southeast Asian Studies

Suga, Masumi and Ichiro Susuki (2012) "Japan May Take Indonesia to WTO Over Curbs on Metal Exports," *Bloomberg News,* June 12

Sullivan, Gregory M. and Kusuma Diwyanto, (2007) "A Value Chain Assessment of the Livestock Sector in Indonesia," Jakarta: Agribusiness Market and Support Activity, United States Agency for International Development

Suryadarma, Daniel, *et al.* (2006) "From Access to Income: Regional and Ethnic Inequality in Indonesia," SMERU Working Papers, May

Suryadarma, Daniel (2011) "The Quality of Education: Intertemporal Standing and Attempts at Improvement," Chapter 6 in ed. Chris Manning and Sudarno Sumarto, *Employment, Livings Standards and Poverty in Comtemporary Indonesia,* Singapore: Institute of Southeast Asian Studies

Syrquin, Moise and Hollis B. Chenery (1989) "Patterns of Development: 1950-1983" *World Bank Discussion Papers* no. 41, The World Bank TPI (2011) *Corruption Perceptions Index 2011*, Berlin: Transparency International

Tadjoeddin, Mohammad Zulfan (2011) "The Economic Origins of Indonesia's Secessionist Conflicts," *Civil Wars*, vol.13, pp.312-332

Tadjoeddin, Mohammad Zulfan and Syed Mansoob Murshed (2007) "Socio-Economic Determinants of Everyday Violence in Indonesia: An Empirical Investigation of Javanese Districts, 1994-2003," *Journal of Peace Research*, vol. 44, pp.689-709

Tedjasukmana, Jason (2007) "Indonesia's Perilous Skies," *Time*, www.time.com, January 5

Tampubolon, Hans David, Nurfika Osman, and Rendl A. Witular (2012) "MP3EI Infrastructure Projects Flounder as Government Fails to Act," *The Jakarta Post*, August 31

Tan, Deyi (2011) "Indonesia Infrastructure A US $250bn Opportunity," Morgan Stanley Research, Singapore, May

Taylor, Michael (2011) "Battle Over Huge Coal Deposit Highlights Risks in Indonesia," *The Jakarta Globe, Business*, October 10

Temple, Jonathan (1999) "The New Growth Evidence" *Journal of Economic Literature*, vol.37, no.1, March, pp.112-156

Temple, J. (2000) "Education and economic growth," HM Treasury seminar on Economic Growth and Government Policy, October 12

Thee, Kian Wie(2002) "The Soeharto Era and After: Stability, Development and Crisis," in eds. Howard Dick et al., *The Emergence of a National Economy – An Economic History of Indonesia, 1800–2000*, Crow's Nest (Australia): Allen and Unwin. [*The Emergence of a National Economy, An Economic History of Indonesia, 1800-2000*, Honolulu: Allen & Unwin and University of Hawaii Press]

Thee, Kian Wie (2003) *Recollections–The Indonesian Economy, 1950s–1990s*, Singapore: Institute of Southeast Asian Studies, (ISEAS)

Thee, Kian Wie (2006) "Indonesia's First Competitition Law: Issues and Experiences," in eds. Lee Cassey and Cheong May Fong, *Competition Policy in Asia–Models and Issues*, Kuala Lumpur: University of Malaya

Thee Kian Wie (2010) "Indonesia's Economic Crises and the Prospects for Rapid and Sustained Growth," *Indonesian Institute of Sciences* (P2E-LIPI), Jakarta

Thee, Kian Wie (2012) *Indonesia's Economy Since Independence*, Singapore: Institute of Southeast Asian Studies

Thee, Kian Wie (2012) "What Can Be Done for Moving Indonesia Forward?" Center for Economic and Development Studies, Indonesian Institute of Science, Paper prepared for this study, May

Thee Kian Wie and Siwage Dharma Negara (2010) "Survey of recent developments," *Bulletin of Indonesian Economic Studies,* vol. 46, no. 3, pp. 279-308

Thomas, Kelly (2012) "Supply chain segmentation: 10 steps to greater profits," *CSMP's Supply Chain Quarterly,* no. 1

Tinbergen, Jan (1952) *On the Theory of Economic Policy,* 2nd edition [Volume 1 of *Contributions to Economic Analysis,* Amsterdam: North-Holland]

Tinbergen, Jan (1954) "Centralization and Decentralization in Economic Policy," *Contributions to Economic Analysis, VI,* Amsterdam: North- Holland Publishing Company

Toha, Risa (2012) "The Threat of Group Inequality and Ethnicized Politics in Indonesia," Paper prepared for this study, Harvard Kennedy School Indonesia Program

Tomsa, Dirk (2008) *Party Politics and Democratization in Indonesia: Golkar in the Post-Suharto Era,* London and New York: Routledge

Transparency International (2011) *Corruptions Perceptions Index 2011,* Berlin: Transparency International Secretariat

UNDP (2012) *Africa Human Development Report 2012, Towards a Food Secure Future,* New York: United Nations Development Programme

USAID (2008) "Indonesian Port Sector Reform and the 2008 Shipping Law," United States Agency for International Development, Jakarta, August

USDA (2013) "World Agricultural Supply and Demand Estimates WASDE-516 – March 18, 2013" United States Department of Agriculture World Agricultural Outlook Board, Washington D.C.

Unditu, Aloysius and Leony Aurora (2008) "Indonesia Seizes as Capital Deteriorates," *Bloomberg,* November 22

Unditu, Aloysius, Francezka Nangoy, and Tito Summa Siahaan (2012) "Indonesian Market Plunges as Investors Move to Sidelines," *The Jakarta Globe,* May 27

United Nations (1996) *Human Development Report 1996,* New York: Oxford University Press for the United Nations Development Programme

Urban Age (2009) *Cities and Social Equity Inequality, territory and urban form Detailed Report,* London: Urban Age Programme London School of Economics, July

Vallikappen, Sanat and Berni Moestafa (2013) "World's Most Profitable Banks in Indonesia Double U.S. Returns," *Bloomberg,* (www.bloomberg.com), February 5

van der Eng, Pierre (2005) "Capital Formation and Capital Stock in Indonesia, 1950-2007," *Working Paper* No. 2005/24, Research School of Pacific and Asian Studies, Australian National University

van der Eng, Pierre (2009) "Total Factor Productivity and Economic Growth in Indonesia," *Working Papers in Trade and Development,* No. 2009/01, Australian National University, January

van Klinken, Gerry (2007) *Communal Violence and Democratization in Indonesia: Small Town Wars,* New York, NY: Routledge

Varela, Gonzalo, Erique Aldaz-Carroll and Leonardo Iacovone (2012) "Determinants of Market Integration and Price Transmission in Indonesia," World Bank East Asia and Pacific Region *Policy Research Working Paper* no. 6098, June

von Luebke, Christian (2011) "How Much Longer Can Elites Hide Their Privileges From View?" *Inside Indonesia,* April 10

Varshney, Ashutosh, Mohammad Zulfan Tadjoeddin, and Rizal Panggabean (2008) "Creating Datasets in Information-Poor Environments: Patterns of Collective Violence in Indonesia, 1990-2003," *Journal of East Asian Studies,* vol. 8, pp. 361-394

Vel, Jacqueline (2007) "Campaigning for a New District in West Sumba," in *eds.* Henk Schulte Nordholt and Gerry van Klinken *Renegotiating Boundaries: Local Politics in Post-Suharto Indonesia,* Leiden: KITLV Press, pp. 90-120

Vianello, Fernando (1998) "labour theory of value," in eds. John Eatwell, Murray Milgate and Peter Newman, *The New Palgrave A Dictionary of Economics,* vol. III, London: Macmillan Reference Ltd., pp.107-113

Wall Street Journal (2012) "Jakarta's Trade Backsliding," *The Wall Street Journal* online, July 18

Wardi, Robertus and Kristantyo Wisnubroto (2012) "High Cost to High Seas Shipping in Indonesia," *The Jakarta Globe,* May 14

Warr, Peter (2011) "The effect of research on agricultural productivity in Indonesia," Final Report Small research and development activity, Australian Center for International Agricultural Research, Canberra

Warr, Peter (2011) "Food Security vs. Food Self-Sufficiency: The Indonesian Case," Arndt-Corden Department of Economics, Australian National University, Departmental Working Papers 2011-04

Warr, Peter (2012) "Research and agricultural productivity in Indonesia," Paper presented at the Australian Agricultural and Resource Economics Society, 56th conference, Fremantle, Feb 7-10

Watanabe, Ryo (2000) "EFA 2000 Assessment, Draft Country Report, Japan," [available on www.unesco.org/education/wef/countryreports/japan/contents. html accessed December 14, 2009]

Welsh, Bridge (2008) "Local and National: Keroyokan Mobbing in Indonesia," *Journal of East Asian Studies,* vol. 8, pp. 473-504

Wijayanto (2011) "The truth about corruption in Indonesia," *The Jakarta Globe,* Scene, July 31

Wilkinson, Steven (2004) *Votes and Violence: Electoral Competition and Ethnic Riots in India,* Cambridge: Cambridge University Press

Williamson, Oliver (1996) *Mechanism of Governance,* Oxford: Oxford University Press.

Willums, J-O (2001) "Life-Long Learning in the New Economy" in (eds) Simon Zadek, N. Hojensgard and P. Raynard *Perspectives on the New Economy of Corporate Citizenship* Copenhagen: The Copenhagen Center

Wimmer, Andreas, Lars-Erik Cederman, and Brian Min (2010) "Why Ethnic Groups Rebel? New Data and Analysis," *World Politics,* vol. 62, pp. 87-119

Winters, Jeffrey (2011) *Oligarchy,* New York: Cambridge University Press

Winters, Jeffrey (2012) "Pathways to a people's president," *Inside Indonesia,* January 21

Wong, Edward (2013) "On Scale of 0 to 500, Beijing's Air Quality Tops 'Crazy Bad' at 755," *The New York Times,* January 12

Wong, Victor and Vivian Yan (2010) "Financial Inclusion in Indonesia, The Summary Document," Case Study for Innoviti, India and PrimaVista, Indonesia, London Business School

Woo, Win Thye and Chang Hong (2010) "Indonesia's economic performance in comparative perspective and a new policy framework for 2049," *Bulletin of Indonesian Economic Studies,* vol. 46, no.1, April, pp. 34-64

World Bank (1981) *Accelerated Development in Sub-Saharan Africa An Agenda for Action,* Washington D.C.: The World Bank

World Bank (1984) *Towards Sustained Development in Sub-Saharan Africa,* Washington D.C.: The World Bank

World Bank (1986) *Financing Adjustment with Growth in Sub-Saharan Africa, 1986-90* Washington D.C.: The World Bank

World Bank (1989) *Sub-Saharan Africa From Crisis to Sustainable Growth A Long-Term Perspective Study* Washington D.C.: The World Bank

World Bank (1992) *Indonesia Growth, Infrastructure and Human Resources,* Country Department III, East Asia & Pacific Regional Office, Report No. 10470-IND, May 26

World Bank (1993) "The East Asian Miracle: Economic Growth and Public Policy," New York: Oxford University Press

World Bank (1994) *World Development Report 1994, Infrastructure for Development,* New York: Published for the World Bank by Oxford University Press

World Bank (1997) *World Development Report 1997, "The State in a Changing World,"* Washington D.C.: Oxford University Press for The World Bank

World Bank (1998) *World Development Indicators 1998,* Washington D.C.: The World Bank

World Bank (1999) *World Development Report, 1998/99 "Knowledge for Development,"* New York: Published for the World Bank by Oxford University Press

World Bank (2002) *Constructing Knowledge Societies: New Challenges for Tertiary Education A World Bank Report,* Washington D.C.: World Bank Education Group, April

World Bank (2003) *Lifelong Learning in the Global Knowledge Economy Challenges for Developing Countries,* Washington D.C.: The World Bank

World Bank (2003) *World Development Indicators,* Washington D.C.: The World Bank

World Bank (2005) *A Better Investment Climate for Everyone,* Washington D.C.: The World Bank

World Bank (2005) *Indonesia Brief: Attracting New Mining Investment,* Jakarta: The World Bank

World Bank (2006) *World Development Report 2007 Development and the Next Generation,* Washington D.C.: The World Bank

World Bank (2007) *World Development Report 2008 Agriculture for Development,* Washington D.C.: The World Bank

World Bank (2008) *The Growth Report: Strategies for Sustained Growth and Inclusive Development,* Washington D.C.: The World Bank for the Commission on Growth and Development

World Bank (2009) *World Development Report 2009, Reshaping Economic Geography,* Washington D.C.: The World Bank

World Bank (2010) "Subsidies in the Energy Sector: An Overview," Background Paper for the World Bank Group Energy Sector Strategy, July

World Bank (2010) *Indonesia Skills Report: Trends in Skills Demand, Gaps, and Supply in Indonesia,* Report No. 54741-EAP, Human Development Department, East Asia and Pacific Region, The World Bank, May

World Bank (2011) "Geothermal Clean Energy Investment Project," Report AB5963, Project ID: P113078 (available online), The World Bank, Washington D.C., March 29

World Bank (2012) *Indonesia Economic Quarterly Rising to present and future challenges,* Washington D.C.: The World Bank

World Bank (2012) "Trade Development in Indonesia," www.worldbank.org/id/trade, [Report on "Boom, Bust and Up Again? Evolution, Drivers and Impact of Commodity Prices: Implications for Indonesia."]

World Bank (2012) *World Development Indicators 2012,* Washington D.C.: The World Bank

World Bank (2013) "Pink Sheets", www.worldbank.org/INTPROSPECTS/

World Bank/IMF (2010) *Financial Sector Assessment Program Indonesia Basel Core Principles Assessment Detailed Assessment of Compliance,* Washington D.C.: The World Bank and International Monetary Fund, December

World Economic Forum (2012) *The Global Competitiveness Report 2012-2013,* Geneva: World Economic Forum

Wu, Jun Jie and M. Gopinath (2008) "What Causes Spatial Variations in Economic Development in the United States?" *American Journal of Agricultural Economics,* vol.90, no.2, May, pp.392-408

Wynne, Mark A. and Janet Koech (2012) "One-Size-Fits-All Monetary Policy: Europe and the U.S.," *Economic Letter,* Federal Reserve Bank of Dallas, vol. 7, no. 9, September

Yulisman, Linda and Andi Haswidi (2012) "Discourse: Free trade for the sake of fair trade," *The Jakarta Post,* Discourse, January 24 [Interview with Gita Wirjawan, Minister of Trade]

Zoetelief, Jochem (1999) "Perspectives on informal rural finance," *SDdimensions,* Sustainable Development Department (SD), Food and Agricultural Organization of the United Nations, September